REGIONALISM AND THE STATE

To Lise,
For the many wonderful years, and for those to come

7 Day

University of Plymouth Library
Subject to status this item may be renewed
via your Voyager account
http://voyager.plymouth.ac.uk
Tel: (01752) 232323

Regionalism and the State
NAFTA and Foreign Policy Convergence

Edited by
GORDON MACE
Laval University, Canada

ASHGATE

Published by
Ashgate Publishing Limited
Gower House
Croft Road
Aldershot
Hampshire GU11 3HR
England

Ashgate Publishing Company
Suite 420
101 Cherry Street
Burlington, VT 05401-4405
USA

Ashgate website: http://www.ashgate.com

British Library Cataloguing in Publication Data
Regionalism and the state : NAFTA and foreign policy
    convergence
    1. Free Trade Area of the Americas (Organization) 2. Free
    trade - America 3. America - Economic integration 4. United
    States - Foreign economic relations 5. Canada - Foreign
    economic relations 6. Mexico - Foreign economic relations
    I. Mace, Gordon
    337.7

Library of Congress Cataloging-in-Publication Data
Mace, Gordon.
    Regionalism and the state : NAFTA and foreign policy convergence / by Gordon Mace.
        p. cm.
    Includes bibliographical references and index.
    ISBN 978-0-7546-4891-8
    1. Regionalism. 2. International relations. 3. Canada. Treaties, etc. 1992 Oct. 7
I. Title.

JF197.M33 2007
327.7--dc22

2007017565

ISBN 978 0 7546 4891 8

Printed and bound in Great Britain by MPG Books Ltd, Bodmin, Cornwall.

Contents

List of Figures and Tables

Figures

Tables

Notes on Contributors

Guillermo R. Aureano is Lecturer and Internship Coordinator at the Department of Political Science of the Université de Montréal. Associate researcher with the Research Group of International Security (GERSI) from its foundation, he completed post-doctoral studies at the Institut d'études politiques de Paris and served as a consultant to UNESCO and the Department of Foreign Affairs and International Trade of Canada, among others. His main fields of research are drug trafficking, money laundering, and terrorism control policies. Among his recent publications: *La lutte au financement du terrorisme: leçons apprises de la guerre contre la drogue*, *Relações entre as ONGs, as OIGs e o Estado no caso da lutta antidrogas*, and *El uso recreativo de drogas: una visión política*.

Louis Bélanger is Professor of International Relations at the Department of Political Science and the Institute for Advanced International Studies at Laval University. At the time of completing his chapter for this book, he was a Canada-US Fulbright Visiting Scholar at the Paul H. Nitze School of Advanced International Studies (Johns Hopkins University).

Martin Duplantis is a Master Degree Candidate at the Department of Geography of Université du Québec à Montréal.

Michel Fortmann is Professor of Political Science at the Université de Montréal. He is the director of the Research Group in International Security, which he founded in 1996. He is the coeditor with T.V. Paul and James Wirtz of *Balance of Power, Theory and Practice in the 21st Century* (Stanford University Press, 2004). He has written extensively and edited several books on defense policies, arms control, European security and strategic studies. His articles have been published in *International Journal, Études internationales, Canadian Foreign Policy* and *Relations internationales et stratégiques*.

Hugo Loiseau is professor at the École de politique appliquée at the Université de Sherbrooke (Québec, Canada). He obtained his Ph.D. in political science from Laval University (Québec, Canada). His thesis underscores the importance of the diffusion of international norms of democratic civil-military relations in the Americas. His main research interests bear on civil-military relations, cyberspace and Latin America. His current research program focusses on regionalism in the Americas.

Gordon Mace teaches at the Department of Political Science and at the Institute of Advanced International Studies of Laval University, Québec, Canada. He is also director of the journal *Études internationales* and director of the Centre d'études interaméricaines (Inter-American Studies Center) also based at Laval. A student of regionalism and inter-American affairs, he is co-author of *The Americas in Transition: The Contours of Regionalism* (Lynne Rienner Publishers, 1999) and co-editor of *Governing the Americas: Assessing Multilateral Institutions* (Lynne Rienner Publishers, 2007). He obtained his Ph.D. in 1979 at Geneva's Graduate Institute of International Studies.

Nelson Michaud (Ph.D., Laval; post-doctoral studies, Dalhousie University) has been appointed as Director (Teaching and Research) at the École nationale d'administration publique (ENAP) in September 2006. Prior to these responsibilities, he was associate professor of political science and international relations, and Director of research groups at the ENAP. He has published numerous articles in peer-reviewed journals, chapters in collective works, and encyclopaedia articles. He is the author of *Diplomatic Departures: The Conservative Era in Canadian Foreign Policy 1984–1993* (UBC Press, 2001), co-edited with Kim Richard Nossal and of the *Handbook of Canadian Foreign Policy* (Lexington Books, 2006) co-edited with Pat James and Marc O'Reilly. He appears regularly as a speaker and expert commentator in Quebec, Canada, the United States and Europe. His works and many publications lead him to receive a number of prestigious research grants and, in 2005, the Prix d'excellence en recherche for the entire Université du Québec network, and in 2004, the Prix d'excellence en recherche from his institution.

Stéphane Roussel teaches at the Department of Political Science of the Université du Québec à Montréal and holds the Canada's Research Chair in Foreign and Defence Policies. His research deals with the security relationship between Canada and the United States as well as security problems in the Arctic and on the attitude of Quebecers concerning military matters.

Jean-Philippe Thérien teaches at the Department of Political Science of the Université de Montréal, and is Associate Scientific Director of the Centre d'études et de recherches internationales de l'Université de Montréal (CERIUM). His research interests include inter-American politics, development assistance, and North-South issues.

Acknowledgments

This book is the result of a research program initiated a few years ago at the Inter-American Studies Centre located in Québec City. It would not have been possible without the collaboration and support of many people, among them the contributors to the volume. I want first of all to thank them all for accepting to be part of this project and to write a case study linked to the theoretical questions at the base of the research program. This effort is the main factor responsible for the unified focus of the collection which makes the book a different kind of edited volume.

I would also like to gratefully acknowledge the work of our research assistants Nicolas Lesieur, Isabelle Lombardo and Nathalie Watts who were involved at various stages in the evolution of the project and whose meticulous work helped considerably. Thank you to Karen Lang and Chau Nguyen for translation, and a very special thank you to Chantal Lacasse who assisted me in the last phase of the project. Her dedication and attention to details was of considerable help and made it possible to finish the manuscript without too much stress.

Financial assistance for the research program was generously provided by the Fonds québécois de recherche sur la société et la culture and by the Social Sciences and Humanities Research Council of Canada. We are naturally grateful to both institutions for their support to our research team over the years.

Finally, I want to express my gratitude to Kirstin Howgate for her patience and her support for the project, and to Emily Jarvis who supervised with great care the making of the book. Thank you also to James McAllister (Production), Helen Harvey (Marketing), Donna Elliot and Carolyn Court (Commissioning Administration), and Margaret Younger (Assistant Commissioning Editor), the Ashgate team, who worked at various stages to make this project possible. I am of course responsible for any remaining errors in the manuscript.

G.M.

Introduction

Gordon Mace

Ever since the pioneering work of Karl W. Deutsch and Ernst B. Haas in the 1950s, regionalism has been the subject of numerous studies. This vast literature has essentially sought to understand how this phenomenon works: why do governments undertake such a venture and what explains the progress and failure of regionalism? The traditional theorization of regionalism or regional integration[1] used to concur with the liberal current of the realist paradigm, which has dominated the field of international relations for a long time. Indeed, liberal theorists tended to explain regional integration in terms of the behavior of the agent or domestic actors.

The literature on international relations has evolved considerably since the first signs of regionalism. Explanations for international phenomena are no longer exclusively focused on the behavior of state actors; rather, there is an increased emphasis on the growing role of international institutions. The theories of constructivism, as developed in studies on regimes and research on the world economy, indeed showed that structure could also influence or constrain the agent. However, this research intuition has never been systematically tested in studies of regionalism, and even less so using an integration model completely different from the one currently operating in the European Union.

Since little is known about the precise causal relationship between international institutions and national policy choices (Cortell and Davis 1996, 451), the main contribution of this book involves using the study of regionalism to draw firmer conclusions about the analytical link between institutions and government choices. This is no small challenge given that the institution chosen for this analysis, the North American Free Trade Agreement (NAFTA), unlike the European Union, does not have strong regional institutions. NAFTA's normative framework is the only constraint on participating governments at the community level. A further challenge is that foreign policy, the field of government behavior analyzed here, is far removed from NAFTA's central theme.

The introduction is divided into four parts. Part 1 will briefly summarize the theoretical debate on the study of regionalism from the perspective of the agent-structure relationship. We will briefly discuss a number of deficiencies in traditional and recent theoretical approaches to regional integration and will show how certain intuitions of constructivism can help to better understand the regionalism phenomenon. Part 2 will examine the hypothesis of convergence and show how the writings on this concept can contribute to the study of the influence of regionalism on

---

1   In this book, the two terms are used synonymously.

the behavior of the actors therein, mainly the governments of the member countries. Part 3 will provide a justification for the choice to study NAFTA, and, lastly, Part 4 will present a summary of the contributions to this book.

1. Theoretical Considerations

The first models of analysis of regionalism, all focused on understanding European integration, had already established the analytical link central to grasping the phenomenon. These models sought to explain the dependent variable, that is, how the integration process or the structure operated. The explanatory factors, or independent variables, all had a link to the behavior of the agent, whether governments, groups or individuals. As will be seen, present-day research programs on regionalism have remained true to this original theoretical orientation.

Three main approaches dominated the study of regional integration during the 1955–1970 period. Each one sought to explain the evolution of integration based on the interplay of national actors. The neofunctionalists, led by Ernst Haas and Philippe Schmitter (Haas 1958; Barrera and Haas 1969, 150–160; Schmitter 1970, 836–868), viewed integration as a gradual process evolving within a continuum which would ultimately spill over from an initial economic sector into other sectors. The creation of an integration process assumed the existence of favorable preconditions and, once in place, the integration operated essentially as the result of the behavior of the governments of the member countries.

Midway between neofunctionalism and David Easton's systemic analysis, Leon Lindberg's model (Lindberg 1967, 344–387; Lindberg 1970, 649–731) views the integration process as a political system. The model, of course, includes the much-vaunted feedback loop, which in this case does not involve any influence of structure over agent, but only assumes that the system generates information used by the actors to adjust their behavior. The idea, which is similar to that formulated by Moravcsik (Moravcsik 1998), is that community institutions and governments are the main actors of integration, relying on the support offered by the national environment composed of socio-economic groups.

The pluralist model represents the third main approach of this first wave of theorization. According to this approach, developed from Karl Deutsch's work (Deutsch 1954; Deutsch et al. 1967; Puchala 1970, 732–763), integration evolves through transactions and communications between members, especially the elites of the societies that are part of the process. According to the pluralists, governments are not the main actors of the integration process, which evolves according to the exchanges between groups and individuals. In this case, it is still the agent who acts on the structure.

Parallel to the new wave of regionalism that emerged in the early 1990s, a new theorization was developed. Within it, three particular analytical currents seem more relevant to the argumentation developed here. Researchers identified with the "new regionalism" approach (see, among others, Hettne, Inotai, and Sunkel 1999; Mittelman 1996, 189–213; Marchand, Boas, and Shaw 1999, 897–909; Schulz, Söderbaum, and Öjendal 2001, 1–21) essentially seek to understand regionalism in terms of its relationship with globalization. Their theoretical models attempt to explain the dynamic of regionalism through the influence of mega-variables such as the structure of the global system, the nature of relations between regions and the dynamic specific to each region (Hettne 2000, 7–8), or production systems, power relations, socio-cultural entities, and so on (Mittleman 1996, 196–206). The focus is thus on using systemic factors to explain the evolution of regionalism. Some would refer to these systemic factors as "institutions," but institutions so vast and complex that the scientific literature has not been able to establish a robust analytical link between the influence of these institutions and the behavior of integration actors.

A second current, neorealism, essentially seeks to explain the functioning of regionalism (and cooperation) through the behavior of states, which act according to the distribution of gains or in order to have a voice opportunity (Grieco 1995, 21–40; Grieco 1996, 261–305; also see Battistella 2993, 335–338). The third and last current is that of liberal intergovernmentalism, inspired by the work of Moravcsik (see especially Moravcsik 1997, 513–553; Moravcsik 1993, 473–524). It seeks to explain integration through the combined interplay of the pressure of societal actors and the actions of national governments. The societal actors try to make the governments advance their interests with the central institutions, whereas the national governments, as formulated by Putnam (Putnam 1988, 427–460), use the pressure of societal actors in their negotiations with community institutions and other governments while using the interplay of regional negotiations to control the societal actors.

All the theoretical interpretations developed within the framework of neorealism, liberalism and global interdependence therefore have constructed explanations for integration in which integration is only a reaction to the interplay of national actors or the influence of transnational forces. In none of these theories, is it imagined that regionalism could have an influence on the actors that are a part of it.

We must turn to the constructivist research program to find this type of explanation. Indeed, constructivism (see, among others, Onuf 1998, 58–78; Wendt 2000; Checkel 1998, 324–348; Finnemore and Sikkink 2001, 391–416; Zehfuss 2002), particularly a number of central postulates that form the basis of international relations analysis, offers an alternative to the rationalist research program. Of interest to us is the postulate that involves the mutual constitution of the agents and structures that brings constructivists to conceive of international relations as a set of phenomena where agents and structures are mutually constituted in a spiral of identity formation. When applied to the study of regionalism, this conception of international relations helps to introduce an analytical link that had until now been overlooked by the specialist literature. This analytical link concerns the manner in which the regional structure influences the behavior of national actors that are part of this structure.

Our study is thus an attempt to empirically test this scarcely-explored analytical link. Indeed, we want to analyze the influence of a regional structure on the behavior of its member country governments. We have chosen to study NAFTA as an example of a regional structure because it has the distinctive feature of relying on norms rather than on the action of central institutions, as we will see further below. By choosing NAFTA for our case study, we want to see if our intuitions concerning a spill-over effect and the structure/agent link turn out to be true in the case of a regional structure with a low level of institutionalization. We also restricted our examination to NAFTA's influence over the foreign policy of its member countries. The demonstration that NAFTA influences this area of public policy, a subject on which the Agreement is generally silent, would surely constitute a vivid example of the power of a regional structure that has such a low level of institutionalization.

2. The Hypothesis of Convergence

Turning to the problem of how to actually conduct the analysis, the constructivist research program offers few clear leads on how to test research intuitions concerning the interrelation between structure and agent. Quite specific studies have been conducted on certain elements of the research program, such as the life cycle of norms (for instance, Checkel 1997, 473–495; Finnemore and Sikkink 1998, 887–917; Klotz 1995; Florini 1996, 363–389).[2] Carlsnaes also proposed a general model to study the agent-structure relationship in the field of foreign policy analysis (Carlsnaes 1992, 245–270). However, this model does not indicate how to operationalize the analysis of a relationship of influence between a structure and an agent, for instance, regionalism's influence over a governmental actor.

We must thus turn to other research programs and other fields of analysis to borrow the concepts and the method that will allow us to validate our conclusions about the influence of the regional structure. The concept of convergence is thus borrowed from the field of public policy. As Bennett points out (Bennett 1991, 215), the notion of convergence has gained in importance in political science and international relations work as a result of globalization and the upsurge of regionalism.

"The hypothesis of convergence" is based on the postulate that globalization leads to genuine change in the structures of the global economy. These changes in turn favor a harmonization of national institutions and practices (Radice 2000, 721).[3] We will apply the same reasoning with regard to regionalism, and state that the progressive strengthening of central institutions should create strong pressure in favor of a convergence of national policy preferences and regulation regimes in member countries.[4] This argument has also been formulated with regard to NAFTA without, however, ever being supported by a concrete demonstration (see,

---

2   At first glance, it may appear that the study proposed here is really an analysis of the life cycle of norms. This would be the case if we were analyzing the evolution of NAFTA's various norms. However, our study is different because it focuses exclusively on the impact of these norms on the behavior of the actors. Our unit of analysis is thus government behavior, rather than the regional norm.

3   This idea is closely related to the concept of "teaching" developed by Martha Finnemore. Finnemore established a distinction between "teaching" and "learning." The former refers to the pressure applied by central institutions to have norms enforced, while the latter refers to a process of emulation between the participants in a regime or institution. The approach favored in this book is more similar to the notion of "learning." (see Finnemore 1993, 565–597).

4   "Where regional economic integration is well advanced...we might realistically speak of certain convergent tendencies" (Hay 2000, 250).

for instance, McDougall 2000, 287–289; Gabriel, Jimenez, and Macdonald 2003; Milner and Keohane 1996, 4).

Despite a substantial body of literature on the subject and the growing importance of the notion of convergence in the study of comparative policy (Howlett 2000, 307), the study of convergence is not exempt from conceptual and methodological problems (Bennett 1991, 215; Bush and Jörgens 2004, 1; Seeliger 1996, 287). The definition of the concept itself and the manner of concretely studying it remain problematic. In order to clarify the concept and the method of analysis, we must build an operational concept based on notions that already exist in the literature.

By grouping these different elements, we can then define convergence as a process in which two or more elements of two or more actors' policies become similar after a defined period of time. These elements can be of a more specific nature, such as those identified by Bennett (goals, content, instruments, results, or particular style of a policy), or they can be more abstract, such as those used by Hay (*input*, policy, *output*, and convergence process) (Bennett 1991, 219; Hay 2000, 514).

Different processes can lead to a situation of convergence: emulation, networking between elites, harmonization, penetration (Bennett 1991, 220–228), and diffusion (Bush and Jörgens 2004, 6–9). However, according to Seeliger (Seeliger 1996, 289), the following important elements should be taken into account in analyzing convergence: the identification of a relatively specific time period, and the ability to measure, quantitatively or qualitatively, certain characteristics between T1 and T2. The analysis must thus clearly identify the differences and similarities in the actors' behavior – both discourse and actions – between the start and the end of the period.

It is also important to clearly distinguish between convergence and alignment. Convergence occurs when each actor modifies an initial position X and adopts a new position Y that is similar to that of the other actors by the end of the period being analyzed. However, alignment, not convergence, occurs if only one actor has modified its position to bring it in line with that of another. While both cases are interesting, the regional structure may or may not have been the cause of the phenomenon, as this analysis will show.

A research design for the study of policy convergence must thus answer three main questions:

(1) Which elements are converging?
   At what level is the convergence taking place? Discourse or behavior? In both cases, is it only the actors' preferences and expressed goals that are converging, or are the actors' actions and the instruments they set up also undergoing convergence?

(2) How is the convergence occurring?
   Firstly, is it convergence or alignment? Is the phenomenon total or partial, that is, is it only affecting one aspect of the issue? What instruments or means of action are being used by the actor to promote convergence?

(3) How can the convergence be explained? (Brigitte Unger and Frans van Warden 1995b, 1–35.)

If convergence (or alignment) is deemed to be taking place, which factors can explain the phenomenon? Since we are assuming that the NAFTA member countries are undergoing "learning" type of convergence, based on Finnemore's distinction in Note 17, it would be appropriate to determine if the phenomenon is the result of a process of emulation between actors, pressure from elites, or other reasons.

In order to provide valid answers to these questions, we must develop a research design that can clearly identify the variables in play, identify as specifically as possible the observation period for the study, and use case studies that are independent from each other (Seeliger 1996, 2999–304).

Based on the operational definition that we have just formulated, our study should be considered as an analysis of convergence through harmonization. What we are seeking to explain, our dependent variable, is the preferences and behaviors of the governments of the three NAFTA member countries in different fields of foreign policy. The explanatory factor for convergence, our independent variable, is NAFTA, considered here as an institution and a normative framework that may or may not influence the behavior of participating governments. The period used for the analysis varies according to the different case studies, but generally starts in 1995, after the implementation of NAFTA, and ends with the Special Summit of the Americas, which took place in January 2004 in Monterrey, Mexico.

Some may naturally object to the proposed analysis on the basis that observing convergence is not the same thing as proving the influence of regionalism on the behavior of government actors. Indeed, these are two distinct analytical approaches. The study of influence generally implies two ways of analyzing regionalism: a direct and an indirect approach. The first approach involves interviewing the actors to obtain the information that helps to determine whether there is the influence of regionalism. The second approach involves observing the evolution of the actors' position in order to establish whether there is a relationship between this evolution and the regional structure. The number of case studies used and the exploratory nature of this research study led us to favor the indirect approach.

3. NAFTA as a Particular Regional Institution

A substantial body of literature has now been produced on various aspects of NAFTA such as the economic impact of the treaty on the member countries (Bonser 1991; Bulmer-Thomas, Craske, and Serrano 1994; Globerman and Walker 1993; Weintraub 1997; Hufbauer, Schott and Grieco 2005), the contours of the agreement (Barry, Dickerson, and Gaisford 1995; Doran and Drischler 1996; Pastor 2001; Poitras 2001; Hakim and Litan 2002), the role of the political actors (Doran and Marchildon 1994; Pastor and Fernandez de Castro 1998) and the negotiation process that led to the signing of the accord (Bertrab 1997; Cameron and Tomlin 2000; Mayer 1998). This literature shows how, based on their central elements, NAFTA represents a very different model compared to that of the European Union. First of all, the initial objectives were not the same. While the Treaty of Rome immediately established a customs union (Moravcsik 1998, 86) and left open the possibility of a transfer to a common market or even an economic union, the three North American governments decided in favor of a free trade agreement. The signatories of NAFTA never intended that this more modest achievement could be transformed into something else. That was the case because NAFTA was the answer to a very different set of circumstances compared to those that led to the establishment of the European Economic Community. The deal that led to the accord basically consisted of a secured access to the US market in return for partial harmonization of macroeconomic policies (Mace and Bélanger 2004, 116, 107–126).

But the level of harmonization and the scope of NAFTA are both very far from those envisaged and achieved in the European Union. In the economic sector alone, it is true that NAFTA covers a wide variety of aspects related to trade and investment. But the constraints on national policies are much more limited than those resulting from the monetary union established by the Maastricht Treaty. Furthermore, until recently, North American integration has been limited to economic affairs. Links between trade and security started to be envisaged in the second half of the 1990s, but it is only since 2002 that more comprehensive agreements were signed. These agreements were not formally linked to NAFTA and it is only with the Security and Prosperity Partnership (SPP), signed in 2005, that the trade-security nexus was established. This coupling is not altogether clear and indeed the SPP has been criticized as being a "mishmash of disconnected and mostly trivial initiatives." (Paris 2007, A15) In the European Union, by contrast, the integration process is much wider as it contains also a common agricultural policy and measures related to various sectors such as justice, social affairs and defense.

In addition to the initial objectives and scope of the agreements, NAFTA and the European Union also differ considerably when it comes to regional institutions. In the case of NAFTA, many commentators, including Pastor, Abbott, (Abbott 2000, 519–547) and Bélanger (this book), all agree on the extremely limited political delegation existing in this institution in general, and more particularly, when compared to EU institutions such as the Parliament, the Council , the Court and the Commission.

A first glimpse of the limited character of the NAFTA institutions comes from examining the text of the agreement itself. This document of some 700 pages contains only one page on the Free Trade Commission and an additional page dealing with the Secretariat. Article 2001 describes the composition and the mandate of the Commission.[5] The Commission is formed of cabinet-level representatives (trade ministers of Canada and Mexico with the US Trade Representative) and meets at least once a year. On paper, the mandate of the Commission is very broad since it is tasked with supervising the implementation of the accord and overseeing its future development. It also supervises the work of committees and working groups and can resolve disputes that may arise regarding the interpretation or application of the agreement. But in the real-life functioning of NAFTA, as Robert Pastor rightly notes, the Commission is a virtual structure with no permanent location or staff (Pastor 2001, 73–74). Ministers do meet every year to assess the situation but the meetings are quite informal and few concrete decisions are reached.

---

5   The contents of Article 2001 and 2002 can be found on the website of the Department of Foreign Affairs and International Trade Canada at: http://www.international.gc.ca/NAFTA-Alena/chap20-en.asp?#Article2001.

The same can be said of the Secretariat, which in fact does not even exist. As specified in Article 2002, the "Secretariat" is composed of national sections. Each Section provides administrative assistance to the Commission and to the various panels and committees that may have to be created. Each Section receives funding from the corresponding government with the amount determined through informal discussions.

Consequently, in many ways North American integration under NAFTA is essentially a completely different phenomenon from the European integration process but particularly in relation to the role of regional institutions. In the European Union, institutions, and particularly the Commission, have acted as the main engine in the evolution of the integration process. This supranationalism is absent in North America where integration is characterized by what Grispun and Kreklewich have called "deficient institutionality" (Grispun and Kreklewiwch 1999).

This being the case, in what ways can an institution like NAFTA become a source of policy convergence for its member countries? There are two possible processes at work. The first one relates to norms. As Bernier and Roy have noted, the refusal of the NAFTA members to include any form of supranationalism in the integration process made it necessary to devise an agreement which was both extremely precise in its wording and comprehensive in terms of subject matter (Bernier and Roy 1999, 72–73). This means that it is the treaty itself that becomes a normative order, acting as a constraint on the national governments in some policy sectors.

But norms are not the only source of influence. Even if there are no supranational institutions, the decisions of the NAFTA arbitral panels and the work of the various committees and working groups can also create a pressure toward policy harmonization. The overall result, as John McDougall has suggested, is that the combination of the regional normative order and the administrative practices that occurred afterwards could very well create a strong policy convergence effect (McDougall 2000, 280–290). This combination is a distinctive feature of the North American integration model, distinguishing it from the supranational model of the European Union. A model that could very well lead, according to McDougall, to "another form of political integration, and by a different process" (McDougall 2000, 290).

Political integration, however, is not the subject matter of this book. Rather, we want to examine the assumption that an integration model with such "deficient institutionality" as the NAFTA model could, nevertheless, result in a policy convergence effect among the participating governments. Since NAFTA is a free trade agreement, the assumption of a certain convergence in matters of national economic policies does not seem to be too far-fetched. The task of demonstrating a possible convergence effect on foreign policy behavior, on the other hand, is much more of a challenge. This is the very challenge that the contributors to this book will take up in the following pages.

4. Selected Foreign Policy Issues

The case studies chosen for this analysis naturally respond to the logic of analytical construction. As we have just stated, the decision to use only foreign policy cases shows our willingness to test to the maximum our research intuition concerning the influence of an integration process with "deficient institutionality" such as NAFTA on the behavior of its member states. Since some researchers have already suggested that NAFTA has become a sort of "external constitution" for its member countries (Clarkson 2004, 198–228), it is plausible that this integration process has had an impact on the member countries' national economic policies. However, there is less basis to think that it has had an impact on foreign policy behavior. The demonstration of such an impact would imply that NAFTA is a strong institution and this is precisely the hypothesis that we seek to test in this book.

Among the possible range of foreign policy issues, we chose three categories of cases that represent a gradation related to the NAFTA theme. The first category contains case studies of governments' trade policy preferences. Since this sector is closest to the themes covered by NAFTA, naturally it is here that we would expect to find the greatest convergence between the preferences expressed by Canada, the United States and Mexico since the pressure to harmonize would have been strongest.

In Chapter 1, Gordon Mace and Louis Bélanger will make a comparative analysis of the preferences of these three governments with regard to the negotiations for the implementation of a Free Trade Area of the Americas (FTAA). Among the different issues discussed by the 34 governments participating in the negotiations, the authors will focus on three that are key to the North-South dimension of the regional trade agenda: the situation of small economies, agriculture and trade in services. As explained by the authors, these three issues are extremely relevant since the result of the negotiations in these sectors will have enormous consequences for the trade relations between advanced industrial economies and emerging economies. Also, given the differences between the economic development of Mexico on the one hand and Canada and the United States on the other, these issues are also very relevant to the theme of convergence since they oppose the rationality of NAFTA membership to that of economic development.

In Chapter 2, Louis Bélanger will also examine the trade preferences of NAFTA member countries, but this time with regard to hemispheric and transatlantic relations. In the latter case, the author will analyze the different options for trade liberalization with Europe made available to the three North American governments after the signing of NAFTA. In the case of hemispheric relations, it is mainly the preferences of the governments with regard to the FTAA project as a whole that will be studied. By simultaneously studying these two cases, Bélanger will be able to examine how Canada and Mexico in particular have used these policy spaces to externalize their need for voice opportunities.

In the specific context of North America, the economy and trade are becoming increasingly connected. This has of course been the case since the tragic events of September 11, 2001, but the linkage existed well before, with security agreements signed in the latter half of the 1990s. With regard to the North American dynamic,

September 2001 simply gave enormous weight to a problem that had existed since the signing of NAFTA and which had started attracting more attention. The problem consisted in determining how to ensure the preservation and growth of trade flows while at the same time protecting North America from threats to its security. Given the close link between security and trade, it is easy to imagine that security policies would constitute a second sector in which NAFTA would influence the preferences of the three North American governments.

We have thus chosen two case studies of the security policies of Canada, Mexico and the United States. Nelson Michaud will focus on the three governments' broad security and defense policies, while Stéphane Roussel, Michel Fortmann and Martin Duplantis will deal more with border protection and the issue of the security perimeter. In Chapter 3, Michaud will offer a comparative analysis of the three bilateral security and defense relationships that frame and give meaning to the security dynamic in North America. After reviewing the NAFTA provisions that deal with security, the author will describe the evolution of each one of the security relationships in the North American context. By studying these policies and mechanisms, Michaud will evaluate the progress of multilateralism as it relates to a possible influence of NAFTA.

In Chapter 4, Roussel, Fortmann and Duplantis will study the behavior of the three governments with regard to non-military security. More focused on the deeper relationship between Canada and the United States, this chapter will draw on the concept of public security and will thus deal more specifically with the policing function of the three North American states. The authors will show that a process of socialization to increased securitization was already underway before September 2001 and will analyze its link with NAFTA.

Beyond trade and security policies, regional institutions such as NAFTA can also have a convergence effect in foreign policy fields that are less related to free trade. This phenomenon is not exclusive to NAFTA, since other institutions, like MERCOSUR for instance, have established a link between trade and democracy. We thus formed a third category, which includes cases of foreign policy issues that are far removed from those covered by NAFTA. If we succeed in identifying a convergence between the national preferences in each of these cases, and linking this convergence to NAFTA's influence, we will thus have shown that the integration process can genuinely extend its influence beyond its specific sphere of action.

Three cases were chosen for this category. Chapter 5 will look at the issue of democracy and human rights. In this chapter, Jean-Philippe Thérien will compare the foreign policies of Canada, Mexico and the United States in relation to an issue that has been very prominent in the inter-American agenda since the early 1990s. In examining the evolution of the inter-American regime of citizenship, Thérien will analyze the preferences of the three North American governments with regard to major instruments for the promotion of democracy before and after the signing of NAFTA in 1994. The examination of the three governments' foreign policies will then be compared with the development of NAFTA.

Chapter 6 will deal with the preferences of North American governments with regard to the inter-American anti-drug cooperation strategy. The author of this chapter, Guillermo Aureano, will first review the construction of the inter-American drug control system. He will examine some of the main mechanisms, including the Multilateral Evaluation Mechanism (MEM), as well as Plan Colombia, set up by the United States. In each case, the author will present the context of the different measures and will analyze the preferences of the three North American governments in order to determine whether or not NAFTA has had an effect on them.

Finally, Chapter 7 will closely examine the case of Cuba. As is known, Cuba has long been a bone of contention in the relations between the United States on the one hand, and Canada and Mexico on the other, since the two latter countries have for many years maintained a policy favorable to Cuba. In this chapter, Hugo Loiseau will first make a comparative analysis of the diplomatic relations of the three countries with the Cuban regime, before and after NAFTA. He will show how each government has positioned its policy, in particular with regard to the key issue of democratization. Loiseau will further seek to explain the reasoning behind these positions. As was done in previous chapters, the author will then analyze the role of NAFTA as a potential convergence factor.

All these studies will provide a comparative analysis that is admittedly incomplete, since it does not cover every field of foreign policy, but that will nonetheless prove interesting by virtue of the issues that have been addressed. The diversity of these issues will make for a rich and fruitful comparative analysis. Finally, in the last chapter, conclusions will be drawn with regard to the phenomenon of convergence in the preferences of the three governments, but especially, with regard to a link between this convergence and the existence of NAFTA.

Chapter 1

Convergence or Divergence Effects? NAFTA and State Preferences Towards the FTAA

Gordon Mace and Louis Bélanger[1]

Even though negotiations for the establishment of a Free Trade Area of the Americas (FTAA) have now been stalled for more than three years, the FTAA negotiations remain an interesting case study for examining NAFTA's impact on the policy preferences of its member governments. One reason is that the initial intention of the US government, shared to a point by its Canadian counterpart, was to use the NAFTA as a model for the future FTAA.[2] Another reason is that among the foreign policy issues included in this book, the FTAA negotiations constitute the theme most closely related to the content of the NAFTA. Consequently, it is here that a potential convergence effect should be the most robust because we are dealing more or less with the same economic agenda. The assumption therefore is that governments' preferences should, logically, be made more explicit and observable in the context of these trade negotiations than on issues such as drug control or democracy for example.

A third reason for selecting this theme is related to the fundamental feature of the FTAA negotiations which is the profound asymmetry (Briceno Ruiz 2001, 396–402) between the countries participating in the process. Suffice it to mention that the FTAA project includes two member countries of the G8, the United States and Canada, with a GDP per head of more than $24,000, a cluster of mid-level countries with a GDP per head ranging from $3,030 (Brazil) to $6,110 (Mexico) and $7,550 (Argentina) (Economist Intelligence Unit 2002, 79–80), and a group of very small economies with a GDP per head of less than $900.[3] This unique and complex situation which brings together two countries of the first world and a host

1   The authors would like to thank their research assistants Nathalie Watts and Nicolas Lesieur for their work at data gathering and analysis. They would also like to express their gratitude to the Social Sciences and Humanities Research Council of Canada and the Fonds québécois de recherche sur la société et la culture for their generous funding of this research program.
2   Washington had to change its position at the opening of the official negotiations in 1998.

3   Another way to put it is by stating that the US GNP is around 10 times that of Brazil, 22 times that of Mexico, almost 100 times that of Venezuela and 4 times that of the region as a whole (see Smith 1999, 41).

of semi-industrialized and low-income countries creates significant challenges for the governments involved in the process, and particularly for the governments of North America when it comes to dealing with problems of disparity and unequal development.

This central feature of the FTAA project explains our selection of cases when examining the convergence issue in North American governmental policies in the FTAA negotiations. We have selected three case studies in which we will examine the policy proposals of Canada, Mexico and the US. These are: the situation of small economies, agriculture, and trade in services. As will be explained later on in the paper, the treatment of each of these elements in a multilateral trading negotiation such as that of the FTAA will have enormous consequences on a trade relationship involving advanced industrial economies and emerging and less-developed ones.

Our study follows closely the analytical framework just presented in the introduction of the book. According to that framework, a study of policy convergence must be able to answer at least three central questions: (1) what converges?; (2) how does convergence take place?; and (3) why does it occur? (Unger and van Waarden 1995, 1–35 cited in Howlett 2000, 307.) In order to provide answers to these questions, we use a research design that can be summarized in the following way. The dependent variable is the policy preferences of the three member governments of the NAFTA in relation to the FTAA which we consider as a foreign policy issue. Our independent variable is the NAFTA envisaged here as an institution as well as a normative framework that may or may not act as a constraint for the behavior of each participating government. The time period for this study starts in December 1994 when the FTAA project was announced during the first Summit of the Americas and ends in January 2004 at the Special Summit of the Americas held in Monterrey.

In the following sections of the chapter, we discuss each of the three case studies selected for the analysis. We adopt a presentation which is similar for the treatment of each element. First, we try to summarize the basic significance of each case as it is discussed in the framework of the FTAA. Then we track the evolution of the position of each of the three North American governments and we compare them. Finally, we try to establish the degree of convergence among the three NAFTA countries in relation with each case study and we try to provide a provisional assessment regarding the influence of the NAFTA factor in relation to the degree of convergence arrived at.

The Situation of the Small Economies

Before getting to the analysis of the specific case studies, a few words are necessary concerning the general attitude of the three NAFTA governments concerning the FTAA project as a whole. It is well documented that both the United States and Canada have always strongly supported the idea of a comprehensive and inclusive FTAA but the government of Mexico never came out strongly and officially in favor of the FTAA prior to January 2004. During all the pre-negotiation phase as well as in the course of the negotiations themselves, the Mexican government always kept a low profile and never took firmly position in favor of the FTAA. It is only at the Monterrey Summit that Mexican President Vincente Fox officially declared that Mexico fully supported the FTAA and was in favor of an inclusive agreement adopted in conformity with the initial calendar (Pansza 2004, 3A).[4]

Although it came late, this declaration of support was important in the sense that it finally brought Mexico in line with the position of its two neighbors concerning the FTAA project at least prior to the Trade Ministerial of November 2003. However it is at this meeting that the US government decided to modify its position in the face of Brazilian opposition. At Miami in November 2003, Washington did not reduce its support for the FTAA but decided to accept a less comprehensive and less inclusive version of the initial project. As a result, one could conclude that the general positioning of the three governements towards the FTAA project after November 2003 was still not converging at least in what concerns the scope of the project.

Coming now to the situation of the small economies, the fundamental problem of small economies participating in *laissez-faire* free trade areas (FTA), as identified many years ago,[5] is the near impossibility to compete with the much larger and more diversified economies participating in the same FTAs. Large economies, because of bigger markets, more-developed business firms and better access to capital, will naturally tend to reap most of the benefits of an FTA as economic activity will tend to concentrate there. As a consequence, the smaller economies lose ground and asymmetry grows.

This situation was clearly evident in one of the first integration schemes established in Latin America, the Latin American Free Trade Association (LAFTA).[6] As a way to help solve this problem, the United Nations Conference on Trade and Development (UNCTAD) adopted the principle of special and differential treatment at its 1964 conference.[7] A central feature of the North-South dialogue of the 1960s and 1970s, what came to be known as the principle of preferential treatment, was at the basis of the adoption of the Generalized System of Preferences (GSP) in 1968 (SELA 1997a). At the subregional level, particularly in Latin America and Europe, preferential treatment became an important element of integration processes taking the form of various measures related to tariff and nontariff barriers, safeguards, rules of origin, financial and technical assistance, investments and services.[8] Measures of preferential treatment are still present in the MERCOSUR and in the remodelled integration processes of CARICOM and the Comunidad Andina.

---

4 Mexico's support for the FTAA was again voiced strongly at the Mar del Plata Summit in November 2005.

5 See, among others, Andrew Axline (Axline 1977, 83–105) and Lynn Mytelka (Mytelka 1979, chapter 1).

6 LAFTA was established in 1960 and benefited mostly to Argentina, Brazil and Mexico, the big three. It was moribond less than 5 years after its creation, after being under attack by Chile, Colombia and other mid-level countries, and was transformed into the Asociacion latino-americana de integracion (ALADI) in 1980 which did not give much better results.

7 The UNCTAD was established in 1963 under the leadership of Raoul Prebisch, a foremost Latin American economist and founding father of the 'structuralist school' in Latin America.

8 For a more complete treatment, see Fernanda Masi (Masi 2001) and SELA (SELA 2001; SELA 1997b).

At the international level, the situation started to change in the 1980s with the adoption by the United States government of the concept of 'reciprocity' (Cline 1982; Bhagwati and Patrick 1990). In adopting reciprocity, the Reagan Administration was targeting more Japan and the European Economic Community (now EU, the European Union) than Third World countries. Nevertheless, reciprocity was adopted as the general principle governing GATT/WTO multilateral negotiations starting with the Uruguay Round and, in so doing, displaced preferential treatment as the dominant feature of international trade at least concerning trade with developing countries (SELA 1997a).

The philosophy of reciprocity became therefore the governing principle of the international trade scene from the early 1990s on. From the Uruguay Round to the APEC to the NAFTA, a new generation of trading arrangements was appearing characterized by the absence of measures of preferential treatment. Even in the South American MERCOSUR, the measures of preferential treatment were extremely limited dealing almost exclusively with longer timetables.

Coming now to the FTAA, it was clear that the initial attitude of the NAFTA governments would not be very favorable to the idea of the special treatment despite the Summit of Miami's Declaration of Principles acknowledging '...the wide differences in the levels of development and size of economies existing in our Hemisphere'. The initial US opposition to discuss preferential treatment in the framework of the FTAA was understandable since Washington had been advocating the principle of reciprocity for more than ten years. The US government was also in the process of replacing preferential trade treatment with tariff reciprocity as the foundation of its Caribbean policy (Grant 2000, 2). Finally, the US government opposed all form of special treatment for Mexico in the NAFTA negotiations even in the area of trade in services where the Mexican negotiators wanted to have the asymmetrical position of Mexico recognized (Cameron and Tomlin 2000, 94; Masi 2001, 7). Consequently, it would have been illogical at the time for the United States to accept a principle for the FTAA that it had just refused in the NAFTA framework. US opposition to formal inclusion of special treatment in the FTAA negotiations will be upheld at least until the Santiago Summit of 1998 where again US negotiators will oppose acceptance of special treatment for smaller economies as a separate area of negotiation (Girvan 2000, 84).

Canada's position was also relatively clear from the start and was reiterated in the March 2000 response made by the government to a report tabled by the Permanent Committee of the House of Commons on Foreign Affairs and International Trade. Ottawa's position was the following: 'Canada's view is that all FTAA signatories must assume the same rights and obligations. However, we recognize the particular challenges of smaller economies and support the provision of technical assistance, and, on a case-by-case basis, the inclusion of measures in the FTAA to ease the transition of smaller economies, provided these are specific and time-limited' (http://www.dfait-maeci.gc.ca/tna-nac/e-comm-summ-e.asp). The insistence on the case-by-case and on the specific and time-limited character of the measures that might be considered indicated that the Canadian government was in favor of applying the general principle of reciprocity in the framework of the FTAA and refused to accept any reference to special treatment as a permanent, structural component of the eventual agreement. Ottawa was willing to negotiate some measures in favor of the smaller economies but only on a transitory basis. One reason for this attitude had to do with the difficulty of defining the concept of 'small economy'. Depending on the criteria used, 26 of the 34 countries taking part in the FTAA negotiations could be considered as smaller economies (FOCAL 2000, 4) and the burden could become heavy for a country like Canada depending on the nature and scope of the measures eventually adopted.

The Mexican government, for its part, did not have a clear and well-knowned position on this subject prior to 2001. The initial Mexican reaction was an extremely cautious one and was expressed by the Secretary of Commerce, Jaime Serra Puche, when he said that Mexico had 'rational and legitimate concerns' about establishing an FTAA on the basis of a NAFTA expansion to all the countries of the Americas (except Cuba) not considering their level of development. Some countries wouldn't fit on that basis (as reported in Gonzalez and Chabat 1996, 49). It is true that the Mexican government had offered some form of financial special treatment to Central American countries through the San Jose Agreement but that agreement was signed in the mid-1980s. The FTAs that Mexico has concluded since the mid-1990s however, including those with the small Central American economies such as Costa Rica and Nicaragua, are modelled on the NAFTA and therefore contain limited measures of special treatment (Briceno 2001, 400). The message sent by these FTAs was that Mexico, as was the case for Canada and the US, supported the principle of reciprocity for trade relations in the Americas. This absence of a clear position on the part of the Mexican government concerning preferential treatment in the early stages of the FTAA negotiations must be understood in the context of Mexico's preference for the current institutional design of economic integration in the Americas. Without an FTAA, Mexico would find itself at the center of a complex of trade agreements that would establish the country as a bridge for economic relations between North and South America (see Figure A3 in Wilkie, Contreras, and Komisaruk 1995, 1190). An envious location compared to being simply a member of the FTAA. Which would explain that Mexico has not taken a 'very proactive role' (Keith 2002, 11) or, in the opinion of some, has 'done little to dispel the perception that it was playing a 'spoiler' strategy' (Mackay 2002, 12).

Things started to change in 1998 with the establishment of the Consultative Group on Smaller Economies at the San Jose Trade Ministerial but more so with the advocacy by Caribbean governments in favor of officially including the theme of preferential treatment for smaller economies in the upcoming discussions. In addition to the difficulties related to size and lack of resources and expertise, the Caribbean governments underlined the problems resulting from the generalization of the principle of reciprocity in international trading arrangements and the negative effect this would have on many sectors of the Caribbean economies such as banana for example. In turn, these apprehended economic difficulties would impact severely on local governments' capacities to deal with increasingly important problems such as illegal migration, environmental damage and organized crime responsible for increasing narcotics and weapons trafficking (Clissold 1998, 3–5).

This campaign brought the CARICOM member countries, supported by the Comunidad Andina, to ask that the Trade Negotiation Committee include preferential treatment as an official theme in its discussions. The proposition was accepted by the other participating governments at the vice-ministerial meeting of April 2000 after a substantial discussion. Preferential treatment was also introduced officially as an object of discussion in the Declaration following the Toronto Trade Ministerial of 1999. Finally, the Quebec Summit of April 2001 reaffirmed the need to take into consideration the various levels of development of member countries and specific measures were included in the Plan of Action to that effect. But a CARICOM proposal for the creation of a regional investment fund was not accepted.

The first concrete collective measure following the engagement taken at the Quebec Summit was the Hemispheric Cooperation Program (HCP) proposed by the United States and accepted by the participating governments at the Quito Trade Ministerial of November 2002. The HCP is a trade capacity-building program implying essentially technical assistance ($140 millions in 2003) to help governments negotiate the FTAA, to help them comply with the trade commitments agreed, and to help them 'benefit from free trade' (Miller 2002). The HCP was certainly a noteworthy effort originating from Washington but it was a limited effort given the importance of the problem.[9] It was also criticized because it was not open only to smaller economies and it would be administered mostly by US agencies. So it is difficult to see how the HCP would make a big difference particularly after the FTAA is in place.

The Bush Administration also took two unilateral steps. The first was the signing of the Trade Act of 2002 which renewed the Generalized System of Preferences enabling 3,500 products from 140 developing economies to enter the US free of duties. The Act also expanded the Caribbean Trade Partnership Act by liberalizing apparel provisions and it extended and augmented the Andean Trade Preference Act whose list of duty free products was augmented to some 6,300 (Franco 2002; Zoellick 2002, 10). The other initiative was Washington's unilateral offer of February 2003 in preparation for the Miami Trade Ministerial that the US Administration wanted to see serve as springboard for the last stretch of the negotiations. The proposal included offers in five areas but two concern more directly the smaller economies. As to what pertains to trade in goods, the United States government was proposing to eliminate all tariffs by 2015 and offered immediate, reciprocal elimination of tariffs in sectors such as chemicals, construction and mining, environmental products, steel, and medical equipment. For smaller economies, the US government proposed to open its market faster so that members of CARICOM would obtain immediately duty-free status for 91 percent of their exports to the United States. The figure would be 69 percent for Central America, 61 percent for the Andean countries and 58 percent for the MERCOSUR countries (Government of the United States – United States Trade Representative 2003). The proposal concerning agricultural trade, for its part, also took into account the different levels of development of FTAA members. The CARICOM countries for instance would immediately have 85 percent of their agricultural trade with the US duty-free.

---

9   According to Brazil's Ambassador to the United States, Rubens Barbosa, a dozen or so governements did not participate to all the phases of the FTAA negotiations because of the costs involved and the lack of expertise (Monsen 2002).

There was apparently no reaction on the part of the Canadian government to the US offer of February 2003 but, as said before, Canada did agree to the establisment of the HCP at the Quito Trade Ministerial. Furthermore, Ottawa did support Jamaica's demand for the establishment of an 'adjustment fund' to help smaller economies (*The Jamaica Gleaner* 2001) and accepted that these countries could take more than a decade to eliminate their tariff barriers (http://www.dfait-marci.gc.ca/tna-nac/FTAAreport-full.fr.asp).

These gestures illustrated that the Canadian position had shifted slightly in favor of more openness towards the situation of the smaller economies. But Canada was still supporting the entrenchment of the principle of reciprocity and would accept to negotiate some measures of special treatment only on an *ad hoc* basis thereby refusing to institutionalize the preferential treatment in the FTAA. If this position is maintained to the end, it will represent a truly important change in Canadian foreign policy towards the developing countries as compared to the Canadian attitude at the time of the North-South dialogue ot the 1970s.

In the case of Mexico, the change in regime following the 2000 election has apparently brought some modification to the Mexican position regarding preferential treatment. The clearest signal came at the Quebec Summit of April 2001, only a few months after Vicente Fox came into office, when the new Mexican President called for the establishment of a 'social cohesion fund' (*La Jornada* 2001). Monies for the fund would come from a percentage of annual military spending by each national government. This proposal was not precisely linked to the situation of the smaller economies in the framework of the eventual FTAA but they would clearly be the main beneficiaries of such a fund. The Fox government also supported the creation of the HCP but it was at the same time, and until very recently, a staunch and vocal supporter of the NAFTA and, by extension, of the principle of reciprocity.

So what to think of all this? The partial conclusion is that there has been a small but perceptible change in the position of the three NAFTA countries with regards to the position of the smaller economies in the FTAA framework. Up to 1999, the three governments were strong advocates of the principle of reciprocity and opposed whatever institutionalized measures of preferential treatment for the low-income countries of the region. Since the Toronto Trade Ministerial of November 1999, there appeared to be a certain openness on the part of the three countries with regard to special treatment as each governement proposed or supported measures in that sense. What remains uncertain concerns the status of these measures and what would be the final equilibrium point for the FTAA on the continuum between reciprocity and preferential treatment.

This said there was a change in position toward a common acceptance of some form of special treatment and this change occurred for all three NAFTA governments. Was there a NAFTA effect that could explain this common trajectory? On the basis of the information available, it is clear that there was no alliance or common negotiation strategy on the part of the three countries as the Mexican government had refused the constitution of a NAFTA bloc during the prenegotiation phase of the FTAA. But looking at the negotiation process itself and taking into consideration the bilateral FTAs that all three governments have concluded with hemispheric partners since 1994, it is evident that a NAFTA effect does exists in the sense of a normative framework acting as a guide for action. This is because the level of obligation and precision of the NAFTA is so high[10] that it becomes difficult for its member governments to negotiate anything that would be incompatible with NAFTA provisions without creating significant harmonization problems.

But at the same time there was a strategic positioning factor at play that was most evident in the case of the United States and Mexico. With regards to the United States, it is clear that Washington had to adjust its bargaining position in relation to the situation in the multilateral trade negotiation and particularly to the agenda of the Doha Round. This implies not only a necessary harmonization in terms of contents but it has also a strategic component in terms of the larger negotiations between the US, the EU and Japan. Concerning Mexico, there is first of all a question of image as the government will try to use the FTAA negotiations to re-position Mexico as a leader in Latin America. This implied shaking off a North American label applied to Mexico as a result of the signing of NAFTA and, secondly, not leaving the field open to Brazilian influence. But maybe more importantly, the Mexican government may have wanted to use the FTAA negotiations to sort of renegotiate some aspects of the NAFTA in relation to which Mexico had to make costly concessions because of its limited bargaining power. But before drawing too firm conclusions, let us see what is the situation in the areas of agriculture and services.

Trade in Agriculture

Agriculture still represents a significant component of international trade. For the United States alone, agricultural exports generated $57 billion in direct revenues in fiscal year 2003 plus $84 billion in related economic activities such as packaging, transport marketing. One in three acres in the US is planted for export with the result that the United States, dollar for dollar, exports more wheat than coal, more fruits and vegetables than household appliances, more meat than steel, and more corn than cosmetics. Every $1 billion in exports creates 15,000 thousand jobs and agricultural exports in developing country markets are expected to grow faster than elsewhere because of larger increases in income. What is more, the proportion of high-value products in this sector for US exports is now higher than the value of bulk commodity shipments (Government of the United States 2002d; Government of the United States 2003d).

At the same time, agricultural production is one of the most protected in the world. The EU provides more than $60 billion in domestic support while US subsidies for agricultural production reached a historical high of $30 billion in 2000 which represents 60 percent of all the revenues generated by agriculture in the United States. The EU and the United States also use export subsidies in a significant way and the global tariff for imports of agricultural goods worlwide is 62 percent. In addition, governments also make extensive use of non-tariff barriers such as sanitary and phytosanitary measures along with other 'trade remedies' (Jank 2001; Government of the United States 2002d).

---

10 On this point see the excellent analysis in Frederick Abbott (Abbott 2000, 519–547).

The current situation in world agriculture results in part of the acceptance by the GATT of a general derogation to its article XI following a demand by the United States in 1955. The EEC would follow later on and all this was accepted on the basis of a general assumption in relation to food security. Agriculture was an economic sector different from the others and national governments had the right to protect their population against food dependance. This is why the first agreement on agriculture in the GATT/WTO regime came only during the Uruguay Round of negotiations as a result mostly of the pressure imposed by the Cairns Group (see for example Cooper, Higgott, and Nossal 1993, chapter 3). An agreement that came after difficult negotiations and which left many items open for discussion for the current Doha Round of multilateral trade negotiations.

Trade in agriculture is also very important in the Western Hemisphere which has replaced Asia in 2002 as the top destination for US food and agricultural exports. But it is also an extremely contentious subject pitting mostly the United States against its hemispheric partners especially, but not only, the smaller economies where agriculture still dominates the local economy and where production is limited to one or two items. Essentially, the problem is one of market access where the smaller economies, but also Brazil and other larger countries, accuse the United States of extensive use of protectionist measures, mainly anti-dumping measures, to severely restrict access to its market for agricultural products coming from the rest of the region.

This problem has first been tackled in the framework of the Canada-US Free Trade Agreement (CUSTA) of 1988 whose main provisions were the elimination of agricultural tariffs between the two countries over a ten-year period and the prohibition of use of export subsidies in bilateral trade (although preserving the Canadian system of supply management and marketing boards) (Doern and Tomlin 1991, 76–77). It was then included in the negotiations of the NAFTA which, in the case of agriculture, resulted more or less in three separate bilateral agreement. The provisions that concerned the Canada-United States relationship were basically the same as those included in the CUSTA. The portion of the agreement dealing with the Mexico-US relationship essentially created five categories of products for trade liberalization: immediate liberalization which concerns 57 percent of agricultural trade between the two countries, five-year transition (6 percent of bilateral trade), ten-year transition (23 percent), fifteen-year transition (1 percent of bilateral trade) and highly-and-super-sensitive products. Rules of origin apply the *de minimis* rule which allows a product to benefit from free trade within NAFTA if less than 7 percent of the value of the product is made up of foreign ingredients. Finally, a special safeguard provision is included to protect against the damaging effects of import 'surges' (Avery 1996, 113–115). A noteworthy remark is that the NAFTA provides a special treatment for Canada and the United States in relation to exports of grains to the Mexican market. Because Mexico produces little grains of its own, it imposes a tariff of only 15 percent (to be gradually reduced to zero) for wheat coming from its NAFTA partners compared to 67 percent for other suppliers (Goldstein 2001).

This said, what is at stake when it comes to agriculture in the FTAA negotiations and how did the three NAFTA governments position themselves on this issue? The main issue was one of agenda setting: will the negotiation focus exclusively on market access or will it deal also with trade-distorting measures?

The first concrete US proposal concerning agriculture in the framework of the FTAA came only in February 2003. The proposal dealt basically with market access. The United States proposed four timelines for liberalization almost similar to what exists in the NAFTA: immediate, up to five years, up to ten years and beyond ten years for sensible products such as sugar and oranges. No products were excluded from the negotiation and Washington also proposed to eliminate non-tariff barriers, to reduce regulations and to increase transparency in food safety and customs procedures. In the eventuality that such a proposal be accepted, 56 percent of agricultural imports from the Hemisphere would be duty-free immediately when the FTAA took effect and, in the case of the CARICOM countries, the percentage would be as high as 85 percent (Government of the United States – United States Trade Representative 2003; Government of the United States 2003c).

The US proposal to its FTAA partners was essentially a market access proposition and did not include offers on export subsidies, export taxes, and trade-distorting subsidies (for domestic support) that were included in the US 2002 proposal to the WTO for global agricultural trade reform (Government of the United States 2003b; Government of the United States 2002b). Quite clearly, the US government considered that the major battle concerning trade subsidies and trade remedies would be fought with the EU and the appropriate forum for that is the WTO (Horlick and Palmer 2001).

The Canadian government has stated that its position in the FTAA negotiations on agriculture is exactly the same as the initial position that Ottawa made public in August 1999 for the upcoming negotiation at the WTO. Canada would first of all seek greater market access essentially through tariff reduction. The government would also seek an agreement to eliminate all export subsidies and make sure that these are not replaced by other types of governmental programs such as exports credits and promotion and development of export markets. As to what pertains to domestic support, Canada was seeking the elimination or the maximum reduction possible of all support measures to domestic production and would ask for a ceiling concerning all types of support for domestic production. Finally, the Canadian government was proposing that the use of all sanitary and phytosanitary measures measures should be based on scientific norms and international standards. It should be noted also that Ottawa demanded that state commercialization monopolies be maintained with rules of functioning compatible with the rules concerning market access.[11] This goes against the position of the US government who wants these monopolies dismantled.

When it comes to FTAA negotiations on agriculture, the Mexican negotiation strategy is one of the most interesting to watch. In a 1997 trade policy review on Mexico, the WTO recognized that the economic liberalization program put in place

---

11 The Canadian proposition for the chapter on agriculture in the framework of the FTAA can be found at http://www.dfait-maeci.gc.ca/tna-nac/ftaa_neg-f.asp. For the Canadian proposal on agriculture at the WTO, see Government of Canada (Government of Canada 1999).

by the Mexican government had resulted in major adjustments in the agricultural sector. All non-tariff measures have been converted into tariffs or tariff quotas as required by NAFTA and the WTO while state subsidies for domestic production were reduced (*SICE Foreign Trade Information System* 1997). These changes may explain a certain convergence between the Mexican and Canadian position on agriculture at the WTO concerning the elimination of export subsidies, the use of sanitary and phytosanitary measures and the compatibility of state support for domestic production with commitments made in the framework of the WTO. On the other hand, the Mexican position differed from the Canadian one with respect to the support given by Mexico to preferential treatment in favor of less-developed countries.[12]

The Mexican government did not table any document stating its position on agriculture in the framework of the FTAA negotiations. But the chances are that the ambiguity existing in Mexico's WTO position will be even more apparent in the FTAA negotiations. The reason is that the Mexican agricultural community has been more and more critical of NAFTA's provisions on agriculture and their impact on the Mexican farmlands. Mexican farmers were hopeful that the NAFTA would open the US market for their products. They found to their dismay that while US grains exports to Mexico were growing steadily Mexican exports of tomatoes and sugar to the United States were the object of trade restriction mesures on the part of the US government. The Mexican agricultural community also believed that US growers encouraged discriminatory marketing order schemes and that sanitary and phytosanitary measures were applied for protectionist purposes only (see Huenemann 2001, 3–4).

This is why political opposition to the agricultural provisions of the NAFTA has mounted significantly in Mexico during the past two years. In retaliation to US action, Mexican producers have been using anti dumping measures more frequently (Weintraub 2003, 3). At the beginning of 2003, agricultural organizations of the Permanent Agricultural Congress (CAP) and 15 of the 24 states' Secretaries for Agriculture have called for the renegotiation of the agricultural provisions of the NAFTA (*Reforma* 2003a; *La Insignia* 2003). Despite Canada's formal refusal to reopen the NAFTA for negotiation (*Reforma* 2003b) and President Fox's unwillingness to do so (Reforma 2003c), the CAP organizations maintained their demands for renegotiation or suspension of the agricultural provisions of the NAFTA. In reply, Mexico's Secretary for the Economy, Fernando Canales Clariond, said that new mechanisms were needed inside or outside the NAFTA framework. In the meantime, he stated that the Mexican government would not hesitate to use 'aggressively' defensive measures such as safeguards and anti dumping measures (*El Economista* 2003). Consequently, the internal pressure for improvement of the agricultural situation was so strong in Mexico that it was logical to expect that the Fox Administration would use the FTAA negotiations to clarify rules and redress what was perceived as negative effects of the NAFTA. Such an eventuality would put Mexico in direct opposition to the United States.

---

12 The Mexican position at the WTO can be found at: http://www.wto.org/spanish/tratop_s/agri_s/ngw138_s.doc.

Therefore, it is clear that the NAFTA effect was at play in the positionning of the three NAFTA countries in relation to negotiations on agriculture in the FTAA framework. But it played differently for each government and not in the sense of convergence. The case of Canada is the most straightforward in the sense that the major influence appears to be compatibility of FTAA rules with the NAFTA-WTO normative framework. Canada's main goal in relation to trade in agriculture is to improve market access worlwide while at the same time preserving state monopolies regulating internal production. The strategy is harmonization of Canadian positions in both FTAA and WTO negotiating forums which means that Ottawa was also pushing for reduction of export subsidies for domestic production in the framework of the FTAA.

The US situation was naturally more complex with a high stakes bargaining strategy given that the United States and the EU are the two most important players in this area. More than in the case of Canada, Washington used the NAFTA-WTO normative framework as a guide for FTAA negotiations. The US government was willing to discuss all aspects related to market access in the FTAA negotiations but wanted to exclude from that forum export subsidies and support measures for domestic production because it was convinced that the only appropriate setting for that is the WTO.

Subsidies and other trade-distorting measures are fundamentally a problem involving the US and the EU. Consequently, the United States will not consider significant changes outside of the WTO negotiations because trade remedy laws constitute a strategic bargaining chip for Washington (Horlick and Palmer 2001, 5). For Bergsten (Bergsten 2002), this is more or less the role played by the 2002 US Farm Bill who, according to some, would make the situation 'immeasurably more complicated' given the substantial increase in agricultural subsidies contained in the bill (Mackay 2002, 11). As written in a governmental document, 'The 2002 US Farm Bill – which authorized up to $123 billion in all types of food-stamp, conservation,and farm spending measures over six years – made clear that while the United States will respect WTO limits, it will not cut agricultural support unilaterally' (Government of the United States 2003a).

It is evident therefore that the US position on agriculture in the FTAA negotiations was part of a more global bargaining strategy, and that strategic positioning also comes into play as an explanation for US behavior. This is also true for the domestic politics factor as illustrated by researchers of the Department of Agricultural Economics of Mighigan State University. They show how well organized and how well represented farm organizations are in the US agricultural policy making process and how, finally, the US position on agricultural trade issues is the product of a 'massive politics of accomodation' (Browne, Schweikhardt, and Bonnen 2000, 19). Consequently, US agricultural trade bargaining was truly a two-level game resting for the most part on the *ad hoc* political coalition existing at the time of the negotiation.

Finally, in the case of Mexico the NAFTA factor was also at play alongside domestics politics. Contrary to Canada and the United States, however, it is less NAFTA as a normative framework that played a role than NAFTA as a gains-related factor. As seen before, there was an acute perception in farm and policy circles in Mexico that the NAFTA had not benefited the Mexican agricultural sector as it should have done. A major reason for this has to do with US protectionist measures. Consequently, the Mexican government might very well have used the FTAA negotiations to try to regain what was perceived as 'losses' resulting from the NAFTA particularly in terms of added constraints to US behavior.[13] The more so since there was increasing pressure from farm producers and organizations to redress the situation. So the combination of domestic pressure and gain-seeking appear to be at the basis of the Mexican bargaining stance with respect to agriculture in the FTAA negotiations.

Trade in Services

Positive vs. negative listing

At the multilateral level, services have been the object of negotiation for the first time during the Uruguay Round, with very limited success: the General Agreement on Trade in Services (GATS) is almost unanimously viewed as the weakest of the WTO family of agreements, its principal achievement being standstill bindings (see Sauvé 1997, 429–455). Yet, when one considers the growing importance of the service industries in the economy, it clearly appears that no significant advance in global trade liberalization will be made unless the resistances to the removing of trade barriers in service areas are overcome. In the industrialized countries of Europe and North America, service industries account for 60 to 70 percent of the GDP, and an even more important percentage of the work force.[14] Even middle-income countries in South and Central America now depend on the services sector for more than 50 percent of their GDP (Mann 1999). Still, global trade remains dominated by trade of goods. For the United States, the world's most important exporter of services, this sector accounts for only 30 percent of all its exports. This gap between the importance of services in the economy and its share of global trade is not due to protectionism alone. After all, the technology that renders many services like banking, insurance, and the like, easy to deliver abroad is still new. But it remains that, compared to the general abolition of tariffs and non-tariffs barriers applicable to manufactured goods, the services industry is a highly protected one. Thus, it is estimated that liberalizing trade in services would significantly boost the global economy.

But, liberalizing trade in services among developed and developing countries is not an easy task. The technology gap between industrialized and industrializing countries, added to the exclusion of southern providers of services from the main markets for high-quality services, have given services industries in the North, and particularly from the US, huge comparative advantages in term of labor availability

---

13 Interestingly from the point of view of our research design, such an outcome would represent an inversed relationship in terms of what influences what. Rather than NAFTA influencing Mexican preferences in the FTAA negotiations, it would be a case of Mexico using the FTAA negotiations to try to modify some of the NAFTA provisions.

14 In the United States, service industries account for 63 percent of the GDP and 80 percent of the employment. (Government of the United States – United States Trade Representative 2002e, 2).

and productivity (Mann 1999). This means that liberalizing that sector would, in term of trade income, be mostly beneficial to the North. In the case of the US, economist Catherine Mann has evaluated that successful negotiation of a multilateral agreement on services is key and urgent for maintaining at a sustainable level the country's trade deficit (Mann 1999). Conversely, industrializing countries know that their industry will need time to sustain the competition from northern providers and would like to benefit from some kind of asymmetrical treatment in trade agreements on services. This is what Mexico, unsuccessfully, asked for when it negotiated the NAFTA (Cameron and Tomlin 2000, 94).

To these two fundamentally different postures toward the liberalization of trade in services, correspond two approaches toward coverage in the negotiation of trade agreements; the 'positive list' approach and the 'negative list' approach. The positive list approach is the one adopted for services in the WTO. According to this more conservative and progressive approach, the rules of liberalization apply only to the sector (and mode of supply) for which states have taken specific commitments. Progressive liberalization is achieved through future rounds of negotiation where sectors not initially committed are scheduled for discussion. This is the path chosen by MERCOSUR members in order to benefit from a ten-years transition period: 'Annual rounds of negotiations based on the scheduling of increasing numbers of commitments in all sectors (with no exclusions) are to result in the elimination of all restrictions to services trade among members' (Stephenson 2001, 178).

The negative list approach, which is similar to the approach generally adopted in the case of trade in goods, has first been applied to services during the NAFTA negotiation, at the firm request of the US. Under this approach, the rules of liberalization cover all sectors or measures not specifically excluded from coverage by their inclusion in list of reservations. This is a much more brutal modality, which basically establishes a level playing field as the basis for negotiation, while the positive list approach favors progressiveness and asymmetrical treatment as paths toward liberalization. Since the negative list approach was clearly introduced in the NAFTA negotiation by the US,[15] our starting point here is a convergence, with Canada and Mexico accepting Washington's position on this topic.

A convergence tempered by Mexico's southern sensitivity

At first sight, the history of trade negotiations in the Hemisphere since the signature of the NAFTA, at the bilateral and subregional levels, as well as the North-American governments' respective initial offers at the FTAA negotiation table, would give credit to the hypothesis of NAFTA as having a no-return convergence effect on Mexico and Canada. Both countries have, it is true, negotiated a set of agreements with regional partners that take up the negative list model. But, a closer look at the modalities negotiated so far shows, in the case of Mexico, a willingness to adapt

15 We already stated that Mexico demanded asymetrical treatment. As Canada is concerned, we can simply say that the CUSFTA did not have a negative list approach for services and that there was no reason for Ottawa to adopt the new approach apart from accepting a request from Washington.

the negative list approach in a way that permits a more progressive and, eventually, asymmetrical liberalization process in services.

Since the opening of the Doha Round of multilateral negotiations, the US is positing itself as the champion of liberalization in the services area (Government of the United States – United States Trade Representative 2002). This has evident consequences on Washington's attitude toward the FTAA negotiation. The US proposal of February 2003 clearly stood for a negative list approach. Such an approach does not totally preclude asymmetrical treatment as we have seen in the case of NAFTA. The US-Chile trade agreement, signed on 6 June 2003, demonstrated that Washington was ready to tolerate some level of asymmetry through the use of reservations. A look at this treaty shows that the annexes listing non-conforming measures in cross-border services and investments, including financial services, fill a total of 34 pages for US reservations as compared to the 86 pages needed to list Chilean reservations (United-States-Chile Free Trade Agreement 2003). It nevertheless remains a status quo, NAFTA-like, agreement, establishing initially the terms of liberalization instead of planning for progressive liberalization. Interestingly, the US-Chile agreement doest not establish any committee on cross-border trade in services, of the like it establishes for trade in goods or in the special case of financial services. Thus, the US position on trade in services is unsurprising; it consists in a reaffirmation of the negative list approach with pressure made for limiting as far as possible other parties' use of reservations.

In its initial FTAA offer, communicated in February 2003, Ottawa also made a strong commitment in favor of the negative list approach, which is presented as the norm for Canada in all regional or bilateral investment and services negotiations (Government of Canada 2003c). The lists of reservations presented by Canada distinguished between standstill reservations on existing measures and general reservations applicable to existing as well as future measures in sectors like social services or transportation. Overall, the number of reservations appeared limited and there was no mechanism for phasing out of any kind of transitional measure entrenched in the proposal. Canada's proposition in the FTAA context was coherent and very similar with the text of the Canada-Chile Free Trade Agreement. It is important to note, however, that the Canada-Costa-Rica FTA, thus a treaty with a much smaller and less developed economy than Chile, limits itself, as services are concerned, to a reaffirmation of the GATS obligations and to a commitment to consider the need for further disciplines in three years.[16]

If Mexico's myriad of post-NAFTA bilateral and subregional FTAs are generally regarded as an extension of the NAFTA approach to trade in services (see Pinera Gonzàlez 2000, chapter 6), Sherry Stephenson judiciously points out that, as services are concerned, Mexico has shown a willingness to go further:

All of the agreements signed by Mexico [after NAFTA] (although not the subsequent agreements negotiated by Chile) contain an article stipulating 'future liberalization', whereby parties are to negotiate the liberalization and removal of nonconforming measures

---

16 The text of both treaties are available on the Government of Canada's site at: http://www.dfait-maeci.gc.ca/tna-nac/reg-en.asp.

listed in the annexes; the articles thereby introduce a marked element of dynamism into these agreements (Stephenson 2001, 179).

Indeed, such a measure has two important consequences. On the one hand, it removes the 'status quo' dimension of the NAFTA model: all excluded sectors or measures can, in the future, be subjected to negotiation. On the other hand, the inclusion in the structure of the agreement of the possibility to pursue the negotiation *ex post*, certainly opens the door to the planning of a smoother, transitional, process of liberalization that would much more easily accommodate demands for asymmetrical treatment. Examination of the treaties signed by Mexico indicates that this second kind of implication is one Mexicans were looking for. First, some of the agreements have been signed even in the absence of finalized lists of reservation, as in the cases of the Bolivia-Mexico and the Mexico-Nicaragua FTAs, for which no lists have been published yet. This clearly indicated, on the part of Mexico, a willingness to be flexible and to accommodate smaller countries demands for a gradualist process of liberalization. Second, when lists of reservations are effectively negotiated, Mexico is taking advantage of the possibility of future negotiation by making an extensive number of reservations. For example, the lists of reservations for Mexico pertaining to services and investments fill almost 200 pages in the case of the Mexico-Triangulo Norte FTA (Tratado de Libre Comercio México-Triagulo Norte 2001). This is more than the double of the pages needed to list the Mexican reservations in the NAFTA.

Based on its recent experience in negotiating treaties with southern, less developed, countries, we can therefore say that Mexico was advocating the 'negative list' NAFTA model of liberalization for trade in services, but was open to adapt this model in order to accommodate the need for gradual liberalization and, even, asymmetrical treatment in favor of the southern economies of the Hemisphere. The US and Canada, for their parts, demonstrated a much more rigid attachment to the NAFTA model in their proposals, even if Canada, as shown in its negotiation with Costa-Rica, may not have been as aggressive as the US in its effort to open the southern markets to North American services suppliers.

The introduction of secondary ruling mechanisms for services: Implications and rationale

Our analysis suggests that, on the basis of NAFTA being the common denominator for the three north-American countries' proposals for the FTAA, the most innovative attitude taken so far was the one taken by the Mexicans. By introducing a provision on future negotiation in the post-NAFTA treaties they signed, the Mexicans have, as services are concerned, attacked one of the fundamental architectural features of the NAFTA; its status quo logic. In order to appreciate the signification of this, it is worth remembering that NAFTA's institutional design is characterized by a combination of extraordinary high levels of precision and comprehensiveness in the treaty itself with a quasi absence of secondary ruling mechanisms (Abbott 2000, 524).This means that NAFTA simply does not allow for a political delegation aimed at insuring the future of cooperation; that no future mandatory round of negotiation is scheduled, and that if residual questions or problems arise, they have to be treated or renegotiated on an *ad hoc* basis by regular diplomatic channels. The farther the Commission, established under Chapter 20 of the NAFTA, can create secondary ruling is by clarifying some provisions of the treaty, as it has been the case in 2001, but not without difficulty, with Chapter 11 on investment (Government of Canada 2001e).

As we have seen, in the case of services, the Mexican bilateral and subregional FTAs modify this order of things by forecasting future rounds of negotiations on sectors that have been originally excluded from coverage through the use of reservations. This is quite innovative because, the usual method for liberalizing in successive rounds is the positive listing approach. Now, the same provision appeared in the chapter on services in the second Draft Agreement of the FTAA:

Future Liberalization

1. Through future negotiations called by the Commission [Responsible for the Administration of the Agreement] [to be held periodically], the Parties shall [jointly] broaden the liberalization achieved in the different service sectors, with a view to eventually eliminating the remaining restrictions [set out in the Article on Reservations or Commitments].

2. The removal of the remaining restrictions shall include the progressive reduction and/or dismantling of the nonconforming measures set out in Section A, together with the progressive incorporation into Section A of the sectors, subsectors, and activities set out in Section B.[17]

Such a provision opens the door for a smoother, gradual process of liberalization, but at the same time aims at achieving, in the long term, a more complete liberalization. Why would Mexico go that way?

First, on the one hand, since the presidential election of 2000, the Mexican government has been very critical of the status quo logic on which the NAFTA has been build. Mexican President Vicente Fox proposed right after his election the creation of a North American common market and was calling for the negotiation of an European-style economic community which would transform the NAFTA in a dynamic structure as well as permit an enlargement of the trilateral cooperation to areas such as immigration, labor, regional development and monetary policy. Caught in a very asymmetric power relation with the US, Mexico suffers from the lack of provisions for secondary ruling in the NAFTA since it means that Washington has no obligation to consider its demands dealing with uncovered sectors of the original agreement. This can explain, not only how sensible Mexico can be toward the demand of smaller countries for a more flexible and dynamic framework of cooperation than the one provided by NAFTA, but also its vested interest in transforming the NAFTA model in this way.

---

17 Section A refers to the list of reservations for existing measures (standstill), while Section B refers to the list of sectors, sub-sectors or activities for which existing as well as future measures are excluded from coverage (*Free Trade Area of the Americas, Second Draft Agreement, Chapter on Services* 2002).

Second, on the other hand, it is clear that this path toward, at the end of the day, radical liberalization of the services sector must be seen as an indication of the confidence post-NAFTA Mexico has attained in its capacity to use the competitive advantage gained by its liberalization, to gain from the opening of other Latin-American markets. Thus, having been in a way forced to enter in the NAFTA on a same level playing field, Mexico is not ready to accept traditional forms of preferential agreements in favor of its southern competitors in the area of trade in services.

Concluding Remarks

What does this preliminary analysis tell us concerning the behavior of the three NAFTA countries in terms of convergence in the framework of the FTAA negotiations? And how did the NAFTA influence came into play?

What was basically at stake in the negotiation over preferential treatment was the institutional design of the future FTAA. The Canadian and US positions were in favor of enshrining the principle of reciprocity and accepting only *ad hoc* measures of preferential treatment. In the case of Mexico, the initial position was also in favor of reciprocity but with the Fox Administration there was a shift toward institutionalization of preferential treatment for low-income countries.

In the negotiation on agriculture, the main issue was one of agenda-setting and concerned the status of subsidies in the forthcoming negotiations. The United States was willing to discuss all aspects related to market access but refused to discuss trade-distorting measures outside of the WTO framework. Canadian preferences were in favor of eliminating export subsidies and support for domestic production but believed that the main forum for this is the WTO. Mexico, for its part, has not made public any formal position but all signs lead to believe that the Mexican government will want to introduce in the discussion all aspects related to subsidies.

With regards to trade in services, the Canadian and US positions were relatively straightforward as each government was in favor of the negative list. The Mexican position was more ambiguous since the government supports the negative list on a general basis but has demonstrated an openness to progressive liberalization in some of the FTAs signed with some of its neighbors.

It appears consequently that the level of convergence is not as high as might have been expected initially. The explanation lies in the fact that the behavior of each government has been influenced by a different combination of factors. In the case of Canada, which seems to be the most straightforward, it is clear that there was a direct NAFTA influence but combined with the WTO. NAFTA and WTO rules appeared to reinforce each others to create a strong normative framework which acted as a guide for the Canadian strategy in the FTAA negotiations.

With regards to the United States, the NAFTA also played an important role as a normative framework guiding US behavior in the FTAA negotiations, which was to be expected in a way given the US negotiating style of building on previous international agreements. But two other factors also influenced US behavior. One is strategic positioning and is most evident in the negotiations on agriculture. Here,

Washington's refusal to discuss subsidies and trade-distorting measures was linked directly to the fact that the US believed that this issue can only be settled in the WTO framework because the central players are the US and the EU. Making concessions in the FTAA framework could harm the US bargaining position with the EU. The other factor was domestic politics which was coming into play again most evidently in the negotiations on agriculture as witnessed by the 2002 Farm Bill.

Finally, a most interesting case is that of Mexico where we find a NAFTA influence at work but in terms of gains more than in terms of normative framework. In all three sectors, but more evidently in relation to preferential treatment and agriculture, indications are that Mexico tried to use the FTAA negotiations to make gains that were not possible in the NAFTA context because of Mexico's limited bargaining power or to recoup for perceived losses resulting from the NAFTA. In addition to gains, there was also a domestic politics factor influencing Mexican behavior particularly in negotiations on agriculture. This became very evident in 2003 with political pressure mounting in Mexico to have the government renegotiate the agricultural provisions of the NAFTA. Given the possible negative consequences of reopening the NAFTA, the Mexican government would presumably have used the FTAA negotiations to try to redress the situation.

Consequently it would seem that even in economic-related matters such as those discussed in the NAFTA and FTAA frameworks, the NAFTA has not produced the level of convergence that was anticipated at the start of this analysis at least with regards to Mexico and even with regards to Canada in relation with certain agricultural issues. One of the reasons may have to do with the closed structure of the NAFTA which does not permit a renegotiation of the initial agreement obliging therefore participating governments to use other fora to clarify or change existing rules. The more so in this case since, as noted previously, Mexico is the NAFTA country to lose more with the establishment of the FTAA because it will cease to be the bridge between North and South America.

Chapter 2

Diverging Preferences:
The Impact of NAFTA on the Member States' Trade Policies

Louis Bélanger

The entry into force of the Canada-United States Free Trade Agreement (CUSTA) in 1989 and the North American Free trade Agreement (NAFTA) in 1994 institutionalized Canada's and Mexico's economic integration to the United States to such a level that one could easily predict that future Canadian and Mexican trade policies would inevitably be aligned to the US one. After all, NAFTA meant for both countries to be entangled in the world's most extensive and complex web of trade and trade-related rules with the world's most powerful economy.[1] Such a convergence could have taken the form of a unidirectional adoption by Ottawa and Mexico City of Washington's preferred options. It could also have been the result of some kind of a process of negotiated convergence, with NAFTA constraining the US to formulate its future trade policy from a North-American standpoint, therefore permitting Canada and Mexico to influence it. The three North American partners could even have used NAFTA as a common platform for upcoming trade negotiations between them and other countries or regional groupings. Wasn't NAFTA itself an enlargement of the previous CUSTA? Other partners could have joined NAFTA, thanks to the agreement's accession clause (*NAFTA*, Art. 2204). Or they could have negotiated a separate agreement with the new NAFTA bloc. These expectations, it must be said, are totally in line with experiences from other regional trade groupings. Apart from the often mentioned European example, free-trade areas such as CARICOM, the Andean Community, the Central America Common Market, and, of course MERCOSUR, have all established common external trade policies (See Salazar-Xirinachs 2001, 45–86).

---

1   As Frederick Abbott described it: 'NAFTA is among the most highly detailed international trade agreements ever negotiated between governments. It comprises twenty-two chapters setting forth specific obligations on trade in goods, services, financial services, investment, intellectual property rights, technical barriers to trade, sanitary and phytosanitary measures, safeguards measures, and dispute settlement. It incorporates a panoply of annexes that elaborate the extent (and limits) of obligations by reference, among other things, to the internal legislation of its parties. NAFTA is broader in scope of coverage (...) than the WTO agreement, and it is comparable in level of detail to the WTO agreement. NAFTA was drafted at a level of detail substantially higher than the EC treaty (...)' (Abbott 2000, 524).

On many accounts, events during the immediate post-NAFTA period were fuelling this interpretation of a convergence effect. For example, months after the entry into force of NAFTA, proposals for the negotiation of a EU-NAFTA trade agreement were made (Duesterberg 1995, 71). Also, Chile formally asked for NAFTA accession in 1995 while Argentina did not hide its intention to be considered next in line. On another front, the three North American partners openly pushed for a negotiation of a Free Trade Area of the Americas (FTAA) that would use NAFTA as a blueprint (Mace et al. 2003, 129–158). NAFTA, it seemed, would logically become both the main vehicle and the model for the three countries' future regional and bilateral trade policies.

Years later, however, we must acknowledge that this anticipated impact of NAFTA never fully materialized. There has been no enlargement of NAFTA through its accession clause. Instead, the three countries have separately negotiated bilateral deals with Chile, which have not resulted in its accession to NAFTA.[2] The FTAA negotiation was officially launched in 1998, but the proposal put forward to structure the talks on the basis of NAFTA was rejected by MERCOSUR (Mace et al. 2003, 129–158). Furthermore, nine years later, the FTAA negotiation has collapsed and, following Mexico's example, the Bush administration has multiplied bilateral initiatives with Central American and Andean countries (Bussey 2004). As for the relations with the EU, the prospect of a common Transatlantic Free Trade Area (TAFTA) rapidly disintegrated in favor of, again, separate bilateral initiatives. Finally, even if this is a possibility that has been contemplated in the case of the FTAA, the NAFTA partners never presented a common position in any multilateral negotiation.

On substance, it is true that many of the bilateral deals negotiated since 1994 by Canada with other hemispheric trade partners reproduced in good measures the NAFTA treaty. This being said, Canada and Mexico also took their distance from the US on some important issues. For example, the Canada-Chile trade agreement provides a reciprocal exemption from the application of anti-dumping laws and countervailing measures, something that Washington has always refused to concede to Canadians during the NAFTA negotiation. Nevertheless, the converging impact of NAFTA does not match what could have been originally anticipated.

Does this mean that the participation in NAFTA did not have any real significant impact on the member states preferences and strategies in international trade policy? Or, does this rather show that the impact is not the one expected? This paper wishes to explore the second possibility. Apart from minor differences in the way they articulate their positions on issues like agricultural subsidies, remedy laws, cultural exemptions or investments, Mexico, Ottawa and Washington share basically the same economic interests and free-trade philosophy. On the other hand, the often-cited governance deficit or institutional deficiency in NAFTA (Grinspun and Kreklewich 1999, 17–33) has created a situation of growing uncertainty for Canada and Mexico; their commercial destiny is now more than ever linked to the US, yet they have absolutely no control on how the US might indirectly affect the range of NAFTA

---

2   The 2003 Chile-US Free Trade Agreement contains no reference to NAFTA, but the preamble refers instead to the FTAA (http://www.ustr.gov/new/fta/Chile/final/index.htm).

rules by unilaterally negotiating with other partners or by adopting new policies in domains not covered by the 1994 agreement. To limit this uncertainty has become the main trade policy objective for Ottawa and Mexico. And in order to achieve this objective, they have defended a trade policy agenda that differed significantly from Washington's. NAFTA's lack of governance structures and secondary rule-making provisions pushes the two junior partners to use *ex post* opportunities to compensate for what they experience or foresee as a loss in international voice opportunities while the US continues to privilege trade arrangement which allow minimal levels of political delegation and coordination.

The first part of the chapter rapidly presents some theoretical considerations on how the participation in an existing trade agreement should affect one state's attitude toward future trade partnerships. The second part offers a brief overview of NAFTA's institutional design and the dynamic it induces. The chapter's thesis is then applied to two areas of post-NAFTA trade negotiations: the western-hemispheric and transatlantic ones.

Diverging and Converging Effects of Trade Cooperation: The Role of Power Asymmetry and Institutional Design

Theories of International Relations and International Political Economy develop different views on how membership in already existing institutions like regional free trade agreements affects states' preferences when they negotiate new treaties or renegotiate existing ones. Basically, however, almost all institutionalist theories – that is, theories that take institutions as an independent factor in the explanation of states' preferences and behaviors, such as functionalism, liberal institutionalism and sociological institutionalism would insist, albeit for different reasons, on the converging effects of existing institutions on policy preferences. On the other hand, these theories have little to tell us about possible diverging effects. Realism, on the other hand, predicts the opposite: the effect, when there is one, should lead to diverging strategies. Grieco's amended realist theory of international cooperation, however, suggests that this diverging effect is for a good part dependant on the specific design of the existing institution. In the context of this research, such a proposition deserves our attention.

Functionalism sees international institutions as responses to the needs created by transnational forces and integration (Deutsch et al. 1968; Haas and Schmitter 1964, 705–737). Accordingly, existing international institutions will impact on future institution-making when they first impact on the level and form of economic and cultural integration. This is what functionalist authors refer to as the 'spill-over effect'. Therefore, a functionalist reading of NAFTA will take good measures of the acceleration of regional economic integration that followed the entry into force of the agreement and predict that such a deep integration pattern should lead to policy convergence and institution-building.

Rational institutionalism, for its part, considers that states' views on international institutions are primarily determined by the net benefits they expect to obtain from cooperating with others. That is why, according to rational institutionalist theorists like Keohane (1984) and Weber (2000), states care a lot about the transaction costs linked to the creation and operation of international institutions. Because institutions are costly, states will try to make the best use of already existing ones. That means that they would rather extend the mandate or enlarge the membership of existing institutions than create and operate new ones. According to this approach, trade agreements like NAFTA, that surpass in scope and depth any previous arrangement and have been very costly to negotiate,[3] should then be used by member states as a common framework for future cooperation.

Sociological institutionalists do not consider states as rational actors, but rather as cultural phenomenon. They see the institutionalisation of world political and economic relations as part of a global process of weberian rationalisation of the social through iteration and diffusion of institutional innovations that advance the management of human affairs by liberal rule of law, scientific knowledge and technology (Thomas et al. 1996, 325–347). Clearly, a sociological institutionalist view of NAFTA would focus on its unprecedented high level of technical precision and legalism. It is thus as a new, universally applicable, common standard for the institutionalisation of free-trade that sociological-institutionalism would expect NAFTA to have converging effects, rather than because of its economic benefits or because it provides a common forum for coordination.

Thus, generally speaking, institutionalist theories see existing institutions as favoring future institution-making and predict that members of an institutional agreement should develop converging views on subsequent opportunities for institutionalization. This, of course is a very broad assertion in need of important qualifications since, as mentioned, the converging effects of existing institutions depend for each theory on variations of different factors like level of integration, transaction costs, or level of legalism. But, it can nevertheless be said that when these theories have a lot to say on the converging effects of membership in institutions like NAFTA, they have much less to tell us about possible diverging effects.

Realism, on the other hand, considers international institution-making as unnatural for states, which, according to realist premises, should grant supreme value to the maximisation of their autonomy and independence. Even more so when the institutions' finality, as it is the case with free-trade agreements, is to facilitate economic integration and interdependence (Waltz 1979). So, when states nevertheless agree to participate in an economic alliance like NAFTA because there are sufficient gains to be made, we should expect the members of that alliance to seek counterbalancing in the future rather than further 'bandwagoning'. However, such a reaction will depend, for a large measure, on the relative power of member states. While dominant states in an alliance may possess enough power to compensate alone for the relative loss of autonomy induced by an institutional arrangement (internal balancing), less powerful states may need to look for others to build some counter-power and deconcentrate their entanglement in institutional frameworks (external balancing). Thus, realism, because it is a theory of power politics, introduces a variable that institutionalist theories tend to neglect, namely the

---

3   On the difficulties encountered during the NAFTA negotiation and high domestic political costs involved, see Frederick W. Mayer (1998).

relative symmetry or asymmetry of capabilities among member states and, by doing so indicates that asymmetry may lead to diverging preferences among the members of an institutionalized alliance, be it a military or an economic one.

An amended realist theory of international economic cooperation, the one developed by Joe Grieco in its effort to provide a realist account of the European Union experience, is of interest here because of the analytical linkages it suggests between power asymmetry and institutional preferences. Less powerful states, Grieco argues, often fear that institutionalized cooperation, even if it proves to be advantageous for everyone, would increase their dependence on a dominant and potentially hegemonic neighbour. For this reason, they usually try to negotiate a form of institutionalization that gives them a certain level of effective voice or 'voice opportunities'. He describes these as 'institutional characteristics whereby the views of partners (including relatively weaker partners) are not just expressed but reliably have a material impact on the operations of the collaborative arrangement' (Grieco 1996, 288).

In international affairs, voice opportunities mechanisms usually take the form of formalized frameworks for *ex post* negotiation. Such institutional features are very important since states cannot count on a common legal system and authority to take charge of the future of cooperation. This is why James Fearon makes this useful distinction between two features of international institutions: the contract itself, through which states co-ordinate their actions; and the governance structures through which states ensure the collaboration needed to enforce the contract (Fearon 1998, 274–275). Grieco mainly considers situations where diverging preferences on institutionalization occur in a bargaining game over a single institution, but there is no reason not to consider the possibility that, in order to redress the balance through voice opportunities in one institutional setting, less powerful states will try to obtain compensation in others.

How all this can help us understand the impact of NAFTA membership on the way the three countries have engaged themselves in subsequent trade negotiations? Grieco's amended realism, suggests an interesting hypothesis. Less powerful states like Canada and Mexico, the theory implies, when they overcome their fear of dominance by a hegemonic neighbour, and opt for institutionalized economic cooperation, will try to compensate the loss in autonomy by looking for institutional designs that offer voice opportunities. At first sight, NAFTA doesn't offer voice opportunities, albeit this is an empirical question in need of further investigations. If it is the case, then we may ask the following analytical question: Are the divergences between Canada and Mexico trade policies and the US ones mainly divergences in institutional preferences related to the enhancement of voice opportunities for the two less powerful NAFTA members?

The remaining of the paper will thus focus on governance structure. I will first explore what NAFTA has to offer in term of voice opportunities in order to verify the level and form of the expected voice deficit to which Canada and Mexico are confronted. In the subsequent sections, I will then try to see how central voice concerns have been in the divergences of preferences toward trade strategies one can establish between Canada, Mexico and the US.

Power Asymmetry and Voice Deficit in NAFTA[4]

NAFTA's institutional design is characterized by a combination of extraordinary high levels of precision and comprehensiveness in the treaty itself with a quasi absence of secondary ruling mechanisms, or governance structure. This specificity has been highlighted by many specialists (see Abbott 2000, 519–547; Bernier and Roy 1998, 72), but its radicalism has not always been understood correctly. One reason for this is probably a certain level of confusion in the interpretation given to the dispute settlement mechanisms (DSM) enshrined in the treaty. The DSMs one finds in NAFTA are designed to rule on disputes pertaining to the interpretation of the agreement. Their mandate is to interpret the law; they do not make the law. If some commentators saw, at first, in the DSM provisions any hope for policy coordination, they were disappointed (see, for example, Weintraub 1994). As Morales found, '(s)o far, all the conflicts handled by either Chapter 18 of CUSTA or Chapter 20 of NAFTA have focused on technicalities or on the interpretation of the agreement' (Morales 1999, 46). Thus, Bernier and Martin's first assessment proved to be the correct one: 'NAFTA is a comprehensive and technical agreement, and its enforcement leaves little leeway for politics' (Bernier and Roy 1998, 73).

This minimalism in political delegation is evident if one looks at the design of the Commission, the political arm of NAFTA. The Commission, the principal collaboration tool provided by the agreement has no competence for renegotiating elements of the treaty or for taking enforcing measures. It is explicitly prohibited for the Commission to establish a centralized bureaucracy, its secretariat having to be restricted to the coexistence of three separate national secretariats [North American Free Trade Agreement 1994, Art. 2002(1)]. Robert Pastor describes the primitive character of the political institutions in these terms:

> The signatories of NAFTA deliberately wanted to avoid establishing any bureaucratic or supranational institutions. (...) The modus vivendi was to create a 'NAFTA Free Trade Commission', which was a 'virtual' structure; that is, it was simply a phrase to describe periodic meetings among the trade ministers of the three countries, 'with no permanent location or staff'. Their meetings were intended to assess the implementation of the agreement, resolve any new disputes, and oversee the work of numerous committees established to address specific issues described in each chapter in the agreement (Pastor 2001, 73–74).

This means that NAFTA simply does not allow for a political delegation aimed at insuring the future of cooperation; even less so for a coordination of the external relations of the three partners. No future mandatory round of negotiation is scheduled. If residual questions or problems arise, they have to be treated or renegotiated on an *ad hoc* basis by regular diplomatic channels.[5] The farther the Commission can

---

4   For a more complete review of NAFTA's institutional design, see Louis Bélanger (Bélanger 2007).

5   The Commission has adopted some technical revisions of the very complicated rules of origin contained in Annex 401. Even in this case, adoption of these modifications is subjected to ratification in each of the parties (See Government of Canada – Canada Gazette 2004).

go on its own is to clarify some provisions of the treaty, as it has been the case in 2001, but not without difficulty, with Chapter 11 (Government of Canada 2001e). And even though, a subsequent panel ruling indicated clearly that such clarifications cannot, in any circumstances, be interpreted as modifications of the original text of the agreement (*In the Matter of An Arbitration Under Chapter Eleven of the North American Free Trade Agreement Between Pope & Talbot Inc. and Government of Canada. Award in Respect of Damages* 2002). Another illustration of the limitation of the Commission's capacity to amend the NAFTA written contract was given by its failed attempt at establishing a permanent North American Trade Secretariat (NATS). At its first meeting, in January 1994, the Commission decided the creation of such a permanent secretariat responsible, among other things, for coordinating the work of the national secretariats. Because Canada and the US inherited, from the two parallel agreements, respectively an Environmental and a Labour secretariat, the NATS was to be established in Mexico City. But, since there are no provisions for this administrative body in the text of the NAFTA, the US Congress never voted the money necessary for its implementation (Grijalva and Brewer 1994, 5).

As I have said, to this extraordinary low level of political delegation corresponds the institutionalization of relatively strong dispute settlement mechanisms. This can be seen as a direct by-product of precision; the concern for writing the most definitive treaty possible demands such mechanisms able to autonomously take charge of the need for *ex post* interpretation (see McCall Smith 2000, 144–145). However, in spite of its high level of precision and its evident ambition to accomplish deep cooperation or completeness, NAFTA has not institutionalized the ultimate delegation mechanism for interpretation and precision, which would be the kind of permanent tribunal Robert Pastor is advocating today (Pastor 2001, 103). The delegation system NAFTA offers is limited to DSMs which do not have the authority of a standing tribunal since only DSMs rulings taking place under Chapter 19 (anti-dumping and countervailing measures) are binding.

How has this specific institutional design been negotiated? Unfortunately, we do not know a lot about how the institutional elements were handled during the NAFTA negotiation compared to substantive issues (Grieco 1996, 288). However, what we do know indicates that the institutional outcome have indeed been the result of a bargaining in which extreme precision was the price the US had to pay for avoiding delegation for secondary ruling, or, simply put, political delegation. A good example of this is provided by the negotiation over the compatibility or not of anti-dumping and countervailing measures with the establishment of a free trade area. Both Canada, during the CUSTA negotiation, and Mexico, during the NAFTA one, went to the table with the clear objective of prohibiting such measures and replace them by a regional competition policy (Cameron and Tomlin 2000).

That meant the creation of a political coordination mechanism for the joint monitoring of the North American market. Washington opposed such a solution and the Chapter 19 finally adopted was a last minute compromise. Under NAFTA, each country maintains its own trade remedy laws and anti-dumping and countervailing measures determination procedures, but actions by national agencies are subject to challenge and review by a binational panel system which substitutes for domestic court appeal recourses. Here, completeness is obtained by, in a sense, incorporating the three countries' bodies of remedy law into the orbit of the Agreement, and this was clearly chosen as a substitute for politico-administrative delegation. Part of the compromise was the acceptance by the US, under Chapter 15, of future negotiations on this issue of common competition policies. But these *ex post* negotiations stalled rapidly (see Cameron and Tomlin 2000 as well as Winham and DeBoer-Ashwort 2000, 35–52). So, what we have here is a good example of an issue that Canada and Mexico would have wanted to be dealt with collectively through permanent policy coordination and which, in front of American resistance, gave instead rise to extended precision and judicial delegation.

This short overview of NAFTA's institutional design demonstrates that, in view of amended realism, Canada and Mexico experienced an important voice deficit when entering with the US in the NAFTA trade alliance. As less powerful partners, they entered in a highly comprehensive contract without securing appropriate institutional mechanisms to compensate for their new dependency. Moreover, it is also quite evident that the preferred option identified in the literature in such a situation, which is obtaining compensation through the modification of the existing institution [referred to by Aggarwal as the 'control' option (Aggarwal 1998, 195–213)], is not immediately available at a reasonable cost. I now turn on extra-regional trade relations, first transatlantic, and then hemispheric, to see in what measure Canada and Mexico have externalized their need for voice opportunities and how it can account for the divergence of their trade policy from the American one.

NAFTA and the Future of Transatlantic Trade Cooperation

The signature of NAFTA posed an immediate challenge to the future of the transatlantic relations of each of the North American countries. Prominent personalities in Canada and the US like Jean Chrétien, Henry Kissinger and Newt Gingrich, as well as EU Commissioner Leon Brittan endorsed at that time the idea of negotiating a free trade agreement between the European Community and the newly created North American commercial zone: a Transatlantic Trade Agreement (TAFTA) (Crawley 2000, 9–34). This ambitious project never left the ground, but it prompted different reactions and bilateral initiatives, which permit to identify some clear differences in the trade policies of Ottawa, Mexico, and Washington. This field of inquiry is also interesting in the context of this research because the rationale behind much of what has been proposed or accomplished appear to be much more political than economical, at least on this side of the ocean. NAFTA, substantially had the effect of diminishing the relative share of European exportations and importations in the overall North American countries' trade, but it did not affect negatively the absolute level of commerce. Moreover, the transatlantic movement of goods and services being already highly liberalized, additional liberalization would not permit important absolute gains. For example, a study made by the Canadian government showed that the advantage for Canada of a complete liberalization of trade with Europe, *including agriculture*, would produce a gross increase of the GDP estimated at US$236 millions. This means less than half of one percentage point (Government of Canada 2001d, 39).

As I have just mentioned, US officials considered, right after the signature of NAFTA, different options for trade liberalization with Europe. In preparation for the EU-US Madrid Summit, in December 1995, some scenarios were examined, including an all-encompassing TAFTA (Preeg 1996, 110). At the Summit, Bill Clinton and Jacques Santer did not announce the launching of negotiations of a comprehensive TAFTA, but of a more limited 'New Transatlantic Marketplace' (NTM) as part of a 'New Transatlantic Agenda' (NTA) (*The New Transatlantic Agenda* 1995; *Joint EU-U.S. Action Plan* 1995). In 1998, a draft proposal for the NTM circulated among Europeans. It came short of a NAFTA-like trade area, but nevertheless proposed an elimination of tariffs on industrial products by 2010, a free trade area in services, a mutual recognition or harmonization of national regulations and standards, and an agenda for liberalization beyond levels fixated by existing agreements in government procurement, intellectual property and investment (Hindley 1999, 50–51). The NTM proposal was coldly received by Europeans and was finally vetoed by France.[6] In May 1998, the US and the EU agreed on a new agenda, 'The Transatlantic Economic Partnership' (TEP), that reinforced the 1995 NTA and, as part of this agenda, a Draft Action Plan is negotiated by the European Commission and submitted to EU members. Subjected, again, to strong resistances among Europeans, the Action Plan is nevertheless signed by Washington and Brussels on November (Government of the United States – United States Mission to the European Union 1998). The TEP Action Plan reiterates about the same general goals as the failed NTM, but without fixating datelines and specific actions. What it plans is future discussions and better coordination of views at the multilateral level, but no formal negotiations agenda and liberalization processes (Hindley 1999, 46).

It is very interesting to note that even the failed NTM was designed in a way of reducing to a minimum the level of delegation and voice articulation mechanisms. For example, the NTM plans to achieve mutual recognition of inspection, testing and certification of products without creating any institutional bodies for negotiating and deciding on minimum standards, nor for binding dispute settlement. Mutual recognition or harmonization would simply be achieved 'by developing a framework of convergence of law, procedure and practice involving the various legislative and regulatory bodies, as well as for the application of the principle of mutual recognition' (cited in Hindley 1999, 51). As Hinley puts it, the NTM proposal limited itself to suggest an institutional umbrella that was so light that it did not add much to what could be achieved without it, and even that was probably too much for the US (Hindley 1999, 53–54).

The TEP institutional setting takes the 1995 NTA structures 'as its point of departure' (United States Mission to the European Union 1998, para. 4). The NTA already created a Senior Level Group composed of two representatives of the EU presidency, two representatives of the European Community and two representatives of the US State Department, which oversees the implementation of the Agenda and prepares the twice-yearly EU-US Summits. The TEP Action Plan, adds to it a 'TEP Steering Group' which do not have a mandate for negotiation, but for exploring the possibility of negotiating specific agreements in the sectors covered by the Action

---

6 On European reactions, see Hindley (1999, 50–51).

Plan, like procurement, standards or intellectual property. 'In the framework of sectoral agreements, where commitments would be entered into, *says the Action Plan*, specific organisational arrangements will be established as appropriate.' (United States Mission to the European Union 1998, para. 4).

While the US and the EU hesitantly discussed over minimalist frameworks to monitor their trade relations, Mexico and the EU embarked in a much more ambitious partnership. In 1995, Mexico and Brussels officially launched bilateral negotiations and it was agreed that the future trade agreement would be embedded in a complex mechanism of cooperation that would include three pillars: political dialogue, commerce, and cooperation (Sanahuja 2000). The cornerstone of the new EU-Mexico institutional setting is the 1997 so called 'Global Agreement' (European Communities 2000c, L276/45–61). Basically, this Global Agreement enumerates a series of broadly defined objectives (the 'Trade' title comprises only four articles) and mandates a Joint Council to negotiate arrangements in specific areas. So far, the Joint Council has approved Decision No 2/2000 covering trade in goods, including government procurement, competition and intellectual property, and Decision No 2/2001 covering trade in services and investment. The Joint Council is a permanent ministerial-level body to which the parties have delegated the power to progressively write down their mutual contract and amend it. Article 47 of the Global Agreement states:

> The Joint Council shall, for the purpose of attaining the objectives of this Agreement, have the power to take decisions in the cases provided for herein. The desisions taken shall be binding on the Parties which shall take the measures necessary to implement them... (European Communities 2000c, L276/53).

In addition to this delegation for secondary ruling at the level of the Joint Council, one can also find in the decisions several mechanisms indicating the willingness of the Parties to establish permanent cooperation. For example, Decision 2/2001 mandates the Joint Committee to take decisions or make recommendations on trade and trade-related matters (European Communities 2001, L70/20–21); Decision 2/2000 includes a provision for further negotiations if any party offers additional advantages to a third party in procurement (European Communities 2000b, L157/24); the same decision establishes a permanent mechanism of cooperation between the European Commission and the Mexican *Comision Federal de Competencia* to coordinate their competition policies;[7] and, overall, the Global Agreement and the Decisions taken so far have given birth to seven Special Committees responsible for assisting the Joint Council in different trade areas.

Canada has been, at the same time, the most ardent supporter of a TAFTA and the one among the three NAFTA partners to accomplish the less in terms of bilateral relations. NAFTA had not yet come into force when Canadian Trade minister Roy MacLaren proposed the negotiation of a Canada-EU trade agreement as a first step toward an inter-regional TAFTA (Wolfe 1996, 353–380). Repeatedly, in the following years, Prime Minister Jean Chrétien will officially propose to the European

---

7   *Annex XV to Decision No 2/2000 of the EU-Mexico Joint Council of 23 March 2000* (Competition-mechanism of cooperation).

Union to launch discussions over a NAFTA-EU free trade zone. It became rapidly obvious, however, that both the EU and the US had no appetite for a TAFTA and the Canadians realized that their only option was to prevent Brussels and Washington to negotiate a bilateral agreement that would cause them prejudices. Thus, Ottawa reacted to the EU-US NTM project by negotiating a similar agreement with the EU. According to Donald Barry:

> The Canada-EU agreement was similar to its US-EU counterpart, with only one noteworthy departure – in addition to a joint trade study, Canada and the Union would 'consider with the United States, on a case-by-case basis, trilateralization...for subjects contained in the New Transatlantic Market Place' (Barry 2000, 296).

Then, when the EU and the US resumed their trade talks around the TEP proposal, Canada once again failed to convince one or the other to trilateralize the negotiation and had to duplicate the EU-US template. This lead to the signature, in December 1998, of the EU-Canada Trade Initiative (EUCTI). While it tried to cope with the risk of marginalization implied by the bilateral talks between Washington and Brussels, Ottawa regularly renewed its call for a real bi-regional free trade agreement. But the Canadian government had to resign itself. In December 2002, Canada and the EU announced their intention to negotiate a bilateral trade agreement of a new kind, and on March 3, 2004, the European Commission has agreed on a blueprint for official negotiations of a EU-Canada Trade and Investment Enhancement Agreement (TIEA), which, as far as we know, and as the NTM, would essentially be a framework for cooperation between respective regulating authorities (European Commission 2004a).

As in the case of hemispheric trade negotiations, transatlantic relations have been an area of extra-regional trade policies where our three 'amigos' have manifested diverging preferences. While the US constantly tried, from 1994 to present, to advance proposals aimed at alleviating some remaining irritants in their trade with Europe but cautiously avoided serious institution-building, Canada and Mexico were eager to engage in comprehensive trade agreements with the EU. But, again, Mexico and Canada preferred very different paths. Canada's first option, as in the case of the FTAA, was to develop a framework of cooperation with Europe, the proposed TAFTA, which would be based on NAFTA itself. When it became clear that this option was not available, Ottawa made all it could to match the advancement of the EU-US cooperation, not without showing its frustration, therefore maintaining favorable conditions for an eventual trilateralization. This strategy had converging consequences: in following the path traced by Washington and Brussels, Ottawa was forced to limit itself to mere replicas of the agreements designed by the two commercial superpowers. So, if Canada and the US have expressed diverging preferences regarding the future architecture of transatlantic trade relations, in the end, they inherited very similar outcomes. Mexico, for its part, never manifested any interest in the TAFTA discussions. It chose to enter into bilateral negotiations with Europe and obtained a trade agreement, which provides high level of delegation to governance structures.

Post-NAFTA Hemispheric Trade Policies

On the surface, it would seem that the three NAFTA partners have always been equally enthusiast promoters of the FTAA project. However, at different phases of the negotiations, important differences between them have been manifest in positions and attitudes toward the overall institutional design of an eventual hemispheric free trade zone. This divergence of perspective has become more evident since the almost total collapse of the FTAA talks during the Miami ministerial meeting in November 2003. The relative easiness with which, on this occasion, the US has bended before Brazil and abandoned the objective of a single comprehensive agreement to embrace the watered down 'FTAA *à la carte*' option was in a sense revealing of how feeble Washington's interest for real hemispheric trade governance has always been. This about-turn pushed an infuriated Canadian government to take the lead, with the Chileans, of a group of states that tried, without success, to rescue what can be saved from the FTAA original project.

The US attitude toward a truly comprehensive free-trade treaty for the Americas has always been ambiguous. The project is often described as an American initiative. In fact, there are good reasons to think that when George Bush Sr. announced its 1990 'Enterprise for the Americas Initiative', he only had a very vague idea of the implication of the allusion it contained about the possible negotiation of a hemisphere-wide free trade agreement.[8] Four years later, after the successful NAFTA negotiation but its difficult adoption by Congress, when a new American President invited the leaders of the hemisphere to the first Summit of the Americas in Miami, the Latin-American states had to strongly insist to obtain that their host accept to put trade at the top of the agenda (Wiarda 1995, 43–68). The Clinton Administration obliged, but made it clear that if a hemispheric free trade agreement should be contemplated, it would have to take NAFTA as its cornerstone (see Feinberg 1997).

Not eager to share its NAFTA-secured access to the US market with other Latin-American Countries, Mexico has never been an enthusiast supporter on the FTAA (see Keith 2002, 11, and Mackay 2002, 12). But voice has also been a concern. Mexico was opposed, right from the beginning to a FTAA built by coordinating the NAFTA and MERCOSUR zones, fearing that, on the one hand, Brazil would then be considered as the only major spokesperson for Latin-American countries in such a scheme, and, on the other hand, that its voice would not be heard if mediated by Washington given the absence of voice opportunities in NAFTA. This was also the reason why Mexico refused that the NAFTA countries presented themselves at the negotiating table as a bloc, like it has been the case for MERCOSUR as well as the CARICOM and the Andean Community.

Mexico's concern for secondary ruling procedure is also apparent in the design of the numerous post-NAFTA free trade agreements it negotiated with other hemispheric partners. For example, compared to NAFTA, the 1998 Chile-Mexico Trade Agreement adds some modest, but nevertheless significant, powers to the Commission. The Chile-Mexico Commission can modify, in addition to the rules

---

8   For a more complete analysis of the US attitude before the official negotiation were launched, see Louis Bélanger (1998, 95–109).

of origin and the dates settled for tariff reduction, the list of reservations on market access, granted that any such decision is approved by governmental decree in Chile and published in both countries' Diaro Official [*Tratado de Libre Comercio entre la República de Chile y los Estados Unidos Mexicanos*, Articulo 17–01 and Anexo 17–01(3)]. Moreover, if Mexico's myriad of post-NAFTA bilateral and subregional FTAs are generally regarded as an extension of the NAFTA approach to trade in services (Gonzàlez 2000, Chapter 6), Sherry Stephenson judiciously points out that, as services are concerned, Mexico has shown a willingness to go further (see Mace and Bélanger, this book):

> All of the agreements signed by Mexico [after NAFTA] (although not the subsequent agreements negotiated by Chile) contain an article stipulating 'future liberalization', whereby parties are to negotiate the liberalization and removal of nonconforming measures listed in the annexes; the articles thereby introduce a marked element of dynamism into these agreements. (Stephenson 2001, 179)

Typically, such articles mandate the Commission to launch future negotiation for the elimination of all remaining reservations.[9]

Canada, unlike Mexico, is not really concerned about sharing its privileged access to the American market with the less developed economies of the region. Moreover, Canada can only envisage marginal economic gains from a better access to South American and Caribbean markets, which account for about 1.5 percent of its foreign trade. Thus, Ottawa's strategic interest in using hemispheric free trade negotiation as a mean to obtain voice benefits was less tempered by fears of loosing substantive benefits. This may explain why Canada was, in the first place, the country that insisted that NAFTA include an accession provision. As for the FTAA, Canada's 1995 White Paper on foreign policy clearly stated that the government expect it 'to encourage outward-looking and cooperative US economic policies' (Government of Canada 1995, 15) and former Prime Minister Jean Chrétien made public calls for hemispheric solidarity to counter-balance American power (*Le Devoir* 1995). Thus, Canada, contrary to Mexico, backed the initial US view of the FTAA as a 'NAFTA enlargement' process.

However, right from the start, this conception of the FTAA prompted strong oppositions, not only from Mexico but also from the MERCOSUR countries. The Miami Declaration finally stipulated vaguely that the heads of states and governments were committed to: '...build on existing subregional and bilateral arrangements in order to broaden and deepen hemispheric economic integration and to bring the agreements together'.[10] In front of this opposition, during the next four years of pre-negotiation that separated the Miami Summit from the 1998 San José Ministerial

---

9 'Artículo 10–09: Liberalización futura: A través de negociaciones futuras a ser convocadas por la Comisión, las Partes profundizarán la liberalización alcanzada en los diferentes sectores de servicios, con miras a lograr la eliminación de las restricciones remanentes inscritas de conformidad con el artículo 10–07(1) y (2).' (*Tratado de Libre Commercio entre la Republica de Chile y los Estados Unidos Mexicano*, art. 10–09).

10 A choice of words that was much more representative of the Brazilians' view (cited in Rosenberg and Stein 1995, 10).

Meeting, the US promoted the idea of a FTAA that would be built on a partnership between NAFTA and the MERCOSUR. Now both Canada and Mexico were opposed to this 'NAFTA-MERCOSUR coordination model'. At the 1995 Denver and 1996 Carthagena Ministerials, Canada pleaded against it, arguing that the South American and the North American integration models were too different for thinking of a merger. Ottawa's reaction is also understandable on the basis of the implication of a bloc-to-bloc structure for its voice opportunities. Such a bipolar coordination model, in the absence of any satisfying voice opportunity mechanism inside NAFTA, risked equating, for Canada (as for Mexico), to a delegation of authority to Washington. Canada thus preferred to become the proponent of an approach originating from the OAS, which called for the WTO-like negotiation of a brand new agreement among all participating countries (Hall 1997, A1). From a Canadian and Mexican standpoint, the creation a new, hemispheric-wide, agreement instead of a patchwork solution meant not only a direct hold on the negotiation process, but the prospect of the creation of richer governance structures to cope with the complexity of a free-trade zone counting 34 members, widely different in terms of economic and political level of development.

The US finally rallied the proposal sponsored by the Canadians (Mace et al. 2003, 137–139). But, Washington then proposed a negotiation structure that foresaw a step-by-step liberalization scheme made of a composite of initiatives. According to that plan put forward in preparation of the 1998 San José Ministerial, countries would have first commit themselves to accelerate the implementation of WTO disciplines, then they would adopt business facilitation measures, and after that they would conclude partial agreements on matters on which there is a consensus (Otteman 1998, 18–20). This 'early harvests' mechanic was opposed by MERCOSUR countries, which wanted a single-undertaking negotiation and wait for a complete assessment of the bargain before committing themselves. Canadians, for their part, first backed the American position on sequential negotiation and early harvests, but took their distances when the discussion on these issues threatened the project, and put on the table a compromise – to simultaneously negotiate all domains – around which all finally agreed (Mace et al. 2003, 150).

Once it has become evident that it wouldn't be possible, in a way or another, to use NAFTA as the institutional bedrock of the new agreement, the US manifested its willingness to negotiate a brand-new agreement, but one with an institutional design that would offer a minimal level of voice opportunity to other states. This preoccupation was obvious in the way Washington dealt with the key question of special treatment for smaller economies (see Mace and Bélanger, this book). Since the opening of the talks, Washington showed a strong opposition to any accommodation that would enshrine in an eventual FTAA measures which would permit to administer a preferential treatment system aimed at offering to the smaller and less developed economies the time and favorable conditions to adapt to, and profit from, trade liberalization. The US maintained as long as it could the position of strict reciprocity – that is, all FTAA signatories must assume the same rights and obligations (Miller 2002). When, at the 2001 Quebec City Summit, a consensus nevertheless emerged that the FTAA would not happen unless some kind of special treatment would be adopted, the US promptly reacted by announcing unilateral or quasi-unilateral measures, having for effect to extract from the FTAA process special treatment programs (see Mace and Bélanger, this book). Washington's staunch opposition was not only driven by principles, but also by its fear to see the FTAA institutional design evolving from a strict free trade agreement to an international organisation responsible for international development.

As we have seen, the story of the FTAA negotiation has in good part been dominated by the U.S attempt to obtain the benefits of commercial liberalization, while resisting to developments that would result in the institutionalisation of governance structure. It was thus not as surprising as it seemed to see the US quickly seizing the ball when Brazil made its about-turn before last November Ministerial meeting in Miami. The resulting US-Brazil proposal of a restructuring of the negotiation process that would produce a double-track liberalization system – with two negotiating tables: one for the negotiation of a basic minimal agreement binding the 34 countries, and one for one or several plurilateral and optional agreements on higher levels of obligation in different sectors – can be interpreted as a return, for the US, to a lighter commitment closer from its first-best option. Just before the opening of the Miami ministerial, the US Trade Representative coincidently announced Washington's decision to launch a series of bilateral negotiations with Colombia, Panama, and Peru, and then Bolivia and Ecuador. Added to the NAFTA and existing, or near completion, bilateral FTAs negotiated by Washington with hemispheric partners, this means that the US would in a near future be at the center of a network of 14 free trade partnerships replicating the NAFTA institutional design. The result may be less ambitious than the FTAA in terms of liberalization, but it also means much less engagement for the US and equally less voice opportunities for its trade partners.

Overall, Mexico and Canada, even if they embarked with the US in the FTAA negotiation, developed diverging attitudes on how the hemispheric trade agreement should be negotiated and should operate. While the US proposals showed a clear desire to avoid entangling governance structures, Mexico fought hard to preserve an autonomous voice in the process and developed views on institutional designs that would add voice opportunities in a future trade agreement. Canada, for its part, clearly looked at the FTAA as a way to recuperate, through new institutions and internal alliances, some of the autonomy and voice opportunities lost in the NAFTA. This is coherent with its original, first choice option, of a FTAA through NAFTA enlargement as well as its enduring efforts to counter US attempts to minimize the institutional coherence and scope of the project.

Conclusion

NAFTA should have brought Canada's and Mexico's trade policy to converge with the US one. This is what institutionalist theories would have predicted. And this is what could have been expected at the time of the agreement's ratification, in view of the precedents created by existing free trade areas in other regions of the world and by the NAFTA itself as an extension of the previous CUSTA. But, as we have seen, the converging effect, when there was one, has taken an unforeseen path. The reason is that NAFTA is equipped with inadequate, embryonic governance structures that do not foster coordination of the member-states' respective trade policies. This choice of institution, coupled with the asymmetry of power between the member states, created a deficit in voice opportunities for Canada and Mexico. Because of that, NAFTA induced diverging interests and preferences in trade policies among the three North-American states. These divergences were less about the substance of trade than about institutional strategies and trajectories, albeit Mexico has demonstrated more concern than Canada for the preservation of its preferential access to the US market. While the US entered in post-NAFTA trade negotiations demonstrating a clear willingness to obtain liberalization but not at the cost of entangling governance structure, the two other partners deployed strategies aimed at institutionalizing negotiation processes and trade cooperation mechanisms in ways that would produce opportunities for voice and coalition-making from which they expect to benefit.

To achieve this, however, Mexico and Canada choose different paths and preferred different institutional trajectories. The Mexicans preferred balancing through independent extra-regional institution-making, and the less successful Canadians preferred expanding NAFTA and making room for intra-alliance balancing. Mexico's sensitivity to the relative advantage given by NAFTA to its firms over other Latin American competitors may explain why it has been reluctant to contemplate any enlargement scenarios, be they directed toward other hemispheric countries or Europe. The Mexicans also demonstrated suspicions over the possibility of the NAFTA countries operating as a single bloc during trade negotiations. Thus, Mexico clearly opted for direct extra-regional relations in its quest for distinct voice opportunities. Canada, on the other hand, didn't show the same level of suspicion and was willing to engage with extra-regional partners through the NAFTA bloc. Ottawa thus seemed to look for a NAFTA that would open itself to other partners, by way of accession or enlargement, thus permitting Canada to exert intra-alliance balancing strategies. Unfortunately for Canada, considering European reactions to TAFTA-like initiatives and the near collapse of the FTAA negotiations, this first-best option did not succeed.

Chapter 3

Security Policies in the NAFTA Environment

Nelson Michaud

The events that unfolded after September 11, 2001 have made us consider security questions under a new light. A light that allows very few shades of grey, a light that, held by President George W. Bush, does not leave much room for uncertainty: "Every nation, in every region, now has a decision to make. Either you are with us, or you are with the terrorists" (Bush 2001, 1349). Moreover, the dissuasion of any "future military competition" (Bush 2002, 29) coupled with the doctrine of "preemptive strikes" outlined in *The National Security Strategy* (Bush 2002, 15) leave us with the impression of forces from the entire continent – in fact, from the whole world – joining the American effort. Time collapses reality in a way that events from a not so distant past seem to be forgotten.

In terms of security policies, there is no doubt that September 11, 2001 left a scar that is now engraved in the marble of history. Absolute priority is given to these questions and, if there was a need for it, more than ever, the realist mantra calling for the defense of the national interest understood in terms of power prevails. The question now seems to be settled, at least for the foreseeable future.

Is this need to act collectively the sole result of the terrorist attacks of September 2001? Or is it rooted more deeply in a continental perception towards security questions? Already, the United States counted on a strong partnership with Canada through NORAD that complemented NATO.[1] Incentives to open the security agenda to include Mexico in order to ensure a thick continental security wall already existed for relations among the three countries had intensified through the economic realm with the adoption and implementation of the North America Free Trade Agreement in 1994. In other words, would low politics lead the way for a better integration of policies in the field of high politics? In itself, such an influence goes against the realist tide that factually has characterized American foreign policy over and above ideologies (Mearsheimer 2001, 25).

Although surprising at first, such a turn in American foreign policymaking is not impossible. After all, at the beginning of 2001, Henry Kissinger wrote that "America is obliged for the first time to devise a global strategy stretching into indefinite future. Fate has propelled a nation convinced of the universal application of a single

---

1   Joel Sokolsky underscores that "Although there were operational links between NORAD and NATO, the Americans never regarded NORAD as a NATO command" (Sokolsky 1995, 176).

set of maxims into a world characterized by a multiplicity of historical evolutions requiring selective strategies" (Mearsheimer 2001, 25).

The question of NAFTA's influence can also be supported in part by the fact that the door leading to hemispheric cooperation in terms of security was already open. Indeed, multilateral action has started, being fuelled by the concept of the protection of democracy. For instance, in 1985, countries members of the Organization of American States agreed to amend the organization's charter with the Carthagena Protocol that put the promotion and strengthening of representative democracy at the core of the organization's priorities. Canada subscribed to this by having the OAS Secretary General authorize the creation of the Unit for the promotion of democracy, which allowed, among other actions, the intervention that was necessary to settle the uprising in Haiti (Michaud and Bélanger 1999, 385). Several actions followed suit, a key one being the adoption of the Washington Protocol in 1992, which stipulated that a member shall be suspended from the organization if its democratic government is taken over by force. This principle was extended at the Québec Summit of the Americas where it was decided that non-democratic countries would not be member of an eventual Free Trade Area of the Americas.

No doubt, the footing for better cooperation in the field of security policies is present. However, reaching for a common goal can be done individually as it can be the result of a joint effort. Hence, the hemispheric agenda does not necessarily mean a security agenda common to all countries and even less an integration of security policies. It is therefore an excellent field where to test if we are witnessing a convergence or an alignment of policies.

Multilateral security policymaking therefore needs to be better understood in some regards: Did NAFTA influence the security policy agenda in Canada, the United States and Mexico? The question is no doubt worthy of interest for the United States where a stiffer resistance is theoretically expected; however, it has as much relevance regarding the other partners in the trade deal for they might be expected to follow the hegemon's lead. It is the aim of this chapter to bring some light, if not an answer to this question.

Theoretically, this problem reaches the heart of the debate that splits realists and neo-liberals as it serves, at the same time, as a good benchmark for the evaluation of constructivist conclusions. Two aspects of this debate are directly called upon: the segregation between high and low politics, that is, security and non-security issues, and the importance of institutions in policymaking. Since the impact of the constructivist approach on this analysis has been eloquently presented in the introduction of this book, I will only briefly complement it with some "realist vs neo-liberal" perspective. This will provide a useful scale from which to measure if convergence has happened in matters of security in the NAFTA environment, and if such is the case, what does converge, how is this convergence carried, and why do we see the phenomenon surface.

Going back to the basis of the approach I have chosen to conduct my analysis, we must first know that, looking at high and low politics, realists admit that other spheres of influence exist, but security issues must prevail. In addressing this question, Morgenthau refers to "the autonomy of the political sphere" (Morgenthau 1985, 13). Mearsheimer, for his part, is even more explicit: "Offensive realism recognizes that great powers might pursue non-security goals, but it has little to say about them, save for one important point: state can pursue them as long as the requisite behavior does not conflict with balance-of-power logic, which is often the case" (Mearsheimer 2001, 46). In other words: "Security trumps wealth when those two goals conflict" (Mearsheimer 2001, 48). Conversely, neo-liberals consider that the question is not one of exclusion, but one of hierarchy within priorities, both aspects of wealth and power combining to define the bahavior of a given state (Keohane 1984, 21).

For the purpose of this study, these considerations need to be read in light of the role each school gives to institutions, that is "collections of interrelated rules and routines that define appropriate actions in terms of relations between roles and situations" (March and Olson 1989, 21). On the one hand, realists like Kenneth Waltz consider that institutions affect the prospect for cooperation only marginally (Waltz 1979, 115–116). Complementing this line of thought, Mearsheimer documents this evaluation by the fact that "There is little evidence that [institutions] can get great powers to act contrary to the dictates of realism [...] The United States is the most powerful state in the world, and it usually gets its way on issues it judges important. If it does not, it ignores the institution and does what it deems to be in its own interest" (Mearsheimer 2001, 364–365). On the other hand, neo-liberals advocate that "institutions can change the incentives for countries affected by them, and can in turn affect the strategic choices government make in their own self-interest" (Axelrod and Keohane 1993, 112).

I will start the exploration of the question raised by the integration of North American security policies by postulating that security in North America, is dominated by the United States; and that, consequently, security questions are dealt within bilateral relationships where the hegemon is almost certain to dominate, whereas in a multilateral relationship, it exposes itself to the uncertainty inherent to the dealings and bargaining with several partners. Therefore, should the multilateral setting of NAFTA exercise some influence over the security policy making, it will be translated by a sliding from bilateralism towards multilateralism. Should the security policy making environment remain solidly in the bilateral framework, then the NAFTA multilateral influence will remain questionable.

Based on realists' theoretical conclusions, I will hypothesize that, contrary to other policy fields explored elsewhere in this book, security policymaking has not been influenced by NAFTA. The findings will be supported by a sequential analysis of the three bilateral relationships: United-States – Mexico, Mexico – Canada, Canada – United States, for bilateral relationships is what we expect to change over time, should the NAFTA policymaking framework be transferred to the field of security policies. Since issue areas such as drug trafficking and the continental security perimeter are addressed in the chapters by Aureano, and then Roussel, Fortmann and Duplantis, they will not be considered in the present chapter. These analyses will be flanked by a quick overview of the security dimensions covered by NAFTA and by the role that is played by integrative structures aiming at continental security.

NAFTA and Security

The first observation we can make from the reading of the agreement is that there is no specific chapter dealing with security matters. This does not mean that the North American Free Trade Agreement completely ignores security related issues. In fact, the question is taken care of through three clauses. The key one is Article 2102 (Chapter 21), which specifically addresses national security. It has to be read in conjunction with Article 607 (Chapter 6) that deals with national security measures in terms of energy, and Article 1018 (Chapter 10) that concentrates on exceptions to government procurements.[2]

These articles are broad and allow the contracting parties to accommodate their behavior from what is generally prescribed in the Agreement. In fact, the free trade area thus created differentiates itself from other forms of regional integration – such as custom unions or common markets – by the fact that contracting parties, while eliminating tariff and non-tariff barriers, keep their independence in trade policymaking towards third parties (see Nyahoho and Proulx 2000, 778). We should keep in mind that these elements could bear some importance in how security questions are being dealt with on the continent.

Thus, Article 2102 guarantees some form of sovereignty by stipulating that nothing in the Agreement shall be construed "to require any Party to furnish or allow access to any information the disclosure of which it determines to be contrary to its essential security interests", "to prevent any Party from taking any actions that it considers necessary for the protection of its essential security interests" and "to prevent any Party from taking action in pursuance of its obligations under the United Nations Charter for the maintenance of international peace and security". This general guarantee of sovereign decision making is reinforced by Article 607, which allows an exception to the trade of energy or basic petrochemical goods "to the extent necessary to" defense needs and agreements, and by Article 1018 that allows some defense and national security procurements to remain tacit.

As one can see, the Agreement per se does not offer any mechanism that would allow a better integration of the security and defense policymaking. Moreover, the spirit behind these articles encourages, to some extent, an independent behavior for each signatory party. Security matters are not dealt with the same way other trade issues are. This is not much surprising for values such as autonomy of the hegemon or sovereignty of the lesser powers are dear to the participants: they would settled for nothing less. As a consequence, it can be said that the Agreement itself allows bilateral relationships, much more than it helps in bringing multilateralism. Hence, the importance of studying the three bilateral relationships among the contracting parties is reaffirmed.

The United States-Mexico Relationship

Although it can be said that "the U.S. military relationship with Latin America and the Caribbean goes well beyond security assistance programs, exercises and

---

2   Full text of these articles can be consulted in the *Appendix* of this chapter.

deployments" (Just the Facts 2003), and although Mexico is the Latin American state closest to the American boarder, the bilateral relationship that exists between these two continental actors is not the most intense one can find. Cope qualified it as a "long-standing but distant relationship" (Cope 1996, 179). Among the recent continental security developments, the establishment of NORTHCOM no doubt includes Mexico, but it can hardly be related to the free trade deal, many other factors having prompted the need for the new structure.

Historically, military exchanges between Mexico and the United States meant for the latter, the invasion of the former's territory, which ended in "a devastating loss of territory to the United States as a result of the Mexican American war" (Randall 1995, 77). These events produced in Mexico an enduring nationalist sentiment that surfaces from time to time and that in part explains the low level of defense and security integration between the two countries. In fact, in the immediate aftermath of September 11, 2001, Mexico was put "in the difficult position of having to weigh its pacifist foreign policy against its new relationship with the United States [...] Mexico has to choose between its decades-old defiance of U.S. force and the new reality that its economic and political future lies with the United States" (Government of Mexico – Presidencia de la Republica 2001).

Some warming had been witnessed during World War II. In order to face the common enemy of fascism, both countries established the Joint Mexico-US Defense Commission that would hardly be in use after that period, though still in existence. However, this can be considered as a momentary rapprochement. The prevailing sentiment is one of careful politeness. For instance, when President Kennedy implemented his program *Alliance for Progress*, with the objectives of providing economic and military aid to countries having to counter left-wing guerrilla movements, Mexico declined the invitation to join in. During the 1970s, under the Presidency of Luis Echeverria, in an attempt to balance American influence, clear efforts were made by the Mexican government to diversify its international relations. This included a recognition of Castro's government in Cuba, which was not to favorably predispose Americans towards closer military openings and cooperation with their southern neighbors. And, for a time, offshore resources allowed Mexicans to dream of coupling this political affirmation with a higher level of economic sovereignty.

The early 1980s presented friction points on all of these sensitive matters, and other were added to the list. The United States' attitude towards Central American countries did not please Mexico, pulling the trigger of the defense of sovereignty; a major economic crisis, fuelled by the fall of crude oil prices, put Mexico in a disadvantageous position; and drug trafficking increased significantly, Mexico being used as a springboard to hit the American market. Mexico did not see the United States from a favorable angle, neither did Washington perceived Mexico City approvingly. In fact, "Mexican deviations from US preferences may have been an irritant prior to the election of Ronald Reagan as President, but under Reagan they were seen as serious defections" (Government of Mexico – Presidencia de la Republica 2001).

As it sometimes happens, a point was reached where antagonisms forced cooperation and it is in this light that the "Salinas opening" occurred. Characterized by the new President's rejection of revolutionary principles, this opening took place in several areas including political, economic, even religious spheres. One of the key achievements that can be credited to this new approach is NAFTA.

Some will find a causal relationship between NAFTA and a US-Mexico defense and security alignment. Among them is the American Secretary of Defense, William Perry, who grounds this cooperation… in 1992, that is, over a year before NAFTA was concluded. In a visit to the Mexican Department of Defense – the first one ever by an American Secretary of Defense – Perry states that his goal and the goal aimed at through his encounter with his Mexican counterpart is "to help our nations forge closer security ties […] So let us build a new bilateral security relationship based on openness, trust, cooperation and mutual respect" (Perry 1995). Interestingly enough, Perry goes from a multilateral deal to a bilateral security agenda that he considers as the "third leg" of the Mexican-US relationship – the two others being of a political and economic nature.

As a result, a specific opening was made to have Mexican officers being trained in US military academies. However this endeavour was not unanimously received for some have seen in it the expression of a lack of Mexican sovereignty, which is not without reminding us of the nationalist values that used to slow down any form of alignment. However, this did not prevent some analysts to establish a clear link between NAFTA and security policy alignment. For instance, Cope admits that "NAFTA has created a conductive environment for reshaping bilateral military relations and that both defense establishments have seized the opportunity" (Cope 1996, 205). For his part, James Rochlin goes one step further as he insists on the US-Mexican military integration. For this author, "As the military has occupied a more pervasive role in Mexico, the United States has become more influential over Mexican military. NAFTA has meant both economic and military integration" (Rochlin 1997, 171).

Despite these encouraging signals, one must admit that there was still some resistance south of the Rio Grande and it would be misleading to expect, as a result of these initiatives, a major integration of US and Mexican military efforts. One front where more important progress is made is the one related to drug trafficking as Guillermo Aureano outlines in his chapter. Apart from that, one must acknowledge that Mexico is not a prime recipient of American military aid.

In fact, among Latin American countries, Mexico ranks behind Columbia, Bolivia, Peru, and Ecuador, both in terms of people trained and amount invested by the United States. As the table below clearly shows, US military aid to Mexico indeed went downward from 1997 to 2001, where a slight increase was noticed.

When compared to economic and social aid, military and police aid is no doubt more important, as shown in the next figure. However, we see that it is not consistent and the post 9/11 factor no doubt plays an important role in the increase observed, a phenomenon not present in the immediate post-NAFTA era.

This coolness should be put into context. As Bélanger properly outlined, Mexico plays a secondary role in continental defense (Bélanger 1998, 5). Moreover, it can be explained by other factors. First, from a historical point of view, Mexico continued to oppose a reinforcement of multilateral military cooperation out of its nationalistic concerns for the sacrosanct principle of the non-intervention. To the examples I have

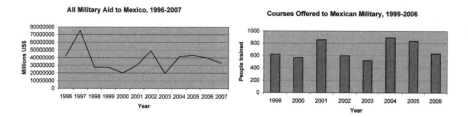

Figure 3.1   US military assistance to Mexico (1997–2002)

Notes: Data show military assistance to Mexico reduced somewhat from 1997 levels. But
              aid amonts have long since stabilized, and documents predict a moderate increase
              in 2001 and 2002.

Source: http://ciponline.org/facts/1101jtf.htm. With kind permission from the Center for
International Policy.

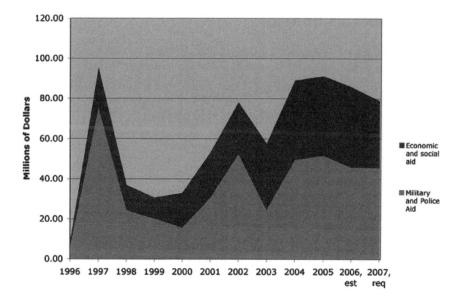

Figure 3.2   US aid to Mexico (total) (1996–2007)

Source: http://ciponline.org/facts/mx.htm#military. With kind permission from the Center for
International Policy.

already referred to, we can add the fierce Mexican opposition to the 1995 attempt
by the Inter-American Defense Board to interpret specific tasks within a broadened
mission, an event that occurred in the immediate aftermath of Mexico's signature of
NAFTA. Mexico perceived it as an arrogation of functions which were beyond the
Board's juridical competency. Second, another element that cannot be neglected is

the domestic factor. As Moreira notes, "the existence of internal problems in Chiapas did not allow the Armed Forces to face a serious identity conflict in Mexico. The old principles that focused on the internal defense could still be applied" (Santana Moreira 1997).

Finally, should NAFTA really play a role in the integration of defense and security policies, the effort would not be only on a bilateral basis between the United States and Mexico. It would extend to Canada as well. There are no signs of such an opening. In fact, Secretary Perry's speech, although it refers to a "new era", nevertheless anchors the Mexican-American defense relationship in strong bilateral and not multilateral terms. NAFTA may have helped some opening, for some time or on some fronts towards a better cooperation in security operations between Mexico and the United States. However, from the evidence gathered thus far in this research, we are at best, much closer to the beginning of an alignment, than we are to any form of convergence. It is therefore difficult to conclude that security policies benefited from the continentalization economic process. An exploration of the Canadian-Mexican relationship is in order, however, to validate if indeed Mexican-American bilateralism did not move into trilateralism.

The Mexico-Canada Relationship

What is found under this second bilateral relationship corroborates the lack of intent to move towards a multilateral effort. In fact, despite a "three-fold increase in bilateral trade and investments" (Government of Canada 2003a), the bilateral relationship between Canada and Mexico in terms of security and defense policy is surprisingly low. It is therefore difficult to find an opening towards multilateralism when bilateralism is barely present. At most, Mexico's sporadic involvement in multilateral peace operations could favor some operational exchanges between the two countries' militaries. However, although their action might happen to be within the confines of the Americas,[3] this cannot be considered as an example of military and security cooperation or integration influenced by NAFTA.

There are reasons to believe that a different outcome might have been expected. There is, of course, the NAFTA incentive, but it is not the only one. After all, both countries share the same omnipotent neighbor and face its unilateral security decisions without having much influence on their formulation. It seems that this is not enough to encourage a stronger partnership between Canada and Mexico. Concretely, no formal agreement has been signed between the two countries (Instituto Matías Romero de Estudios Diplomáticos 1997), which brought Rochlin to mark the Canadian-Mexican military integration in post-NAFTA as null (Rochlin 1997, 2). For his part, Klepak limits the common ground to similarities of views on security questions and the potential for extending cooperation to security questions (Klepak 1996).

---

3   Theoretically, at least. For instance, Canada, but not Mexico, participated in UN operation MINUGUA (1997) in Guatemala (http://www.un.org/Depts/dpko/dpko/co_mission/minugua.htm) and Mexico, but not Canada, took part in UN operation ONUSAL (1991–1995) in Salvador (http://www.un.org/Depts/dpko/dpko/co_mission/onusal.htm).

This does not mean that the Canadian-Mexican bilateral security relationship is non-existent. Indeed, Canada has one of its four Canadian Defence Attaché (CDA) officers in Latin America based in Mexico City. However, one should not forget that this person covers a wide area, being cross-accredited to Belize, Cuba, El Salvador, Guatemala, Honduras, Nicaragua and Panama. In other words, the location in Mexico seems to be more a factor of convenience than the reflection of a well established partnership between Mexico and Canada.

In this regard, it is interesting to note the Canadian Department of National Defence's blunt statement: "In keeping with the 1994 Defence White Paper, the Department of National Defence (DND) and the Canadian Armed Forces (CF) have been actively expanding their bilateral and multilateral defense and security activities in Latin America and the Caribbean", which could be a promising *entrée en matière*. However, the departmental document goes on, pin pointing that "Most of the activity is with Argentina, Brazil and Chile", three states that are identified as "principal countries" (http://www.dnd.ca/admpol/eng/defence/ca_la_relation_e.htm). Mexico is nowhere to be seen on this list. Even the Military Training Assistance Program that provides "a means through which Canada can broaden its relations with Latin American and Caribbean nations, and contribute to the constructive development of their legitimate defence and security needs" (http://www.dnd.ca/admpol/eng/ defence/ca_la_relation_e.htm)[4] is not extended to Mexico.

The premise of this statement is in itself, revealing: "In keeping with the 1994 Defence White Paper"; nowhere in the 1994 policy document does the word Mexico appear (Department of National Defense 1994) ... This is not an isolated oversight, for other Canadian Defense policy statements also ignore Mexico. This is notably the case with the 2001 *Defense Planning Document*. Although the policy paper presents a section that is clearly dedicated to the defense of North America, the text insists that this will be done "in co-operation with the United States", keeping silent mentions of any other partner (Government of Canada 2001b).[5]

Also revealing of Canada's shy willingness to increase its bilateral relationship with Mexico on security matters, is the speech delivered by Art Eggleton, then minister of National Defense, before the Mexican Defense College, a prime location from where to showcase under a favorable light, defense cooperation, if not alignment, between the two countries. The minister instead stressed the importance of the Canadian-Mexican bilateral relationship in terms of trade and economy, but was surprisingly discreet about defense cooperation. At most, there are some references through a third party, being it the UN or the OAS, but not much is said about the Canada-Mexico security relationship. In fact, the minister throws the ball in the Mexican camp, stating that Canada is ready to consolidate cooperation links with Mexico once Mexico has made more precise its intents on the international scene (Government of Canada 2002e).

---

4   This information was consulted again in November 2006, and had not been updated since 2002.

5   The 2005 International Policy Statement merely reiterates a wish for Canada to better cooperate with Mexico on questions related to sexcurity.

No doubt that NAFTA has influenced the structure of Canadian foreign policymaking. From a trade point of view, it goes without saying; also, structural transformations within the department of Foreign Affairs occurred (see Dosman 1995, 90–92). However, the same cannot be said about security and defense matters. As a good indication, the Canadian Embassy in Mexico website consulted at the time this study was conducted and again in November 2006, referred to defense relations not as a separate topic, but as an item under the political relations. One aspect this sub-section covers is the "assistance to Trade Commissioners, liaison with Canadian industry and establishing contacts with host nation military procurement agencies" (Government of Canada 2003b), which is probably the only trace of a link between the NAFTA and Canadian security policy exchanges with Mexico. More eloquently, of the 44 bilateral agreements signed between Canada and Mexico between 1990 and 2004, none bears upon defense matters (Government of Canada 2002a).[6]

It can therefore be concluded that the Canada-Mexico bilateral relationship was not influenced by NAFTA in a way to turn it into a multilateral modus operandi in the field of defense and security. Consequently, one must understand that the Canadian-Mexican exchanges did not influence the American-Mexican bilateral relationship in order to transform it into a trilateral institution. The weakness of the links in these first two cases might offer the explanation for such non-commitment towards continental integration. It remains to be seen if a stronger relationship, such as the one that exists between Canada and the United States, can pull a multilateral relation out of what seems to be a deeply rooted status quo ante free trade.

The Canada-United States Relationship

Of the three security related bilateral relationships under study in this chapter, the one between Canada and the United States is probably the most intense. For the period this study covered, it translated into 80 treaty level defense agreements, more than 250 memoranda of understanding, and 145 bilateral forums under which defense matters are discussed.[7] Macleod, Roussel, and van Mens see it as "a real bargain" although the price to pay might very well be to "not necessarily share either American perceptions of what constitutes a threat or their view of how a perceived threat should be countered" (Macleod, Roussel and van Mens 2000, 341). Indeed, the links are numerous and, at times, tightly knit, to the extent that some might see the Canada-United States security relationship as totally integrated. In fact, this is

---

6   Of the first 35 agreements, one addresses questions of double taxation, the others being concerned with environmental co-operation, distance education, mining, culture and legal matters. On 27 February 2003, Prime Minister Chrétien announced that Canada and Mexico would sign another 9 bilateral agreements on questions of trade, communications, and money laundering, and organized crime; these agreements covered aspects related to education, telecommunications, governance, continental and foreign affairs (Government of Canada – Privy Council Office 2003).

7   These statistics were given by Lieutenant-General George MacDonald (Government of Canada 2002a).

not the case and there were several ups and downs over the years[8] that lend to think that nothing should be taken for granted on this front.

The Canada-American relationship was among the first foreign rapports Canada established as an autonomous state. It can be traced to the Ogdensburg meeting between President Franklin Delano Roosevelt and Prime Minister William Lyon Mackenzie King. The two men knew and appreciated each other well and the President invited his Canadian friend to this summer place to discuss matters of continental defense in the middle of World War II hostilities. Both countries recognized that their strategic interests were inseparable. The talks on joint defense agreements had started in 1937, but the heat of the war made the issue more prominent. The talks translated into the 18 August 1940 agreement that provided both states with a Permanent Joint Board of Defense. In its advisory capacity, the Board was more a symbol than a policy making body, although it formally sanctioned the plans refined by Canadian and American military authorities. In fact, the Board became a victim of its own successes: the level and quality of cooperation, first allowed by the establishment of the Board, made it redundant to a large extent.

Another major milestone in the establishment of integrated military and security efforts one cannot ignore is the North American Air Defense Command, better known under its acronym: NORAD. The organization can be seen in turn, as a step towards the continentalization of defense policies or a cheap way for Canada to benefit from a protection its own resources would never allow.[9] For his part, Joel Sokolsky goes one step further in his evaluation, stating that "the United States has been fortunate to have on its northern border not just a compliant neighbor sensitive to American security concerns in North America, but an active participant in Western collective defence" (Sokolsky 1995, 173). Of course, NORAD was the creature of the Cold War requirements and of the new warfare technology. This could lead to think that NAFTA might have an important influence on the conduct of the agreement.

Such is not the case. Not that the trade dimension is not important, but, as demonstrated by Denholm Crosby, this happened well before NAFTA. As she underscores, "the Canadian/US defence production industry relationship is one of integration, with the Canadian sector being heavily dependant upon the US market for trade and contracts, integrated in terms of Canadian/US ownership, dominated by a few firms, and with defense policy interests synonymous with those of representatives of US owned firms" (Denholm Crosby 1998, 128).[10] In fact, this is a nice occurrence where the causal relationship should be looked at the other way around: "in the 1980s political decision-makers no longer entertained alternatives and consideration of NORAD and NORAD-related programs was largely on the

---

8 One may think here of the tense relationship between the Kennedy administration and the Diefenbaker government, the Canadian claim of sovereignty over the North West Passage, or the surprise stances of the Trudeau government authorizing cruise missiles testing in Canadian over Canadian territory or of a Mulroney government refusing to engage itself in President Reagan's "Star Wars" project, to name but a few instances.

9 An idea particularly well expressed by John Holmes (Holmes 1982).

10 Statistics clearly show that integration happened well before NAFTA (Denholm Crosby 1998, 125–127).

basis of the economic benefits that could accrue through participation" (Denholm Crosby 1998, 121).

A third nexus of cooperation where Canada and the United States meet is within NATO. The organization was founded in Washington, on 4 April 1949, with the signature, of the North Atlantic Treaty. It is widely recognized that the organization is US dominated. Nevertheless, Canada played some role in its inception,[11] notably by promoting a clause to extend the organization's mandate to non-defense issues, and by having it included under Article 2 of the Treaty.[12] At the time of NAFTA implementation, NATO was to face two new challenges: its expansion and its involvement in settling continental crises in the Balkans. These two challenges rest on a common denominator, that is, the need and the will for new resources. In this regard, Canada and the United States, if they were so inclined, were in a unique position to have the organization consider the addition of a third North American partner.[13] However, this research has found no trace of such intent by either Canada or the United States. Canada, especially, was a strong supporter of an expanded membership, minister Axworthy reportedly having stated that "ideally all states that wish to join should be allowed to do so" (quoted in Anstis 1999, 107). The American position is exposed in the White House document *National Security Strategy of Engagement and Enlargement* and aims at enlarging democratic free market countries in view of supporting a strong American economy. To add to this context, Mexico had to clarify its position towards NATO since the country headed for intensification of its economic relationship with Europe, but this did not seem to lead to intensification of security related links.[14] Nowhere in these instances, is Mexico mentioned.

The three aspects I have retained to illustrate the Canadian-American bilateral relationship are, of course, the proverbial tip of the iceberg. However, they provide a fair representation of this relationship both in its historical continuity and in its wide ranging capacity. Would have it been preferable to opt for more recent developments such as interoperability[15] or the security perimeter discussed in section III of the Roussel, Fortmann and Duplantis chapter? As it was mentioned in other parts of this chapter, it is difficult to consider them as being the direct product of the NAFTA environment, for other major concerns, including the response to the September

---

11 For an interesting overview, see Scott Reid (Reid 1977).

12 This clause clearly reflects Canada's values. It reads: "The Parties will contribute towards further development of peaceful and friendly international relations by strengthening their free institutions, by bringing about a better understanding of the principles upon which these institutions are founded, and by promoting conditions of stability and well-being. They will seek to eliminate conflict in their international economic policies and will encourage collaboration between any or all of them."

13 On Canada's and US's objectives towards NATO expansion, see David G. Haglund (Haglund 2000).

14 On Mexico's options in this context, see Francisco Gil Villegas (Villegas 1999, 266).

15 In his study, Joel Sokolsky (Sokolsky 2002, 12) does not refer once to NAFTA and admits that interoperability is not a question influenced by trade; other studies on interoperability include *The Canadian Forces and Interoperability: Panacea or Perdition?* (Griffiths 2002).

2001, terrorist attacks, came into play. For this reason and also because some of these questions are dealt with extensively elsewhere in this book, they will not retain our attention here.

From this quick sketch of events, two general conclusions can be drawn. First, the long standing pattern of Canadian-American cooperation in the realm of security questions pre-dates NAFTA by over half a century. Moreover, nothing in the recent developments the Canadian-American bilateral relationship has known can be directly linked to any NAFTA provisions. Second, it is interesting to see that none of the three examples chosen here – the Joint Board of Defense, NORAD, and NATO – present some clues that a long-standing, well established bilateralism might turn into a multilateral relationship. We witness no openings to greet Mexico within their ranks.[16]

Integration Mechanisms[17]

As McDougall aptly notes, "One way NAFTA promotes policy convergence is through its institutional structures, including various commissions, committees, and working groups" (McDougall 2000, 287). Such mechanisms facilitate the exchange of information, the networking among actors, and the convergence of policies. In the field of security policies, several of these structures exist, but none are NAFTA related. Moreover, these are not the most open organizations, as one might expect. An overview of the scarce information that is available, does not offer a portrait that is much different from what the bilateral relations have allowed to unveil.

Among the inter-american organizations devoted to security and defense that exist, one may list the sectorial organizations, that is, the Inter-American Naval Conference, the Conference of American Armies, and the System of Cooperation among the American Air Forces. To complement these, there are two organizations with a broader spectrum of interest: the younger Defense Ministerial of the Americas, and the older Inter-American Defense Board.

For its part, the Inter-American Naval Conference is key to the sharing of information among its members regarding operational information, feasibility of training, and on general and/or technical support. This is done, notably, through the Inter-American Naval Telecommunications Conference Secretariat, which is composed of five officers and one non commissioned officer from the member countries. It is noteworthy that neither Canada nor Mexico is a member of the IATNC.[18]

---

16 A thorough search of the web sites of all concerned countries and organizations, as well as a key word search in major newspapers of these countries over the period that extended from 1998 to 2003 point to this conclusion.

17 The author wishes to thank Hugo Loiseau for his excellent research report that is used as the basis for this section. The report was produced when its author was a research assistant at the Centre d'études interaméricaines.

18 The membership lists appears on http://www.iantn.navy.mil/member%20countries. htm.

The Conference of American Armies, for its part, counts the three North American Countries within its membership. Its aim is "the analysis, debate and exchange of ideas and experiences related to matters of common interest in the field of defense so as to heighten cooperation and integration between the Armies and to contribute from a military thinkers' point of view to the security and democratic development of member countries" (Conference of the American armies, http://www.redcea. org/english/home.html). Created in 1960, the Conference predates NAFTA and its achievements over the last ten years include the strengthening of integration and collaboration between armies. However, such endeavor does not seem to be related to any NAFTA effect, but rather rests on the "propagation of military culture and national values" (Conference of the American armies, http://www.redcea.org/english/home.html).

The third sectorial organization, the System of Cooperation among the American Air Forces, also dates from the early 1960s (http://www.sicofaa.org/). Its purpose, through the Conference of Chiefs of Air Forces – its ultimate decision making body – is to promote cooperation amongst its members, mainly from a logistical point of view "through the cultivation of valued personal relationships[...] Personal contacts and the exchange of information and ideas among militaries promote mutual trust and understanding" (Fogleman 1996). The value of this cooperation is particularly important in the fight against drug trafficking. No doubt the organization contributes to a higher level of integration of Air Forces of the Americas, but it can hardly be found any evidence of NAFTA's influence over its operations. Moreover, whilst Canada and the United States are full fledged members of the organization, Mexico merely enjoys an observer's status.

Much more recent is the Defense Ministerial of the Americas. It was established in 1995, following the Miami Summit of the Americas to answer an American wish. In doing so, the OAS transformed its three-year-old Special Committee on Hemispheric Security into a Permanent Committee, intensifying its work on issues related to arms trafficking, conflict prevention and various other programs. The Defense Ministerial of the Americas regroups Ministers from OAS member countries as well as civilian and military officials. It met for the first time in Williamsburg, Virginia, in 1995 and, starting in 1996, on a bi-annual basis to "promote mutual understanding and the exchange of ideas in the field of defense and security" (Government of the United States – Department of State 2002). The Defense Ministerial of the Americas operates on the six following principles, none of them reflecting any link with the NAFTA:

- Uphold the promise of the Santiago Agreement that the preservation of democracy is the basis for ensuring our mutual security.
- Acknowledge that military and security forces play a critical role in supporting and defending the legitimate interests of sovereign democratic states.
- Affirm the commitments of our countries in Miami and Managua that our Armed Forces should be subordinate to democratically controlled authority, act within the bounds of national Constitutions, and respect human rights through training and practice.

- Increase transparency in defense matters through exchanges of information, through reporting on defense expenditures, and by greater civilian-military dialogue.
- Set as a goal for our hemisphere the resolution of outstanding disputes by negotiated settlement and widespread adoption of confidence building measures, all of this in a time-frame consistent with the pace of hemispheric economic integration, and to recognize that the development of our economic security profoundly affects our defense security and vice versa.
- Promote greater defense cooperation in support of voluntary participation in UN-sanctioned peacekeeping operations, and to cooperate in a supportive role in the fight against narcoterrorism (Government of the United States – Secretary of State 2006).

As one can appreciate, the North American economic environment did not seem to have influenced the Defense Ministerial of the Americas, despite the closeness in time of their implementation.

Finally, the Inter-American Defense Board can be seen as the highest level Inter-american security and defense organization in the region. It is the fruit of a compromise arrived at during World War II when the United States did not succeed to reach unanimity among the nations of the hemisphere for breaking off relations with the Axis powers. The aim of the Inter-American Defense Board was to provide a means of systematic communication and coordination between the militaries of the hemisphere, and to serve as a symbol of hemispheric unity. Its original charter specified that it is to serve as an advisory organ, and that its resolutions would be non-binding. No forces were assigned, no formal alliance structure was promulgated, and no command and control structures were instituted. In fact, it can be said that the Board's purpose was primarily political, rather than purely military, offering Latin American countries this warm fuzzy feeling of having a say in hemispheric defense planning, although the United States kept under its control most of the defense activity in the region. Interestingly enough, up until November 2002, neither Canada nor Mexico belonged to the organization. The situation evolved when Canada announced its intent to join it at the November 2002 meeting of the Defense Ministerial of the Americas. In the statement issued at the time, Canadian Ambassador Paul Durand then referred strictly to security issues in order to justify Canada's presence on the Board (Inter-America Defense Board 2002) Now that the Board is under the OAS umbrella,[19] Canada and Mexico are members of it; however, this move cannot be linked with any NAFTA influence, but with wider regional considerations for better and more representative governance of the organization.

The review of these five organizations offers a portrait of diversity in origins, membership, and mandates. However, all present a similar response when considered in light of NAFTA, that is, the lack of influence the economic institution has over these security organizations.

---

19 The transfer happened on 16 March 2006.

Conclusion

In accordance with the general research question this book seeks to address, this chapter looked at NAFTA's potential influence over security and defense policies. There were several ways to conduct this investigation. A research organized around issue areas could have offered an interesting approach, but the difference in the level of involvement each country has in peacekeeping or in non-proliferation, for instance, as well as some issues being specifically addressed in some chapters of this book prevented this author to take such route. Instead, I preferred to explore structural data both in the Agreement per se and in already existing continental institutions and I looked if NAFTA influenced bilateral relationships between United States and Mexico, Mexico and Canada, and Canada and the United States, and turned them into a multilateral setting.

Another difficulty of this research was the timeframe to be considered. In order to adequately evaluate the impact of NAFTA on hemispheric security and defense policies, I had to weigh their evolution up until the terrorist attacks against the United States. For, September 11, 2001, indeed changed the face of things. For instance, Mexico who, for a long time, resisted integration of defense and security policies, hosted countries of the hemisphere, in 2004, for the Special Conference on Hemispheric Security, a result of the talks held in Québec City during the Summit of the Americas. At the time of the invitation, the host country "has argued that the conference should be used to craft a replacement for the Rio Treaty, one that would mobilize the region's militaries to deal with non-traditional security issues, such as disaster-response, alongside traditional defense missions" (Kourous 2002).

These caveats being considered, the research explored the five aspects of provisions of NAFTA regarding security, the three bilateral relationships per se, and, finally, the integration mechanisms already present, but that might have been influenced by the Agreement. From each of these themes, partial conclusions were drawn and all converge to determine no direct institutional influence on policymaking.

Again, the war launched by President Bush against terrorism reshuffled the deck. Mexico is now considered in the continental defense plans through NORTHCOM. As well, when the three country leaders met in Monterey, in March 2002, they advocated the need to harmonize their policies on border security. This being said, none of these initiatives are linked by their defenders to integration under NAFTA. The only implication NAFTA might have on these issues is that the Agreement favored a sharp increase in trade; a border management problem due to security concerns might have an important negative economic impact. In a sense, the relationship exists, but it can hardly be said that security policy integration is not directly related to the NAFTA environment. Before September 11, 2001, if the need existed, it was not a prominent concern. The real development was to come only later, when President Bush, President Fox, and Prime Minister Martin signed the North-American Partnership for Prosperity and Security in March 2005 and, again, if this partnership was aimed at consolidating NAFTA, it was not prompted by the treaty, but by post 9/11 threats that could have weakened the benefits expected from the treaty.[20]

---

20 On this partnership and its implications, see Nicolas Moquin (Moquin 2006).

As a consequence, the answers we can bring to the questions raised in the introduction of this book are easy to formulate. First, from the theoretical perspective, we must say that, in the case of security and defense policies, increasing globalization as expressed through the terms of NAFTA did not render national policies more similar over time. The fact that NAFTA has no central authority might very well be one of the reasons why such institutional influence has not been traced, for there are no real incentives to create a Schengen-like environment, for instance: domestic priorities and the defense of each country's sovereignty were stronger than the tacit incentives brought by the economic treaty. We must therefore conclude that the spill-over effect of the trade policy is quasi non existent if not totally absent in the realm of security and defense policies.

Considering the more specific questions this research is offering us to explore, the conclusions this chapter reaches are also easy to formulate since the issue is settled once we have provided an answer to the first interrogation: from what this analysis has brought, we can say that there is absolutely no convergence in terms of security and defense policies. At most, might we see some basis for some bilateral alignments here and there, but most of them predate the signature of NAFTA. There are some wishes expressed, but these are rarely followed by a determining action. As a consequence, there is no need to consider further the sub-questions related the depth of the phenomenon, its nature (emulation vs top-down), and the instruments used to encourage convergence.

Finally, some might argue that security issues are de facto dealt with through economic prosperity. After all, this is the principle upon which Robert Schuman and Jean Monet built Europe (Robertson 1999, 863). Moreover, Mexico had proved during the 1980s that economic unrest was possible and there were people in Washington that feared the potential political instability that might result out of it. However, the conditions of post war Europe, were not necessarily found in North America. There was no threat to the American hegemon, from within the continent. And, one might add, since NAFTA is an economic arrangement to face competition from abroad, at the end of the Cold War, that is, when NAFTA is implemented, competition from a security point of view is at its lowest point. Although economic stability can foster political steadiness, it could be argued that, in fact, it goes against the need for better integrated security policies, for the threat level is lowered significantly. This explanation therefore does not stand the road.

From these observations, we must conclude that the issue area examined in this chapter does not provide grounds on which to validate a hypothesis based on the constructivist approach: the common institutional construct did not bring on policy changes, as the theory predicts. The only possible answer that remains is rooted in the realist thinking and goes against neo-liberal conclusions as well: indeed, in the specific context this study has analyzed, low politics (economy) did not influence high politics (security). Such prevalence of the realist reading can be explained by the fact that, first, of the three bilateral relationships I have studied, the only two that are significant, although unequally, are dominated by the United States; second, the United States operate its foreign policy within a realist framework; third, as the hegemon, the United States will opt for the bilateral frame where they can dominate

– as demonstrated; therefore, there is no incentive to break the bilateral relationships and turn them into a multilateral setting.

The environment in which these bilateral relations evolve, might have helped to have them slide towards multilateralism. However, as demonstrated, NAFTA per se does not encourage integration of policies for the articles dealing with national security outline exceptions that allow national priorities to prevail. Finally, in terms of integration mechanisms, it was possible to establish that none of the five organizations we looked at carry the influence of NAFTA: in some cases, it is not all three countries that are full members of the organization and in other cases the convergence effort made by the organization predates NAFTA.

Does this mean that there is no room for establishing multilateral cooperation in the field of defense and security among the three North American partners? Joseph Jockel's conclusions offer some interesting guidance:

> Because of enduring Mexican concerns, any conceivable military trilateralism as well as Mexico-US and Mexico-Canada military cooperation could not entail, at least in the short run, classical international security cooperation: coordinating the ability of the military to use force or threatening to use force against other countries. Nor it is likely to involve Mexican collaboration in the architecture of western hemispheric cooperation. Rather it is in a very limited realm of the "non-military" uses of the military in support of civilian authorities, that Canada, Mexico, and the US should explore some new joint approaches (Jockel 1995, 212).

In light of this study, these research avenues have not lost their interest.

Appendix

Articles of the North American Free Trade Agreement that Deal with Security Matters

Article 607: National Security Measures

Subject to Annex 607, no Party may adopt or maintain a measure restricting imports of an energy or basic petrochemical good from, or exports of an energy or basic petrochemical good to, another Party under Article XXI of the GATT or under Article 2102 (National Security), except to the extent necessary to:

- (a) supply a military establishment of a Party or enable fulfillment of a critical defense contract of a Party;
- (b) respond to a situation of armed conflict involving the Party taking the measure;
- (c) implement national policies or international agreements relating to the nonproliferation of nuclear weapons or other nuclear explosive devices; or
- (d) respond to direct threats of disruption in the supply of nuclear materials for defense purposes.

Article 1018: Exceptions

1. Nothing in this Chapter shall be construed to prevent a Party from taking any action or not disclosing any information which it considers necessary for the protection of its essential security interests relating to the procurement of arms, ammunition or war materials, or to procurement indispensable for national security or for national defense purposes.

2. Provided that such measures are not applied in a manner that would constitute a means of arbitrary or unjustifiable discrimination between Parties where the same conditions prevail or a disguised restriction on trade between the Parties, nothing in this Chapter shall be construed to prevent any Party from adopting or maintaining measures:

(a) necessary to protect public morals, order or safety;

(b) necessary to protect human, animal or plant life or health;

(c) necessary to protect intellectual property; or

(d) relating to goods or services of handicapped persons, of philanthropic institutions or of prison labor.

Article 2102: National Security

1. Subject to Articles 607 (Energy – National Security Measures) and 1018 (Government Procurement – Exceptions), nothing in this Agreement shall be construed:

(a) to require any Party to furnish or allow access to any information the disclosure of which it determines to be contrary to its essential security interests;

(b) to prevent any Party from taking any actions that it considers necessary for the protection of its essential security interests,

    (i) relating to the traffic in arms, ammunition and implements of war and to such traffic and transactions in other goods, materials, services and technology undertaken directly or indirectly for the purpose of supplying a military or other security establishment,

    (ii) taken in time of war or other emergency in international relations, or

    (iii) relating to the implementation of national policies or international agreements respecting the non-proliferation of nuclear weapons or other nuclear explosive devices; or

(c) to prevent any Party from taking action in pursuance of its obligations under the United Nations Charter for the maintenance of international peace and security.

Chapter 4

The Missing Link?
Economic Liberalization
and the Strengthening of Territorial
Security in the Wake of NAFTA

Stéphane Roussel, Michel Fortmann and Martin Duplantis

To what degree has the liberalization of trade following the implementation of the 1994 North American Free Trade Agreement (NAFTA) affected its member-states' behavior with regard to security policy? More specifically, has this agreement brought about a convergence in the security policies of the United States, Canada, and Mexico?

While the answer is a resounding yes, it should be qualified, since NAFTA's impact has been rather diffuse and indirect. Policies in the area of non-military security, for example, appear to have converged from 1995 to 2005. This was particularly true, however, when trade was the main priority of governments and trade growth required adjustments in terms of security. When security was the main priority, as was the case after September 11, 2001, the convergence effects of NAFTA tended to fade so that trilateralism in trade no longer extended to security. This observation does not, however, necessarily disprove the hypothesis of convergence, since the boost created by trade growth from 1994 to 2000 created the conditions in which trade flows were able to adjust to a security-dominated environment. Indeed, while certain members of the business community would have welcomed a relaxing of controls following the abrupt strengthening of security measures, this did not occur. Thus, the business community learned to adapt and made the necessary representations to bring trade flows back up to 2000 levels. This is called the "ratchet effect."

Caution must be exercised, however, when attempting to characterize this convergence, especially for the period following the 2001 attacks. In many respects, it is Canada and Mexico that adjusted to the security standards of the United States. This "convergence" could thus be better described as an "alignment" (Mace, Introduction – this book).

The present analysis is divided into three parts. Firstly, we will specify certain elements of convergence, this research program's main problematique, in order to adapt it to the subject under study. Secondly, we will observe the way in which Canada and the United States dealt with the issue of control over their common border, from the establishment of NAFTA to the events of September 11, 2001. Finally, we will do the same for the period extending from the fall of 2001 to 2005.

We have chosen to focus on the relations between Canada and the United States. As will be described below, our research revealed little or no trilateral convergence, thus indicating that the two bilateral dynamics evolve alongside each other but that the principle underlying them is distinct.

Elements of the Problematique

Three questions immediately spring to mind when the problematique of convergence is specifically applied to security. First, to what exactly does security policy refer? If we are to observe a causal relationship between the establishment of NAFTA and the security policies of the three member states, a precise definition of the dependent variable is needed. Furthermore, since regional cooperation on matters of defense is examined separately in the context of this research, a distinction should be made between defense policy and security policy.

Second, what is the nature of the theoretical and empirical link between free trade and security, two fields that at first glance appear to be completely unrelated?

Third, what approach should be used in order to operationalize the notions of convergence and divergence more specifically?

The notion of "security"

Obviously, the notion of security has been considerably broadened over the past twenty years. Although the concept of "national security," which mainly refers to the defense of a state against military attacks from other states, dominated the Cold War, political leaders are nowadays much more concerned with the increase in the number of more diffuse risks posed by cross-border crime, illegal migration and environmental problems.[1] Thus, the concept of national security has been replaced in many cases by the concept of public security, "which refers to protection of persons, their goods and assets, the rule of law and democratic institutional development from threats posed by a variety of crimes, violence and corruption" (Bailey 2004, 236). This concept of security will be used here. This analysis will thus not deal, or will deal very little, with military questions, focusing rather on public security, that is, the joint or parallel action of a set of public organizations (justice, police, immigration, environment) confronted with what are usually called "the new post-Cold War threats" (translation) (Raufer 1998). Using Peter Andreas's terms, we will specifically look at the policing function of North American states (Andreas 1998–99, 592).

---

1 As noted by John Cope (Cope 2001) about the Americas: "The region's new focus is on multidimensional, nonstate, and transnational challenges, ranging from criminal threats such as international terrorism, drug trafficking, and arms smuggling to public policy challenges such as poaching natural resources, illegal migration, environmental degradation, weather phenomena, and natural disasters."

The conceptual relationship between trade and security

This brings us to the second question. To many observers, the relationship between the free trade dynamic symbolized by NAFTA and the national security policies of the three member states is not clear. As Colonel Nunez stated: "Most who deal with NAFTA are loath to discuss the connection between trade and security" (Núñez 2002, 3) and this is true for political scientists as much as for economists. In fact, it can generally be said that the nature of the relationship between trade and security has yet to be defined. Moreover, although many intuitive hypotheses have been proposed, few have been subjected to rigorous testing.

There are many possible reasons to explain this deficiency. According to economists, the removal of tariff barriers was the result not of political initiatives, as in the case of European integration, but rather of market forces. The latter motivated governments to satisfy the demands of businesses and to adjust accordingly to the rules of the trade game. It should thus not be expected that merely practicing free trade can stimulate a dynamic of regional integration on matters of security, as certain optimists suggest (*Bob Zoellick's Grand Strategy* 2002, 35; Fauriol and Perry 1999; Franko 2000; Schulz 2000, 41–46). "The North American Free Trade Agreement has been in effect since 1995 yet until 2002 there was no security structure to match it" (Núñez 2002, 4), and for good reason, given that the political will that should have underlain any such integration mechanism has been simply non-existent, as much in the United States as in Canada and Mexico. At a more practical level, it should be noted that security concerns (in every sense of the word) were almost completely absent from NAFTA, which was designed strictly as a trade agreement. [2]

For political scientists, the same deficiencies exist. Theorists from the integrationist school still seem to cling to the spillover hypothesis (an increase in a given field of activity leads to an adjustment and a proportional increase in related fields), judging that, sooner or later, trade growth will lead to an adjustment of security measures (see Malamud 2001). Handicapped by the blinkers of the realist-structuralist framework, realists also have trouble admitting that trade relations (considered to be in the realm of *low politics*) could have important consequences for national security, if we limit the latter to military and strategic issues.

Instinctively in agreement with this point of view, the public at large and political leaders also think that NAFTA has simply nothing to do with national security in its strict sense: "Policy makers and the public apparently do not connect national security, perceived as armed forces and national defense with NAFTA, which regulates trade, finance and some additional areas" (Bailey 2004, 236).

To restore the theoretical and empirical link between trade liberalization and security, one just has to replace the traditional definition of national security with the idea of public security proposed above. It is indeed clear that trade growth, particularly after the establishment of NAFTA, has had important consequences for regional security, especially with regard to border control. The three NAFTA member countries indeed share land borders that are nearly 8000 miles long, and

---

2   And this being the case, even when taking into the account the articles that marginally mentioned the theme of national security in the treaty itself (articles 607, 1018 and 2102).

are becoming increasingly porous in the face of trade flows that have continually increased since 1994. As the Canada-US Partnership (CUSP) Forum notes, "Since the implementation of the Canada-US Free Trade Agreement (FTA) in 1989 and the North America Free Trade Agreement (NAFTA) in 1994, the volume of two-way traffic across the Canada-US border has increased exponentially. [...] Canada-US trade has more than doubled since the FTA came into effect" (Government of Canada – Department of Foreign Affairs and International Trade 2000, 11–12). With regard to Mexico, US authorities report that:

> The 1,951-mile U.S.-Mexico border is the busiest in the world. Each year, the United States' southern border allows in more than 300 million people, approximately 90 million cars, and 4.3 million trucks. Since the implementation of NAFTA, the number of commercial vehicles crossing the border has increased by 41 percent. Two-way trade has almost tripled and cross-border trade averages more than $650 million dollars a day... (Government of the United States – White House 2007)

It goes without saying that such trade growth constitutes a sizeable challenge for the authorities that are responsible for border control in North America. These authorities indeed have to both facilitate legitimate trade and stop illicit traffic of all sorts, whether it be drugs, weapons, or illegal immigration.

The danger of international terrorism must obviously be added to this already long list, and some even go so far as to include environmental damage as a security risk provoked by the establishment of NAFTA.[3] In this sense, trade liberalization and security are closely related (see Chung-in Moon 1996), and the regulation of borders is probably the security issue most directly related to NAFTA that can be imagined. According to John Bailey: "Safe borders in the conventional sense of land, air and maritime travel and shipping is the most immediately NAFTA-centric security issue" (Bailey 2004, 236). The present analysis thus focuses specifically on the evolving US-Mexican and Canadian border control policies following the implementation of NAFTA.

The European Union or the Warsaw Pact?

This brings us to the third question raised earlier, that is, how to approach the notion of convergence in the field of security policies. Based on the research program proposed here, the notion of policy convergence rests on the idea that an agreement such as NAFTA, by encouraging the intensification of trade, fosters a socialization of actors, gradually leading to a harmonization of policies not only in the sectors of

---

3   As Teofilo Ozuna and Ramon Guajardo Quiroga pointed out in 1991: "Increased demographic and economic growth along both sides of the U.S.-Mexico border as well as increased economic integration between the U.S. and Mexico have led to severe natural resource and environmental problems which often spill across the political boundary. The realization of a U.S.-Mexico Free Trade Agreement will not only increase these problems, but given the expected additional investment that could flow into Mexico, it may create environmental problems in non-border areas as well" (Ozuna and Guajardo Quiroga 1991).

activity covered by the agreement, but also in related fields (Gonzalez and Haggard 1998, 295–332).

The implication of this idea for the public security sector, and more specifically, border control, is that the establishment of NAFTA would have been accompanied by a gradual awareness of the security problems brought on by the liberalization of trade between the three countries. This newfound awareness would have been followed, as hypothesized above, by bilateral or multilateral consultations of ever-increasing intensity, then by a rapprochement or a harmonization of the policies of the three NAFTA member-countries. This entire process would have presumably led to the creation of a number of joint programs and/or organizations with the mandate of implementing the new border control policies. Eventually, the three American states would end up constituting a genuine "security community",[4] as is the case in Europe. This hypothesis is attractive, and many analysts have put forward the idea that the future of regional security lies in multilateralism.[5]

However, there is an alternative to this optimistic scenario. According to this research program, the asymmetric nature of the power relations that exist between the three NAFTA member countries does not necessarily foster a convergence of their foreign and security policies. According to this theory, Mexico and Canada, forced to cooperate on issues considered to be priorities by Washington, are not always favorable to the idea of harmonizing their policies in related areas, because they want to preserve their autonomy and protect their sovereignty. The asymmetry of power relations would also, in this sense, prevent a real convergence of security policies within the NAFTA triangle. This would especially be the case for Mexico, whose bilateral relations with its powerful neighbor have traditionally been fraught with suspicion (Cope 2001, 56).

Another sizeable obstacle to bringing the policies of Washington, Ottawa, and Mexico closer together lies in the very style of American policy toward the other states in the region. Many authors (in particular, Bailey and Cope) have underlined that the way in which the American administration views relations with its neighbors has little to do with what is commonly called multilateralism.[6] According to these authors, the American approach has barely changed in the last decade: it remains

---

4   According to the traditional definition developed by Karl Deutsch, a security community appears when the states therein renounce violence as a means to solving their disagreements. From this perspective, such a community already exists in North America, at least between Canada and the United States. However, the definition is still applied only imperfectly to US-Mexico relations (not to mention trilateral relations…) (see Deutsch 1957; Gonzalez and Haggard 1998; Shirk 2003a, 4–5).

5   As Michael Dziedzic underlines: "The post-Cold War period has been marked by an array of non-traditional security concerns that affect all three North American states in one way or another, including the cross-border flow of illicit drugs, contraband weapons, and illegal immigrants. These 'security' concerns are distinctive because the non-state actors associated with them have tentacles that stretch across national boundaries. Consequently, the three states can address these problems effectively only via coordinated, multilateral action" (Dziedzic 1995).

6   "Multilateralism in international politics means that a state pursues its interests and goals beyond its national borders, not alone, but in cooperation and coalitions with other

the "hub and spoke" system, an approach reminiscent of the organization of the Warsaw Pact. In this framework, the United States deals with each regional "partner" individually, based on their particular interests and the crises that may arise between them (Cope 2001, 54). According to these authors, the signing of the *Security and Prosperity Partnership for North America* in 2005 will change little with regard to security, since not much has changed in the relations between the three countries. According to this hypothesis, rather than forming a collective response to a set of common problems, regional security policies follow the dictates of Washington, which themselves follow the often contradictory initiatives of Congress. It would thus be wrong to talk about policy convergence in this context. Rather, it would be more appropriate to talk about a forced alignment dictated by the American agenda (Clarkson and Banda 2004, 313–347).

Managing Growth: Canada-US Relations (1994–2000)

Most of the authors examining security relations and border issues in North America seem to think that everything started on September 12, 2001. This is not the case. In many respects, the agreements signed and implemented after this date are simply a continuation of pre-existing policies. However, there is a difference in the motives driving this deepening cooperation. From 1994 to 1999 (if not 2000), the main reason was economic; from 2001 onwards, security considerations clearly predominated.

Canada-US relations are more developed than Mexico-US relations. This is noticeable on matters of defense and security. As numerous authors have noted, since the 1930s (and as early as the late 19th century), Canada and the United States have unquestionably formed a "security community" (for example, Shore 1998, 333–367; Roussel 2004). In addition, the two countries are united by a relatively dense network of bilateral security institutions (Permanent Joint Board on Defence, Military Cooperation Committee, NORAD), as well as membership in multilateral ones (North Atlantic Treaty Organization). The strengthening of security cooperation between 1994 and 2001 can thus be seen as a continuation of previous initiatives.

Secondly, the level of integration of the two economies is much more advanced. Since the Second World War, the phenomenon of economic integration has been regulated by a growing number of agreements, the most important one before 1994 being the Canada-US Free Trade Agreement (FTA), signed in 1988. The effects of this integration were thus visible well before the 1990s. The share of Canadian exports going to the United States went from 65 percent in 1970, to 68 percent in 1980, 74 percent in 1989, 79 percent in 1993 and finally 84 percent in 1998. Today, the share of Canadian exports going to the US is 87 percent. Thus, although this trend was already in effect before 1988, the FTA helped to drastically accelerate it. In short, if it is true that economic integration has an impact on security cooperation, it should be possible to observe it along the Canada-US border.

states. The opposite of multilateralism is unilateralism: a policy in which a state relies only on its own strengths" (Centre for Canadian Studies, Mount Allison University).

This does in fact seem to be the case. Between 1995 and 2000, numerous initiatives were launched.[7] The first was the signing of the Shared Border Accord in February 1995, which sought to "promote international trade, streamline processes for legitimate travellers and commercial goods, provide enhanced protection against drug smuggling and the illegal entrance of people, and reduce costs for both governments and users" (Government of Canada – Canada Border Services Agency, 2000). This was followed by the creation of a series of cooperation forums, between the main Canadian and American agencies charged with applying the laws, including immigration agencies and police services. Another important step was taken in October 1999, when Prime Minister Chrétien and President Clinton established the Canada-US Partnership (CUSP). This agreement had three series of objectives: to modernize, harmonize, and cooperate on matters of border policy and management; secondly, to intensify cooperation in order to increase the efficiency of customs and immigration services, to implement the law and environmental protection at the border and beyond; and, thirdly, to cooperate in order to counter common threats from outside Canada and the United States.

In strictly conceptual terms, the next step in the cooperation (or integration) process occurred between December 1999 and October 2000. At the end of 1999, the arrest at the Canada-US border of Ahmed Ressam, an Algerian national living in Canada, accelerated the process. Ressam was accused of planning a terrorist attack against the United States. The matter caused quite a stir in Washington, especially in Congress, which called for tighter controls at the Canada-US border. Some high-level Canadian civil servants reacted by proposing the creation of a "North American security perimeter." Newly-received in Ottawa, the idea was brought up again by American ambassador Gordon Griffin in a speech given in October 2000. This notion referred to a number of joint measures, including the use of leading edge technologies and the harmonization of border management policies (Roussel 2002, 669–70). American public discourse was at the time still strongly tinged with references to economic prosperity, with Griffin drawing an explicit link between trade and border security. However, this speech reflected the importance of refocusing on security concerns.

Among the various motives that have fueled this intense spate of activity, it is obviously difficult to distinguish between those that ensued from the establishment of NAFTA and those related to completely exogenous factors, such as the growing concerns about foreign terrorist threats. According to Chris Sands, it is impossible to separate the two types of concerns, which exist on both sides of the border (Sands 2002, 65, 67). Nevertheless, the author's text leaves the impression that most of the reforms undertaken since 1996 have sought to avoid the implementation of the controversial Section 110 of the *Illegal Immigration Reform and Immigrant Responsibility Act* (IIRIRA). This measure, drafted after the first attack on the World Trade Center (February 1993), required foreigners to register with immigration

---

7   For a detailed review of the initiatives implemented between 1995 and 2000, see Christopher Sands (Sands 2002, 51–64), Stéphane Roussel (Roussel 2002, 680–684), *Building A Border for the 21st Century* (Government of the United States – Department of State 2000, 9–22).

authorities upon entering or leaving American territory. From this perspective, the initiatives mentioned earlier have been only indirectly related to the signing of NAFTA. At the very most, it could be said that the promoters (in government as well as in the private sector) of these initiatives were trying to preserve the trade gains created by NAFTA.

According to Deborah Meyer, four interrelated albeit distinct factors account for the growing attention given to the border in the late 1990s: 1. the significant increase in cross-border traffic; 2. the growth in illegal cross-border activities; 3. a new political awareness of the issue; and 4. the representations of border communities (Waller Meyers 2000, 255–268). With these factors in mind, the effect of NAFTA becomes much more understandable. NAFTA is indeed directly responsible for the first and fourth factors, indirectly responsible for the third, and partially responsible for the second.

Firstly, the phenomenal increase in the movement of people and goods at the border during the 1990s is a direct result of the increase in trade between the two countries, which was itself due to NAFTA. It is precisely to respond to the pressure created by this phenomenon that the *Canada-United States Accord on our Shared Border* was signed in 1995; it involved making up for the obsolescence of customs installations and methods, which were completely overwhelmed by the flow of goods and people. In this sense, these reforms are directly related to the signing of NAFTA.

Secondly, although the security concerns are clearly due to factors unrelated to NAFTA (such as the emergence of an extra-continental threat of terrorist attacks against American territory, or the increase in drugs and weapons trafficking), the increase in traffic generated by NAFTA has made the problem even more complex. Indeed, it is increasingly difficult to identify criminal elements or illegal goods in the mass of regular traffic. It is in large part to solve this problem that the agreements mentioned above were signed.

Thirdly, the establishment of NAFTA has been largely responsible for attracting the attention of the two countries' politicians, media, and public opinion to border issues. Of course, this is partly a result of the two phenomena mentioned previously. However, NAFTA has also contributed directly to the issues by putting the Canada-US border and the US-Mexico border on the same footing. Thus, problems that arise along the southern border can easily (and unconsciously) be transposed to the northern border. Thus, if the Canada-US border has become a subject of concern in Washington, it is partly because of this association, which stems from NAFTA.

Fourthly, and although this is difficult to demonstrate, the emergence of border community activism (including not only citizens and business people, but also the staff attached to border infrastructure, customs brokers, environmental activists, native peoples, and so on) also seems to have been related to the establishment of NAFTA. Indeed, it is only during the 1990s that these groups organized themselves and that their influence started to be felt in a significant way. These communities directly benefited from the increase in cross-border traffic, upon which a growing number of jobs depends.

The evolution of relations between the two societies, if not between the two governments, seems to bear witness to a certain convergence of views. This is reflected in the desire to identify threats and ways to counter them and the importance given to maintaining trade gains. On both sides, there are fierce advocates of keeping the borders open and ardent proponents of more numerous and tighter security measures. The former mainly come from local communities and industry and business representatives. The latter can be found especially among politicians, journalists or civil servants from the organizations concerned with this issue. Thus, many Canadian civil servants will appear before Congressional committees to plead for a strengthening of border controls, while Americans will come to Canada to reaffirm the importance of cross-border links. Moreover, the ease with which the various agencies (immigration, police services, transport) implemented the agreements signed during this period indicates the existence of a degree of common views and a "cooperation habit."

Thus, a socialization process does seem to exist. However, it is difficult to positively identify the signing of NAFTA as the source of this process. In fact, it is probably more accurate to say that it is a continuation of a pre-existing dynamic, which in some cases was long-standing, that was simply strengthened by the increase in exchanges ensuing from free trade.

Furthermore, it should be noted that this convergence has been quite imperfect. It is true that in a large number of cases, the advocates of greater liberalization and the advocates of tighter control are not split along national lines. For instance, Canadian and American business people defend a similar point of view, which is different from that advanced by American and Canadian customs officers. As Chris Sands states, it is simplistic to depict Canadians as being obsessed with trade issues and Americans as preoccupied only by security issues (Sands 2002, 67). However, it is true that certain national differences persist, especially among the political elites in the two capitals. Thus, it is essentially in Washington that the terrorism psychosis came into being in 1996,[8] whereas Ottawa was only marginally interested in this issue. With regard to threat analysis, there were thus clear divergences, which have become more pronounced over the years.

Emergence of the Security Imperative and the "September 12" Effect

In the hours following the attacks of September 11, 2001, the American government proceeded to tighten controls on its northern and southern borders: "*the United States effectively closed its borders by grounding aviation, stopping all vessel movements in its major ports, and reducing to a trickle the flow of people and vehicles entering the United States from Canada and Mexico*" (Flynn 2003, 38). The closing of the border led to many delays in goods deliveries on both sides of the border. Thus, the waiting period for primary inspection, which usually takes about ten minutes per truck, reached as high as 10 to 12 hours. The consequences of these delays were

---

8   Between 1994 and 2001, these calls for greater vigilance led to the formulation of about twenty presidential directives or legislative provisions, the injection of astronomical financial resources, the carrying out of ten or so government studies, and the reorganization of the agencies and organizations responsible for protecting the national territory (Fortmann and Haglund 2002, 17–22).

harmful to the economy of both countries, particularly in the automobile sector, where *"every four hour delay at the Windsor-Detroit crossing costs the Ontario economy $7 million (CDN) in lost production and the Michigan economy $14.3 million (CDN)"* (Government of Canada – Department of National Defence 2005, 10). In order to limit the negative impacts on the economy, the Canadian government reacted quickly by creating an action plan called the *Smart Border Declaration* as well as by completely restructuring certain departments.

In order to avoid delays such as those experienced on September 12, then Prime Minister Jean Chrétien mandated John Manley, Minister of Foreign Affairs, to implement an action plan that would respond to the security imperatives while limiting hindrances to trade. In the following weeks, John Manley met with Tom Ridge, Secretary of the Department of Homeland Security, in order to finalize the *Smart Border Declaration*. The two men ratified the declaration shortly thereafter, on December 12, 2001. Upon ratification, the agreement contained 30 points. However, the *Smart Border Declaration* was later modified and two points were added in September 2002. The program had four main objectives:

1. The secure flow of people
2. The secure flow of goods
3. A secure infrastructure
4. The coordination and sharing of information in the enforcement of these objectives

However, the Smart Border Declaration proposed very few new measures to improve border security. A number of them were from initiatives launched before September 11, 2001. The main principles rested essentially on technological innovations, adding personnel, a customs pre-clearance system, and harmonizing American and Canadian border practices. The most visible initiative on the land border was the NEXUS program,[9] which would accelerate low-risk flows, thus giving customs officers the time needed for longer inspections of other users.

The American government proceeded to restructure some of its agencies, in particular, by creating the Office of Homeland Security on October 8, 2001, then the Department of Homeland Security on October 25, 2002, which grouped together 22 federal organizations. This, moreover, marked the creation of the Custom and Border Patrol (CBP), the successor to the Immigration and Naturalization Service (INS). A number of measures was also implemented on the Canadian side. In addition to the *Smart Border Declaration*, the Canadian government undertook other reforms. The most important change came in December 2003, with the creation of the Department of Public Safety and Emergency Preparedness (PSEPC). This new department is directly responsible for five organizations: the Royal Canadian Mounted Police

---

9   The users of this program must register for the program in their country of residence. Once their application has been approved, the users receive a card that they must affix to their vehicle. When the NEXUS member travellers go to the border, they will be invited to take a lane specifically reserved for NEXUS members. Their license plate will then be scanned by an optical scanner and the information on the visitor will show up on the officer's monitor. The users must show their card and can then proceed without further delays.

(RCMP), the National Parole Board, the Canadian Security Intelligence Service, Correctional Service Canada, and the Canada Border Services Agency (CBSA). With the creation of the PSEPC, the border is now governed by security imperatives, whereas previously, under the Canada Customs and Revenue Agency, it was linked more to trade.

This reorganization of departments meant an "automation of border security" since it was no longer conditioned by trade imperatives and it was approached within the framework of rules set by NAFTA. In other words, "security trumped trade."

The change in priorities that occurred after the September 2001 attacks became particularly obvious when comparing the four main objectives of the agreements signed in 1995 and 2001.

Table 4.1   Comparative table of the main objectives of border collaboration between Canada and the United States (1995 and 2001)

Canada-United States Accord on our Shared Border 1995	Smart Border Declaration 2001
Promote international trade	The secure flow of people
Facilitate the flow of people	The secure flow of goods
Provide enhanced protection against drug smuggling and the illegal entrance of people	A secure infrastructure
Reduce costs for both governments and the public	The coordination and sharing of information in the enforcement of these objectives

The objectives in the 1995 Accord were essentially geared toward establishing an open border and sought to reduce costs and improve fluidity, and while it was mentioned, an increase in the security level was not a priority. In contrast, in the 2001 Agreement, security was the dominant issue in the first 3 objectives. It was no longer a question of promoting the economy, but rather of strengthening security, even if this meant slowing down border flows. It is true that in 1996, the Clinton administration attempted to implement Section 110 of the *Illegal Immigration Reform and Immigrant Responsibility Act* (IIRIRA). The application of this measure would have forced all foreigners to register with immigration authorities upon entering or leaving American territory. This reform provoked an important debate in the United States, as well as in Mexico and Canada. The American government finally abandoned the IIRIRA, because applying such a measure would have led to considerable delays at border crossing points.

The return of "stakeholders" and the "ratchet effect"

The strengthening of security measures and the "September 12, 2001 effect" seriously worried the actors concerned with cross-border traffic, in particular the chambers of commerce and automobile industry representatives in the Windsor-Detroit corridor. Twenty-four (24) different coalitions, mainly chambers of commerce, were looking for effective ways to improve the border's fluidity and security.

Table 4.2   Local initiatives, border communities, regional projects

1.	The Canadian/American Border Trade Alliance
2.	Eastern Border Transportation Coalition
3.	Ambassador Bridge – The NAFTA Superhighway Coalition
4.	Appalachian International Trade Corridor – Route 219
5.	Atlantic Coast Trade Corridor
6.	Central North American Trade Corridor Association (CNATCA)
7.	Discovery Institute – Cascadia Project
8.	Greater Tucson Economic Council
9.	I-95 Corridor Coalition
10.	Quebec-New York Corridor
11.	New England Canada Business Council Homepage
12.	Northwest Corridor Development Corporation
13.	Pacific NorthWest Economic Region
14.	Rocky Mountain Trade Corridor
15.	The Great Lakes Trade Corridor Association
16.	Border Counties Coalition
17.	Border Technology Partnership
18.	Canadian American Business Council
19.	Canadian-American Border Trade Alliance
20.	CANAMEX Corridor
21.	North American International Trade Corridor Partnership
22.	Ports-to-Plains Trade Corridor
23.	The Americas Society – Building North America
24.	Continental One Trade Corridor

The main concern of these groups is the slowing of trade growth between Canada and the United States. One such group is the New York State Smart Border Coalition, which is made up of about twenty businesses that are members of the Business Council of New York State. The aim of this coalition is the rapid implementation of the Smart Border Declaration. Furthermore, the coalition is campaigning against the potential application of Section 110 of the IIRIRA or any other procedure that would slow border traffic at the New York State border. The coalition is essentially made up of a group of local actors, like other such coalitions in Ontario, Quebec or British Columbia. Another example is the Coalition for Secure and Trade-Efficient

Borders that includes around forty associations and businesses brought together by the Canadian Chamber of Commerce. In December 2001, this group published an Action Plan to facilitate trade between the two countries by strengthening security and bilateral cooperation at the border (Coalition for Secure and Trade-Efficient Borders 2001).

For many of these coalitions, intervening in debates related to security represented a foray into something they had never done before. Before 2001, chambers of commerce applied political pressure to improve the border's fluidity, notably by fiercely opposing measures that could slow down cross-border flows. The transformation of their discourse after September 2001 was significant. Rather than maintaining their position, business coalitions spoke out in favor of improving border security, all the while constantly reiterating that these measures must still take into account the imperatives of trade fluidity. In other words, they made sure that the trade dimension of cross-border traffic not be drowned out by the security obsession that was sweeping across the United States at the time.

This change in attitude, of course, was the result of a good understanding of their interests. The idea was to reassure the American government, in order to reduce the chances of seeing unilateral American measures being imposed at the border, which would slow cross-border traffic even further.

As a result of this, trade between the two countries, which had tripled since 1989, suffered a significant but temporary decline in 2001–2003. However, by 2005, trade flows were back up to 2000 levels.

Thus, the negative effects of security imperatives slowly faded, as priority was given once again to trade. However, it was not a return to the previous situation; the issue of security at the Canada-US border was there to stay. The Smart Border Declaration remodeled the modes of inspection to make way for a kind of "selective security."

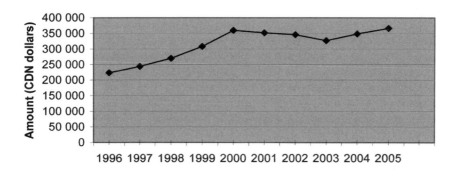

Figure 4.1 Canadian exports to the United States 1996–2005

Source: Constructed by the authors with data taken from the website of Industry Canada at http://strategic.ic.gc.ca.

This new way of operating allowed goods and low-risk people (whose activities are generally related to trade) to cross the border more quickly. This practice is more economical than the systematic inspection of all trucks and containers since the cost of inspecting a single container is $850 ("Interview with A.C. Morancy, Manager, Intelligence Services, Canada Customs" 1999) and requires three agents for five hours. Selective security was made possible through technological innovations. For instance, biometric scanners can recognize data particular to each individual. As regards trade flows, the Canada Border Services Agency equipped itself with VACIS inspection systems, which are gamma ray inspection systems that are able to inspect trucks and containers without having to open them. Nevertheless, only a tiny fraction of goods that cross the border is inspected.

As for non-trade flows, the situation is entirely different. For instance, travelers who cross the border for a reason other than work are subject to more restrictive measures than before September 11, 2001. Some travelers must provide biometric data, whereas others must indicate their precise itinerary, along with reference addresses, which are stored in a computerized database. In addition, travelers from certain countries are now required to have visas to go to Canada, whereas before 2001, they were not. This measure is the result of the pressure put on Canada by the American government to require that visitors from the following eleven countries no longer be exempt from visas: Dominica, Grenada, Hungary, Kiribati, Nauru, Tuvalu, Vanuatu, Zimbabwe, Saudi Arabia, Malaysia and Costa Rica. Since July 2002, Canada and the United States have had a harmonized visa policy for 175 countries. Since January 2006, American and Canadian travelers entering the United States by air from Canada must carry a passport, a requirement which did not exist until then.

The implementation of the "smart border" has continued since 2001, but the feeling of urgency seems to have gradually dissipated. These last few years of security strengthening have slowed down trade between Canada and the United States, but since March 2005, the leaders of Canada, the United States, and Mexico have been engaged in discussions to create the *Security and Prosperity Partnership of North America*. The Partnership's progress report states certain objectives to increase trade flows at the border, in particular the following point: "To promote prosperity by reducing the costs of trade, the United States and Canada decreased transit times at the Detroit/Windsor gateway, our largest border crossing point, by 50 percent." (Government of Canada 2006) Of course, the reference to security is still present, but the concern with increasing flows so as to not harm the economy is also clearly present.

Is it possible to talk about a return to the pre-September 11 situation along the Canada-US border? Certainly not, since the management of the border is now based on the principle of selective security, even though economic imperatives are becoming important again. The difference between the 49th parallel border that existed before September 11, 2001, and the border set up during the five following years is linked to the strengthening of security mechanisms. However, it is a given that these mechanisms must not be implemented to the detriment of trade. In fact, the creation of NEXUS border posts seems to have formalized the distinction between trade flows and other types of traffic.

Thus, it is tempting to speak of a "ratchet effect",[10] that is, a situation in which a field of activity (in this case, trade) is suddenly disrupted by the effort made in another field (security), followed by a period of adjustment and an apparent return to normal. However, this return to normal does not mean a reduction in the measures adopted in the second sector. On the contrary, the notion of the ratchet effect implies that a return to the initial situation is henceforth considered to be impossible.

Conclusion

Two things should be retained from this overview of the evolution of security relations in North America from 1994 to 2004.

On the one hand, there has not been a serious project to institutionalize the management of security problems on a trilateral basis, a project that would constitute NAFTA's security counterpart.

However, although this trilateralization process may seem both logical and inevitable, observers are still waiting to see concrete results (Toupin 2007, A20). There is still very strong resistance to such a project in all three countries, be it because of the asymmetry of power between the members, or because of historical suspicions that are pushing the governments to "compartmentalize" their relations (Roussel and Hristoulas 2004, 41–57).

This observation ostensibly bears witness to NAFTA's limited effect on the way security is approached in North America. It seems to challenge the spillover logic that is often considered to be an inevitable consequence of any regional integration process. Thus, the expected convergence would be rather limited and would be more of an "alignment" phenomenon, with Canadian and Mexican policies coming in line with those of the United States. In many respects, "harmonization" would be a synonym for "Americanization."

However, there is evidence that the integrationist theses should be amended rather than rejected outright. On the one hand, trilateralism is not completely absent from the North American political landscape, insofar as some leaders have often mentioned the idea of creating a "North American security community," before as well as after the September 11 attacks. The very beginnings of convergence can thus be found in public discourse. For instance, in 1998, Lloyd Axworthy, then Canadian Minister of Foreign Affairs, proposed the creation of a North American security community, which would add a human security dimension to the economic space already established by NAFTA. In addition to the environment, natural resources and transports, Axworthy's project dealt with immigration and border management issues, to protect the member countries "against crime, terrorism and the drug trade." (Axworthy 1998) A little over two years later, Vicente Fox's Minister of Foreign Affairs, Jorge Castaneda, raised a similar idea. Finally, in 2005, the signing of the *Security and Prosperity Partnership of North America*, for a time, helped to promote the idea that the three governments were engaged in a true trilateral process.

---

10 For an example of an application of this concept, see R. Higgs (Higgs 1987, 30–33).

On the other hand, the intensification of trade that followed the establishment of NAFTA created the conditions for the emergence of national and transnational coalitions which intervened to reconcile trade imperatives with security imperatives, since they were disconnected from each other after the crisis provoked by the attacks of September 11, 2001. Thus, although convergence may be difficult to observe between governments, it has been more present in some segments of civil society.

Moreover, other indications which are beyond this study's framework are nevertheless worth mentioning here. Trade growth seems to have had similar effects along the Canada-US and Mexico-US borders, that is, an increase in illegal activities and the forming of communities whose prosperity, or even existence, is dependent on transnational activities. Furthermore, the response to these problems along the northern and southern borders of the United States sometimes seemed mutually reinforcing, creating a form of harmonization on a continental scale. David Shirk, who compared the 22 points of the Smart Border Agreement between the United States and Mexico with the 30 points of the Smart Border Agreement between the United States and Canada, showed that the first owed a great deal to the second (Shirk 2003b). However, caution should be exercised on this last point. One of the Canadians' greatest fears is to see the United States express its intention to do the reverse and to apply the measures implemented on the southern border to that of its northern neighbor.

Thus, although the concepts of convergence and integration should not be completely dismissed from the study of the dynamic of security cooperation in North America, they should probably be amended. These amendments involve first recognizing the autonomous nature of the field of security, something which integration theories tend to neglect. Then, the factors which sanction the unequal power relations and allow one member of the community to force its partners to align themselves with its decision should be taken into account. In brief, for better or for worse, the study of security in North America is not yet able to free itself from realist-flavored concepts.

Chapter 5

Democracy and Human Rights in the Western Hemisphere: North American Perspectives

Jean-Philippe Thérien[1]

This chapter compares the foreign policies of the United States, Canada and Mexico concerning the promotion of democracy and human rights in the Americas. It analyzes whether the implementation of NAFTA in 1994 has fostered a convergence of the policies adopted by the three partners of this trade agreement. Through an examination of the behavior of the three governments regarding inter-American norms in matters of democracy and human rights, this study offers an empirical test of the hypothesis, developed throughout the book, that growing economic interdependence brings about mutual adjustments in national policies. In addition, the chapter sheds new light on the impact of international institutions on state preferences. More particularly, it offers insight into how an international institution with a minimalist organizational architecture such as NAFTA can shape the decisions of its members. Finally, by focusing on a specific area of public policy, the following analysis provides new evidence for an assessment of the neo-functionalist intuition whereby regional integration could set into motion a chain reaction that would result in greater cooperation. The "spill-over" hypothesis has at times been implicit in accounts of the recent history of North American integration, but to date it has not been adequately verified (Bonser 1991 and Pastor 2001, 168–169).

The choice of the issue-area to be analyzed – the promotion of democracy and human rights in the Americas – rests on two complementary factors. On one hand, the United States, Canada and Mexico are all major players in the inter-American system. On the other hand, in the past decade or so the promotion of democracy and human rights has gained increasing importance on the agendas of the OAS and the Summit of the Americas meetings. This theme therefore provides an appropriate terrain for comparing the recent evolution of the foreign policies of the three members of NAFTA.

---

1   I am grateful to Marjolaine Pigeon and Nadia Karina Ponce Morales for their research assistance. I also thank Andrew Cooper, Ana Covarrubias Velasco, Lazer Lederhendler, Tom Legler, Jean-François Prud'homme, Isabel Studer Noguez, and Blanca Torres for their comments on earlier versions of this chapter.

It should be noted at the outset that democracy and human rights will be dealt with below as two altogether inseparable notions.[2] According to current thinking, most notably within inter-American institutions, the promotion of democracy helps reinforce human rights, and, conversely, the promotion of human rights supports the development of a democratic order. Following that line of reasoning, it has been argued elsewhere that the activities of hemispheric institutions in the field of democracy and human rights converge toward the establishment of an inter-American regime of citizenship (Cooper and Thérien 2004, 731–746). The notion of the inter-American regime of citizenship makes it possible to interpret what is often referred to as the "inter-American regime of democracy" and the "inter-American human rights regime" as two sides of the same process.[3]

Understood as the ultimate objective of all efforts to promote democracy and human rights, the strengthening of citizenship has been part of the inter-American agenda for over half a century. As early as 1948, the OAS Charter and the American Declaration of the Rights and Duties of Man already defined representative democracy and human rights as key pillars of hemispheric cooperation. During the Cold War, the inter-American regime of citizenship gradually developed, due mainly to the creation of the Inter-American Commission on Human Rights (1960), and of the Inter-American Court of Human Rights (1979). In the 1990s, the regime experienced spectacular growth following the adoption of stricter regional norms in the area of democracy and human rights. These new norms include, in particular, Resolution 1080, the Protocol of Washington, the Democratic clause, and the Inter-American Democratic Charter.[4]

Adopted in 1991, Resolution 1080 requires foreign ministers of OAS member states to meet urgently in the event of an interruption of democracy in a country of the region, in order to undertake collective actions to correct the situation. The Protocol of Washington, which was voted in 1992, allows a two-thirds majority within the OAS General Assembly to suspend a member whose democratic government has been overthrown by force. One of the main results of the Quebec City Summit of 2001, the Democratic clause, established that any interruption or "alteration" of democracy in the region would constitute an "insurmountable obstacle to the participation of that state's government in the Summit of the Americas process" (Declaration of Quebec City 2001, www.americascanada.org/eventsummit/declarations/declara-e.asp) .The Inter-American Democratic Charter, that was adopted a few months after the Democratic clause, represents thus far the most innovative component of the inter-American regime of citizenship. This resolution proposes a holistic view of democracy, in addition to institutionalizing the willingness of American states to

---

2   For a similar viewpoint, see Ana Covarrubias (Covarrubias 2000, 59).

3   The existence of an inter-American regime of human rights is discussed in David P. Forsythe (Forsythe 2000a, 128–132); Jack Donnelly (Donnelly 1998, 72–75); and Tom Farer (Farer 1997, 510-546). References to the concept of an inter-American democracy regime can be found in Richard J. Bloomfield (Bloomfield 1994, 157–159); Heraldo Muñoz (Muñoz 2000, 287–299); and Rubén M. Perina (Perina 2000, 311–376).

4   On the more recent period, see Andrew F. Cooper and Thomas Legler (Cooper and Legler 2006); and Cooper and Thérien (Cooper and Thérien 2004).

intervene the moment an "alteration" of the democratic order occurs in a country of the hemisphere. Beyond these normative gains, the development of the inter-American regime of citizenship also benefited from the creation in 1990, within the OAS, of a Unit for the Promotion of Democracy (UPD) that is especially active in election monitoring and institution-building.[5]

The chapter argues that NAFTA has helped to bring the positions of the United States, Canada, and Mexico closer together with regard to the promotion of democracy and human rights in the Americas. As will be shown, the recent congruence of policies has resulted essentially from a change in Mexico's foreign policy. Since the mid-1990s, the Mexican government has revised its traditional position of non-intervention and has adopted a policy increasingly similar to that of the United States and Canada. In other words, the Mexican government has in recent years modified its conception of sovereignty. One important consequence of this modification is that Mexico is much more ready than before to accept the right of the international community – and therefore that of American states – to intervene on democracy and human rights issues.

The analysis put forward here also suggests that while the significance of the Mexican government's shift of attitude should be underscored, it is somewhat misleading to use the term "convergence" to describe the rapprochement among the policies of the United States, Canada, and Mexico in matters of democracy and human rights. The notion of "convergence" appears confusing to the extent that the policies of the United States and Canada were only marginally affected by the enforcement of NAFTA. It is probably more accurate to refer to Mexico's "alignment" with its neighbors to the North. Moreover, it is clear that the policy change that has occurred in Mexico can be attributed to NAFTA only in a very limited way. All observers agree that the transformation of Mexico's foreign policy in the area of democracy and human rights promotion is due first and foremost to domestic factors. NAFTA can be said at most to have acted as a catalyst in that process.[6]

The remainder of the chapter is divided into three parts dealing respectively with the United States, Canada, and Mexico. Each section begins by discussing the policy applied before 1994 to the promotion of democracy and human rights in the Americas, and then examines the more recent period. Finally, the conclusion attempts to locate the results of this analysis within the broader framework of North American cooperation.

The United States: The Policeman

The United States has been actively concerned with the situation of democracy in the Western Hemisphere for over a century. During that period, US policy has been justified at times by the need to promote free trade and at other times by the imperatives of the war on communism and terrorism. Beyond these changing

---

5   The UPD became the Office for the Promotion of Democracy (OPD) in 2004.

6   This interpretation was for instance suggested by Mexico's former Undersecretary of State for Human Rights and Democracy Mariclaire Acosta, in an interview with the author in December 2002.

motivations, however, US behavior has been guided by the overarching principle that safeguarding US national interests requires hegemonic control over the Americas. NAFTA has done nothing to alter this basic tenet of Washington's foreign policy. In fact, the enactment of NAFTA has quite arguably had a far lesser impact than the end of the Cold War had on US policy concerning the promotion of democracy and human rights in the Americas.

Without reviewing in detail the modern history of US interventions in Latin America, it is nevertheless worth recalling that most of them were carried out in the name of democracy.[7] The 1906 invasion of Cuba at Theodore Roosevelt's behest, for example, culminated in the supervision of an election. Similarly, the General Treaty of Peace and Amity negotiated at the 1907 Washington Conference called upon the leaders of Central America to acknowledge democracy as the only legitimate road to power. US interventionism was slowed by President Hoover's "Good Neighbor Policy" and the outbreak of the Second World War but returned stronger than ever with the onset of the Cold War. From its creation in 1948, the OAS would in this regard provide a powerful instrument to legitimize US foreign policy in the hemisphere. Indeed, for over forty years, the OAS gave the US government a multilateral channel to promote a vision of democracy and human rights that was indistinguishable from the needs of the struggle against communism.

All the crises that successively erupted in Guatemala (1954), Cuba (1960), Dominican Republic (1965), and the Central American isthmus (1980–1989) were interpreted by the United States as situations where communist forces were endangering security and democracy in the region. In each case, the US government's response to the perceived threat was military. Beyond the different forms that US interventionism may have assumed depending on the times and the context, the US administration consistently regarded as non-democratic and potentially dangerous all left-wing governments favoring a redistribution of land and wealth, whereas it accommodated itself to the "cosmetic" democracy of dictators supporting the free market.

It is also significant that the United States has shown the same distrust in the OAS as in other international forums concerning the adoption of legal instruments in the area of human rights. As one scholar noted, US policy towards the inter-American human rights system has historically been "highly selective, which is to say inconsistent" (Forsythe 2000a, 129; Forsythe 1991, 66–98). In favor of the "promotion" yet hostile to the "protection" of human rights, Washington abstained when the Inter-American Commission on Human Rights was established (Leblanc 1977, 70–72). The United States also refused to ratify the American Convention on Human Rights, an agreement adopted in 1969 which is widely viewed as the most important inter-American treaty in the field of human rights. In any case, according to the US interpretation, the Convention cannot be considered legally binding. The launching of the Alliance for Progress by President Kennedy was the only moment in the Cold War when the traditional US approach toward Latin America was seriously

---

7   For an historical overview of US-Latin American relations, see Abraham F. Lowenthal (Lowenthal 1991); Peter H. Smith (Smith 1996); and Howard J. Wiarda (Wiarda 1992).

questioned. A lack of resources and of political will, however, brought about the failure of that otherwise innovative experiment.

With the fall of the Berlin Wall, the inter-American dynamic changed profoundly. The United States soon prevailed as one of the main actors behind the rebirth of the inter-American system and the refocusing of the mandate of hemispheric institutions on democracy (Burrell and Shifter 2000, 40–50). Washington's policy was clearly designed to help consolidate the new democratic regimes of Latin America. But it can also be understood in light of the need to find a regional path to promoting the model of "good governance" advocated by various international agencies across the Third World. According to the rationale of "good governance," democracy constitutes the best regime for ensuring not only peace and security in the hemisphere, but also the expansion of trade and investment. It is no coincidence that the United States' renewed commitment to democracy and human rights in the Americas took shape at about the same time the Initiative for the Americas (1990) and the Free Trade Area of the Americas (FTAA, 1994) were proposed.

In lending its support to the Santiago Commitment, Resolution 1080, the Protocol of Washington, and the Managua Declaration, the United States played a key role in the recent transformation of inter-American doctrine in matters of democracy and human rights.[8] Freed from the geo-political constraints of the past, the United States' hegemonic control over the hemisphere could be transposed within a new regional compromise. On one hand, the Latin American countries have committed themselves to the rule of law. On the other hand, the United States has accepted as never before "the link between the quality of life of the American peoples and consolidating democracy" (see OAS 1993, 109–114).

The United States was among the foremost promoters of the application of Resolution 1080 when crises erupted in Haiti (1991), Peru (1992), and Guatemala (1993). In the case of Haiti, it quickly became apparent that a number of OAS member-states did not share the US inclination for sanctions (Gosselin, Mace and Bélanger 1995, 810). Faced with these conditions, the United States complemented its regional diplomacy with bilateral and multilateral initiatives. In Peru, the US initial firmness was short-lived. In order to oblige a crucial ally in its Andean strategy, the United States was willing to accept the promise of reforms announced by President Fujimori at the 1992 OAS General Assembly (Conaghan 2001, 29). Finally, in Guatemala, Washington's threat of commercial sanctions played a decisive part in delegitimizing President Serrano's *autogolpe* (Millett 1994, 15–16). In sum, the United States certainly contributed to making Resolution 1080 work. This legal instrument, however, was at no time more than another tool to promote its own interests.

---

8   Less important than Resolution 1080 and the Protocol of Washington, that were discussed above, the Santiago Commitment and the Managua Declaration nonetheless deserve to be considered as landmarks in the recent transformation of the inter-American regime of citizenship. Adopted in 1991 (the day before Resolution 1080), the Santiago Commitment linked the renewal of the inter-American system and the strengthening of representative democracy in the hemisphere. The Managua Declaration, which was adopted in 1993, stressed the relationship between civil, political, economic, social, and cultural rights.

The coming into effect of NAFTA in 1994 has done little to modify US policy on the issue of democracy and human rights promotion in the Americas. The United States has continued to strive for the strengthening of the inter-American regime of citizenship along the same lines as what was done immediately after the end of the Cold War. And thanks to the institutionalization of the Summit of the Americas meetings, the first of which was held in Miami in December 1994, that policy was given a new forum to express itself. With an agenda strongly influenced by the US government, the Miami Summit helped to increase the attention paid to democracy in hemispheric cooperation (Feinberg 1997, 166–167). It was, for example, the Miami meeting that popularized the image of the Americas as a "community of democracies" (Summit of the Americas 1995a, 9–10). In an innovative manner the Declaration of Principles adopted at this first Summit linked the issues of democracy, free trade, and sustainable development. More specifically, the declaration recognized that "democracy and development reinforce one another," and that "the fruits of democratic stability and economic growth must be accessible to all" (Summit of the Americas 1995a, 9, 11). The US government also made sure that in the Miami Plan of Action, issues such as corruption, crime, and terrorism would be identified as threats to democracy (Summit of the Americas 1995b, 15–16). The 1994 Summit thus gave the US the opportunity to promote even more vigorously the vision of democracy it hoped to disseminate throughout the Americas.

Since Miami, the United States has actively participated in the consolidation of the inter-American doctrine on democracy and human rights. In this connection, Washington supported Canadian efforts to include a Democratic clause in the Quebec City Declaration. Moreover, alongside "like-minded" countries such as Argentina, Canada, and Costa Rica, the United States took part at a very early stage in the Peruvian initiative aimed at drafting an Inter-American Democratic Charter (Graham 2002, 4). At the first anniversary of the signing of the Democratic Charter, the US permanent delegate to the OAS, Roger Noriega, laid great emphasis on the "poetic justice" of such an accord being realized on September 11, 2001 (Government of the United States 2002a, 1). Referring to the staunch support given by the nations of the hemisphere to the United States' struggle against terrorism, the ambassador added that the Democratic Charter was not addressed solely to the "weakest and smallest neighbors," and that "every country stands to benefit from the solidarity embodied in the Democratic Charter" (Government of the United States 2002a, 2).

The United States has also had to confront the festering of certain conflicts (Haiti, Peru), and the emergence of new crises (Paraguay, Venezuela). In Haiti, the United States managed to return President Aristide to power under the political umbrella of the UN in 1994 (Stotzky 2002, 125–178). However, the carrot-and-stick policy applied by the United States at the bilateral, regional, and multilateral levels has had little success in defeating the corruption, political violence and economic chaos affecting that country. Although the holding of elections in 2006 is generally viewed as an encouraging step for the future of Haitian democracy, the fact remains that in the wake of 9/11 Haiti does not sit very high among the priorities of US foreign policy. Regarding Peru, despite Congress' repeated criticisms of Fujimori's authoritarianism, the US government adopted a wait-and-see approach until the fraudulent elections held in 2000 (Conaghan 2001, 29). Following these elections, the United States tried unsuccessfully to convince the members of the OAS to use Resolution 1080 to deal with the situation. Washington had to be content with sending a high-level delegation to Lima (Cooper and Legler 2006, 67–71). The US objective of regime change was nonetheless achieved when President Fujimori was finally forced to resign in November 2000.

During the Paraguayan crisis of 1996, the United States supported the constitutional regime of President Wasmosy by advocating the application of Resolution 1080 (Valenzuela 1997, 43–55). However, whether the OAS's response was as decisive as that of MERCOSUR in Paraguay's return to democracy remains open to debate. Finally, with respect to Venezuela, Washington has maintained an ambiguous attitude toward the widespread questioning of President Hugo Chávez's legitimacy. At the time of the attempted coup d'état in April 2002, the United States reluctantly supported the recourse to the Democratic Charter to ensure the preservation of democracy in Venezuela (Shifter 2002, B2). When a general strike shook the country a few months later, the US administration officially encouraged the mediation efforts deployed under OAS sponsorship, but it concurrently expressed sympathy toward the opponents of the Chávez government and refused to condemn the calls for a coup d'état (Cason and Brooks, 2002, p. 25). As the most powerful member of Venezuela's Group of Friends, an OAS initiative, the United States subsequently promoted the idea of a recall referendum. However, this strategy backfired when Venezuelans ultimately supported Chávez's maintenance in office in the 2004 plebiscite. More recently, the US government presented as a success Venezuela's isolation at the 2005 Mar del Plata Summit of the Americas, where "all but one country reaffirmed that representative democracy (…) is an indispensable condition for the peace, development, and stability of the region" (US Department of State 2005). Quite obviously, Venezuela stands as the most important test that the new inter-American paradigm of democracy has had to face until now. Among other things, it raises a crucial question: To what extent can Washington put up with a government that does not share its views but that was democratically elected?

On a different front, the United States has made an avant-garde contribution to the democratization of the decision-making processes of the inter-American system by accepting greater participation of civil society in hemispheric debates. The US administration encouraged the involvement of various social groups in the preparations for the Miami Summit and later supported the granting of consultative status to non-governmental organizations in the OAS (Thorup 1995, xiii–xxvi; Shamsie 2000, 11). US policy in this area draws on both the dynamism and the pluralist tradition characteristic of the US civil society, and on the public interest sparked by the FTAA negotiations. The democratization of inter-American politics may eventually lead to a complete redefinition of the regional order. Still, it is clear at this point that for all their openness, the US authorities continue to be more receptive to corporate lobbies that to human rights or environmental groups. In sum, from Washington's point of view, the democratization of the inter-American system seems all the more worthy of encouragement if it serves to strengthen the legitimacy of US positions.

The United States' backing of the inter-American regime of citizenship, however remarkable its recent renewal may be, remains subject to most of the criticisms articulated in the past. First and foremost, the US maintains its narrow conception of democracy. For the US government, democracy continues to be defined primarily as free elections and open competition between political parties. The United States thus pays little attention to the promotion of social and economic rights, in spite of its official support for a host of resolutions that link democracy, peace, and development (Forsythe 2000b, 21). In addition, the United States still refuses to ratify the American Convention on Human Rights and to acknowledge the jurisdiction of the Inter-American Court of Human Rights (Forsythe 2000b, 29). While it claims that its laws and policies are already largely in conformity with inter-American norms, the US position in fact contributes to the weakening of regional treaties and conventions. Lastly, the United States' financial commitment to the inter-American regime of citizenship remains quite limited. In 2001, for example, Washington contributed $6.38 million to the UPD, a trifle when compared to the $1.3 billion that it dedicated to the Colombia Plan (OAS 2000).

To summarize, the United States has for a long time been concerned with the promotion of democracy and human rights in the Americas. Overall, its behavior resembles that of a policeman who feels entitled to enforce his own view of order. Though deeply historical, this characterization of US policy seemed as relevant as ever when, in 2005, the Latin American countries massively rejected an American proposal to create a regional mechanism for monitoring democracy (Legler 2007). The above discussion moreover suggests that NAFTA has done little to alter US policy. NAFTA has, however, helped to bolster the neo-Liberal notion that the best democracy is one that promotes open markets. In this sense, it has certainly strengthened the worldview that was already dominant among the US foreign policy elite.

Canada: The Missionary

Canada shares with the United States the advantage of being the only rich country of the Western Hemisphere. Because of this status, its foreign policy resembles that of the United States in several ways. The history of Canada's involvement in the inter-American system, however, differs extensively from the US experience. As shall be seen here, this difference has at times manifested itself with respect to democracy and human rights promotion. Though it has always been concerned more with the imperatives of order than those of justice in its handling of international affairs, Canada has constantly sought to cultivate its reputation as a "good international citizen" with a deep sense of ethics (Cooper 1997, 71–74, 83–87). As former Prime Minister Lester Pearson noted, Canadians do not ask themselves only "what kind of Canada [they] want," but also "what kind of world [they] want" (Pearson 1974, 32; quoted in Cooper 1997, 74). This style of foreign policy has given rise to a sophisticated discourse in which "Canadian values" – especially the respect for democracy and human rights – occupy a favored position.

Canada became a full-fledged member of the inter-American system only in 1990, when it joined the OAS. Until then its engagement in inter-American affairs had been "irregular" and "inconsistent" (McKenna 1995, 65). Canadian policy had been based on the idea that the country's membership in the OAS could only lead to unnecessary conflicts. Canada had feared that by supporting the United States it would antagonize the Latin American countries and, conversely, by supporting the Latin American countries it would antagonize the United States. To avoid this dilemma the Canadian government preferred to handle its Latin American relations through bilateralism and multilateralism right up to the end of the Cold War. Admittedly, those relations involved democracy and human rights only in a limited way. It should be stressed, however, that well before becoming part of the inter-American "family," Canada had endeavored to demonstrate the autonomy of its foreign policy by adopting distinctive positions, most notably in the cases of Cuba in the 1960s, and Central America in the 1980s.[9]

While the Canadian government was never a cheerleader for Cuban-style socialist democracy, it recognized early on "the right of the Cuban people to seek their own solution" (Ogelsby 1976, 178). Standing in opposition to the policy of political and economic isolation advocated by the United States, Canada, together with Mexico, was alone among the nations of the Americas in not breaking its diplomatic ties with the regime of Fidel Castro. Two decades later, strongly encouraged by Canadian NGOs, the government played an active role in resolving the wars raging in Central America. Although Canada has been occasionally criticized for its lack of policy leadership, there is widespread acknowledgement that it "has effectively promoted democratization" in that region (Spehar and Thede 1995, 143). Canada's contribution has been made concrete through its diplomatic and technical support for the Contadora and Esquipulas II processes, its participation in the ONUSAL and ONUCA peace missions, and its foreign aid programs (Spehar and Thede 1995, 143–144).

From the moment it joined the OAS, Canada's intention of making democracy one of its diplomatic niches became apparent. It was, for example, on the Canadian government's initiative that the UPD was created in June 1990. On the strength of its reputation as an "honest broker" and its expertise in electoral matters, Canada played a crucial role in defining that institution's mandate. It is furthermore significant that to date the UPD/OPD has always been headed by a Canadian. Canada also placed itself resolutely in the camp of the "activist" countries by arguing for the adoption of Resolution 1080 as well as the Protocol of Washington, a treaty the Canadian government was moreover the first to ratify.

During the pre-NAFTA era, Canada supported the use of Resolution 1080 when democracy was interrupted in Haiti, Peru, and Guatemala. Of these three, the Haitian crisis was without a doubt the one in which the Canadian government was most active. It should be recalled that Canada had been heavily involved in the organization of the Haitian elections of 1990, the first free elections in the country's history. Canada later was one of the first states to respond to the September 1991 coup d'état by cutting off its commercial ties and bilateral aid programs. Following the failure of the measures taken by the OAS against the putschist regime of General Cédras, the Canadian government came over to the US strategy, which aimed to resolve the Haitian crisis

---

9   The notion of inter-American "family" was used by Prime Minister Jean Chrétien (Government of Canada 2000).

through the UN. In addition to supporting all Security Council resolutions bearing on Haiti, Canada agreed to be a member of the international civil mission created in 1993 (UNMIH). This multilateral initiative proved, however, to be a diplomatic failure when armed demonstrators dramatically prevented Canadian and US troops aboard the Harlan County from coming ashore in Port-au-Prince. In the aftermath of the Harlan County episode, Canadian diplomacy became unmistakably more hesitant. The low-profile approach was definitely dropped only upon the departure of President Aristide and Canada's decision to supervise the Haitian elections in 2006. Through its various twists and turns, the Haitian case has provided important lessons as to Canada's capacity to act on democracy and human rights issues. On the level of discourse, the Canadian government likes to wrap itself in a cloak of "democratic virginity" in order to promote principles it considers universal (Zylberberg 1995, 114). But when the time comes for action, Canada's leverage is relatively weak, and its foreign policy often remains subordinated to that of the United States.

The traditional proximity of Ottawa's views to those of Washington also makes it possible to understand why Canada, like the United States, has never deemed it necessary to ratify the American Convention on Human Rights or to recognize the jurisdiction of the Inter-American Court of Human Rights. The Canadian government argues that the Convention includes provisions in contradiction with Canadian law and jurisprudence, in particular those related to abortion rights and freedom of expression (Government of Canada 2001c). This overly scrupulous interpretation is not only contested by human rights groups but has also been challenged by a parliamentary committee, which has recently concluded that Canada could easily sign the Convention while at the same time registering certain reservations (Government of Canada – Standing Committee on Foreign Affairs and International Trade 2001). At all events, various experts suggest that the government's attitude regarding inter-American human rights law undermines the "soft power" Canada wishes to exercise in the area of democracy (Rights and Democracy 2000).

As previously noted in relation to the United States, the implementation of NAFTA has had no tangible impact on Canadian policy concerning the inter-American regime of citizenship. The continuity of Canada's policy was made clear as of the Miami Summit, where Canada heartily endorsed the emphasis the US administration was placing on democracy. In recognition of this support, Canada was appointed co-chair, along with Brazil, of the working group charged with verifying that the commitments made at the Summit concerning democracy and human rights were being fulfilled (Shifter and Neill 1996, 3; Mace and Roy 2000, 276).

Canadian leadership was strengthened at the Quebec Summit, often referred to as the "Democracy Summit" (Cooper 2001, 159–171). The adoption of the Democratic clause at that meeting owes a great deal to the skills of Canadian diplomats, who succeeded in overcoming the resistance of the group of "non-interventionist" countries, still powerful within the OAS. As mentioned earlier, the Democratic clause broadened inter-American law by establishing that a simple "alteration" of the democratic order in one of the region's states could entail collective action.[10] It was also at the Quebec Summit that Canada began to take part in the drafting

---

10 The text of the democracy clause is available at www.summit-americas.org.

of the Democratic Charter. Favorable to this accord from the outset, the Canadian government has described the Democratic Charter as one of the "most significant achievements" of the OAS, and as a political mechanism that "signifies the value that we, as citizens of the Americas, place on democracy and the fruits that accompany it" (see Government of Canada 2002c). Careful to avoid any accusations of neo-imperialism, Canada especially stresses the idea that the Charter was elaborated in a spirit of prevention rather than punishment (Government of Canada 2002d).

In response to the political crises that have plagued the hemisphere since 1994, Canada has tried on each occasion to promote regional solutions. In Haiti, despite persistent difficulties in the democratization process, the Canadian government remains resolutely involved in all the major initiatives that have been undertaken by the OAS (see, for instance, OAS 2003a). In Venezuela, Ottawa endorsed the application of the Democratic Charter and continues to encourage ongoing dialogue within the inter-American system. Absent from Venezuela's Group of Friends, however, Canada has been much less influential in that country than in Haiti. This said, it was probably in the resolution of the Peruvian crisis that the Canadian government's role was the most noteworthy. As it happens, Fujimori's contested election in the spring of 2000 took place only a few days before the first OAS General Assembly to be held on Canadian territory. That meeting was to provide the minister of Foreign Affairs, Lloyd Axworthy, with the opportunity to highlight Canada's mediation capabilities. Even though they refused to use Resolution 1080, the members of the OAS charged the Secretary-General of the organization, César Gaviria, and the Canadian minister with a high-level mission to evaluate the political situation in Peru. The mission succeeded in setting up a *mesa de diálogo* where the Peruvian government, opposition parties, and civil society groups negotiated a major program of political reform. One should not overestimate either the role of the OAS mission in the fall of the Fujimori government or the role that Canada played in the overall process (Cooper 2002, 296). Nevertheless, the Peruvian episode clearly allowed the Canadian government to assert its leadership in issues of democracy.

In recent years, Canadian policy has also distinguished itself through its commitment to strengthening the mechanisms whereby civil society can participate in hemispheric affairs. Canada has been one of the foremost advocates of every measure adopted in this connection, whether in the OAS, within the Summit framework, or in the FTAA negotiations. It is telling that the Trade Ministerial of Toronto held in 1999 was the first event in the FTAA process where groups from civil society were invited to organize their own parallel meeting. In 2000, the OAS General Assembly held in Windsor became another first by innovatively allowing members of civil society to discuss with official delegates. Canada also played a leading role in the creation of the Inter-American Parliamentary Forum (IAPF), a network whose goal is "to consolidate democratic values, practices and institutions throughout the Hemisphere" (Governement of Canada 2001a, 48). Finally, on the domestic level, the government has established an office to liaise with social groups concerned by the FTAA. It is difficult to measure to what degree these efforts to democratize Canada's inter-American policy reflect a genuine interest in consultation on the part of the government, or whether they should be regarded primarily as part of a public relations operation. At the very least, however, it can be asserted that

Canadian policy has nourished public debate on the accountability of the decision-making structures of the inter-American system.

Canadian policy on democracy and human rights in the Americas raises criticisms similar to those directed at US policy. First, Canada upholds a conception of democracy that, while less militaristic than that of the United States, remains largely procedural, and leaves little room for the consideration of economic and social rights. Commenting on the Mexican project to include a Social Fund within the FTAA, the Canadian Minister for International Trade, Pierre Pettigrew, aptly summarized the Canadian view when he declared, "We liberalize trade, but we let the governments redistribute the wealth" (author's translation) (Krol 2001, A8). In other words, while it advocates a strengthening of democracy in the region, the Canadian government does not feel especially concerned about the lack of truly equal opportunity across the hemisphere. Furthermore, Canada's financial commitment to the promotion of democracy and human rights has overall been modest. It is revealing, for instance that during the 1990s Sweden contributed more than Canada to the budget of the UPD.[11] As well, the priorities to which Canadian resources in the area of democracy have been channeled – particularly the elimination of anti-personnel mines – have at times been put in doubt (Mace and Roy 2000, 283).

In many ways, Canada poses as a missionary of democracy and human rights in the Americas. This issue certainly represents the sphere of activity where Canada, since joining the OAS, has most methodically striven to concentrate its ideological and political influence. It is thus hardly surprising that Canada is among the countries that have contributed the most to the recent development of the inter-American regime of citizenship. Considering the objectives of this chapter, it is important to emphasize the continuity of Canadian policy throughout the 1990s and the fact that NAFTA had no more impact on Canada's position than it did on that of the United States. By and large, what is perhaps most characteristic of Canadian policy is the persistent gap between the *dichos* [what is said] and the *hechos* [what is done]. As two commentators have observed, "As far as democracy in the Americas is concerned, it appears that the discourse of the Canadian government [...] does not translate into the corresponding concrete action" (author's translation) (Mace and Roy 2000, 284). The ambiguities of Canada's behavior are to a great extent inseparable from the priority attributed by Canada's foreign policy to the maintenance of the established international order. Undoubtedly, given Canada's very real proclivity for negotiation and compromise, Canadian policy on the promotion of democracy and human rights in the Americas cannot be considered a carbon copy of US policy. In the final analysis, however, the "Canadian values" the government claims to promote are rather close to the principles underpinning US hegemony in the region.

---

11 For the 1990–2001 period, the contribution of Sweden and Canada to the UPD amounted to $16 million and $6.3 million respectively (see OAS 2000).

Mexico: The Bricklayer

Of the three members of NAFTA, Mexico is the country where the implementation of the trade agreement has had the most definite impact on policy relating to the promotion of democracy and human rights in the Americas. Though undeniable, the impact has nonetheless been indirect: the opening up of the economy brought about by NAFTA has accelerated an opening up in the political sphere that has in turn led the Mexican government to show more support for the inter-American regime of citizenship.

The particularity of Mexico *vis-à-vis* the US and Canadian situations stems from its very different political and economic history in comparison with that of its two Northern neighbors. Before turning to the details of this history, however, it would be useful to underscore two basic ideas that will inform the following analysis. First, Mexico's foreign policy regarding democracy and human rights is linked far more closely to domestic issues than is the case in the United States or Canada. So while it is clear that NAFTA was not what triggered Mexico's democratization (Cameron and Wise 2004, 319), one can argue that NAFTA did create an opportunity to consolidate both the domestic and international dimensions of Mexican policy on democracy and human rights. Second, over the last two decades Mexico's attitude towards democracy and human rights has been characterized above all by its gradualness.[12] Because the transformation of that policy came about in a slow, incremental, way, the image of the bricklayer provides an apt emblem of the process. In keeping with that image, the coming into effect of NAFTA will have been just one more brick in the construction of a democratic regime *à la Mexicana*.

Mexican foreign policy was traditionally shaped by the principle of non-intervention.[13] This approach was a political consequence of the various foreign interventions that left their mark on the nation's collective memory, the most traumatic one being without a doubt the war that resulted in the conquest of one third of Mexican territory by the United States in the 19th century. The always-difficult relations with the Colossus of the North led the Mexican government to apply a foreign policy based on defensive and protectionist nationalism. At the same time, the attitude adopted on the international level was in line with the domestic needs of the authoritarian Mexican system. More specifically, the defense of the non-intervention principle facilitated the *Partido Revolucionario Institucional*'s (PRI) grip on power for over 70 years. Any external interference, especially coming from the United States, was condemned in advance as an assault on the country's sovereignty. The United States, for its part, accepted the situation in the belief that, given the Cold War environment, Mexico's stability must come before the urgency of political reforms.

Due to its apprehensions about the United States' hegemonic tendencies, Mexico has had a long history of mistrust regarding the OAS. From 1948 on, the Mexican government systematically opposed the idea of granting too much power to the

---

12 This interpretation is in line with the argument made in Jean-François Prud'homme (Prud'homme 2003, 3).

13 For an historical view of Mexico's foreign policy, see Mario Ojeda (Ojeda 1984).

organization, particularly in the military sphere (Ojeda 1984, 67). Its hope was that the OAS would focus on the economic and social development of the region. Because of the Cold War, however, the ensuing events turned into a source of endless frustration for Mexican foreign policy. A number of observers came to see the OAS as the United States' Department of Colonies or as a forum where decision-making was based on "a majority of one" (Ezeta 1992, 25). It is in no way surprising that Mexico's multilateral diplomacy consistently gave preference to the UN system over the inter-American system.

For decades, the Mexican government staunchly defended the primacy of the non-intervention principle in numerous situations where inter-American politics involved democracy and human rights. In the Guatemalan crisis of 1954, for example, Mexico was one of the few members of the OAS to refuse to censure the reformist government of Jacobo Arbenz. In the 1960s, in the face of pressures from Washington, Mexico was the only Latin American country to maintain diplomatic ties with Cuba. Two decades later, Mexican concerns over US interventionism prompted the government to seek solutions to the civil wars in Central America through the Contadora group rather than the OAS. With respect to human rights, Mexico agreed to ratify the American Convention on Human Rights, but only after registering a large number of reservations. Moreover, it has until recently rejected the contentious jurisdiction of the Inter-American Court of Human Rights, objecting that Mexican law adequately protected the rights of Mexican citizens (see Ojeda 1984, 53–65; Heller 2000, 299–309; Heller 1999, 177–178).

Mexican policy within the OAS slowly began to change in the early 1990s. The most telling example of this change was no doubt the Mexican government's support for the adoption of Resolution 1080 and for its earliest applications. At that juncture, however, Mexico still remained hesitant in embracing a pro-active approach toward democracy and human rights. During the negotiations on Resolution 1080, Mexico's yes vote came only at "the eleventh hour" because it wanted at all costs to avoid "[bearing] the onus of being the sole member to 'vote against democracy'" (Bloomfield 1994, 162). In his address to the General Assembly of the OAS, the Minister of Foreign Affairs, Fernando Solana, thought it necessary to reiterate his government's traditional position: "Mexico is opposed to the creation of automatic mechanisms of response in case of abrupt changes in political systems" (author's translation) (Solana 1994, 575). And, even though it sanctioned the use of Resolution 1080 in Haiti, Peru, and Guatemala, Mexico declined to participate in the missions dispatched to these three countries (Domínguez and Fernández de Castro 2001, 60). In 1992, the principle of non-intervention was once again invoked by Mexico to justify its refusal to sign the Protocol of Washington. In the debate on this amendment to the OAS Charter, Minister Solana stressed, "It is not external dictates, but rather the conditions and the decision of each society that allow it to advance and perfect its democratic system" (author's translation) (Solana 1994, 575). Clearly, the evolution of Mexican policy has come about in small steps and not through a radical break with the past.

While the end of the Cold War provided a favorable environment, the gradual transformation of Mexican external policy in the area of democracy and human rights can be explained primarily in terms of the internal political dynamic. In struggling for the democratization of the domestic political system, Mexican civil society forced the government to modify its behavior on the international level. A watershed in that process was the decision of the *Partido de Acción Nacional* (PAN) to go before the Inter-American Commission on Human Rights with charges of election fraud in connection with the elections held in 1985 and 1986 in the states of Durango and Chihuahua. The government of President Carlos Salinas (1988–1994) reacted to the publication of the Inter-American Commission's report of May 1990, by establishing the National Commission on Human Rights (Covarrubias Velasco 1999, 438–439; Domínguez and Fernández de Castro 2001, 106–107). Urged on by opposition parties and non-governmental organizations, the internationalization of Mexican domestic policy gained momentum with the stepping up of the NAFTA negotiations. To preserve the country's positive image, the Salinas administration had no choice but to pay ever more attention to democracy and human rights issues.

The Chiapas revolt, launched the very same day that NAFTA came into effect, intensified even further the intertwining of the domestic and international dimensions of Mexican policy on democracy and human rights. In response to ever-increasing pressures, the Mexican government took a series of unprecedented initiatives. Starting with the 1994 elections, for instance, it authorized the presence of "international visitors." In 1996, major electoral reforms were approved. During the same year, the Inter-American Commission on Human Rights was for the first time invited to make an on-site investigation of accusations of human rights violations. In 1997, a democratic clause was incorporated in the accord signed with the European Union. And in 1998, the Mexican government recognized the jurisdiction of the Inter-American Court of Human Rights, while reserving only the right to expel foreign citizens without trial (see Covarrubias Velasco 1999, 439–440; Covarrubias Velasco 2001, 68–71; Domínguez and Fernández de Castro 2001, 108–110). This series of measures advanced the opening up of the political system and thus fostered the political shift that would take place in July 2000, when Vicente Fox was elected president.

As suggested by the abovementioned evolution of the attitude of Mexican authorities toward the Inter-American Commission on Human Rights and the Inter-American Court of Human Rights, the effervescence of the domestic political scene in the 1990s altered the relationship between Mexico and hemispheric institutions. It should be pointed out, however, that for all that the government of Ernesto Zedillo (1994–2000) did not give up its attachment to the principle of non-intervention in the management of regional affairs. Following the Peruvian elections of 2000, Mexico, along with Brazil, was the fiercest opponent to the OAS's recourse to Resolution 1080. For the Zedillo administration, the use of Resolution 1080 was unjustified since Peru was not confronted with a coup d'état. Mexico's ambassador to the OAS, Claude Heller, explained his country's policy by declaring that the OAS "at no time should be a substitute for the functions which correspond to state institutions" (quoted in Cooper and Legler 2006, 65). It was only after Fox's election that this position was put into question.

Right from his inaugural speech, President Fox stressed the need to deal with the deficiencies of Mexican democracy. Consistent with this concern, he included among his staff a number of individuals known as resolute defenders of human rights, most notably Jorge G. Castaneda, Adolfo Aguilar Zinser, and Mariclaire Acosta (Human Rights Watch 2002, 45). In foreign policy, Fox advocated a "concept of the universality of the principles of human rights, a concept that was anathema to previous Mexican governments" (author's translation) (Human Rights Watch 2002, 48). This approach would soon have major repercussions for the country's inter-American relations.

Mexico's change of policy on issues of democracy and human rights promotion in the Americas was strikingly expressed through its support for the Democratic clause adopted in Quebec City, and for the Inter-American Democratic Charter. In Quebec City, Fox justified Mexico's position on grounds that "the democratic exercise of power [...] will lead to more competitive and progressive economies, and to more just and humane societies" (author's translation) (Government of Mexico 2002a). Before the Inter-American Court of Human Rights, he later added that the Mexican state would henceforward be impelled by a new vision whereby "the intrinsic and inviolable dignity of the human person" constitutes "a fundamental principle having precedence over the notion of sovereignty" (author's translation) (Government of Mexico 2002b). The new philosophy of the Mexican government was consolidated by a variety of measures that contrasted sharply with past policies. At the OAS, for example, Mexico has taken a leadership role to ensure that the fight against terrorism is conducted "in keeping with obligations under international law" (OAS 2002; OAS 2003b). At the global level, in a highly symbolic initiative, the Mexican government used the UN Commission on Human Rights to denounce the human rights situation in Cuba (Prud'homme 2003, 10). And at the sub-regional level, a democratic clause based on the Democratic Charter was included in the development program known as the "Puebla-Panama Plan".

It is still too *early* to measure exactly the implications of the changes made to Mexico's foreign policy since 2000. The government's prudence in the face of the attempted coup d'état in Venezuela suggests that the Estrada doctrine remains a basic reference for Mexican diplomacy. While Mexico was officially in favor of the OAS resorting to the Democratic Charter, president Fox abstained from openly condemning the actions of the putschists. "Mexico," he declared the day after the coup, "will abstain from either recognizing or not recognizing the new government of Venezuela, and will limit itself to maintaining diplomatic relations with that government" (author's translation) (Government of Mexico 2002a). Such ambiguous diplomatic language can be read as a further illustration of the gradualism typical of Mexican foreign policy on matters of democracy and human rights. The Mexican government is certainly more willing now than in the past to accept the idea that collective action can be carried out to defend democracy in the hemisphere. Yet, as demonstrated by its stand as a member of Venezuela's Group of Friends and by its continued refusal to ratify the Protocol of Washington, the Mexican government shows no enthusiasm whatever for the use of sanctions to maintain constitutional order. Precisely what shape Mexico's highly nuanced policy will take in the end, only time can determine. In the meantime, one of the main tests of the depth of the Mexican government's new convictions will be the degree of interest it shows in the democratization of its inter-American policy. To date, the consultation mechanisms it has set up have clearly not met the demands of Mexican civil society as a whole.

As this analysis shows, Mexican policy regarding the promotion of democracy and human rights in the Americas has constantly evolved since the early 1990s. Its strong attachment to the principle of non-intervention has gradually given way to the notion that sovereignty involves certain limits. This change can be linked indirectly to NAFTA, in that Mexico's "market liberalization [...] made an important albeit subtle contribution to Mexico's democratization" (Domínguez and Fernández de Castro 2001, 109). At the same time, the Mexican approach to democracy continues to be imbued with traditional Latin American values. Despite the change observed in recent years it would be naïve to think the Mexican government has completely broken with its former view of international law. Mexico furthermore continues to attach considerable importance to the economic dimension of democracy. In 2005, Foreign Minister Derbez stressed that "democracy without economic and social rights is an incomplete project" (author's translation) (Government of Mexico – Secretaría de Relaciones Exteriores 2005). In the end, it is difficult to evaluate the specific role NAFTA has played in the recent transformations of Mexican foreign policy, as compared to the role of other factors such as the end of the Cold War, the election of Vicente Fox or the vigor of civil society. Ultimately, one of the few things that can be said with any certainty is that the evolution of Mexican policy on the promotion of democracy and human rights in the Americas has been shaped above all by the domestic political environment.

Conclusion

As suggested by the images of the policeman, the missionary, and the bricklayer, there are significant differences among the policies of the United States, Canada, and Mexico regarding the promotion of democracy and human rights in the Americas. In recent years, however, these differences have been attenuated, due mainly to changes in the behavior of the Mexican government. Mexico is today far more open to the idea that the respect for democracy and human rights constitutes a legitimate concern for the international community in general and for the American states in particular. Mexico's position on this issue has thus moved significantly closer to the activist policy long advocated by the United States and Canada.

Our analysis shows the growing similarity among the policies of the United States, Canada, and Mexico relating to democracy and human rights promotion in the Americas. Yet, with reference to the questions raised at the beginning of this chapter, it would be more useful to interpret this increasing similarity in terms of alignment rather than convergence. A convergence of policies is commonly assumed to involve a mutual adjustment in the approach of *all* concerned parties, whereas the congruence that has developed among the US, Canadian, and Mexican policies regarding an inter-American regime of citizenship has been quite asymmetrical. One could, of course, engage in a lengthy debate to determine whether Mexico's new attitude toward the promotion of democracy and human rights in the Americas is due primarily to normative or to material factors, but the basic dynamic appears to be perfectly clear: Mexican policy has moved closer to that of the United States and Canada, while there is nothing to indicate that US and Canadian policies have likewise approached Mexican policy.

In addition, although it may be difficult to establish a formal causal link, this chapter lends credence to the idea that even those international institutions with a rudimentary architecture such as NAFTA can influence the national policies of their member countries. Here, once again, the Mexican case is of particular interest. By focusing on the promotion of democracy and human rights in the Americas, our analysis was directed above all toward explaining how NAFTA was able to act as a catalyst in the recent evolution of Mexico's foreign policy. But it can also be argued that the economic liberalization engendered by the free trade treaty has accelerated the country's political liberalization, not only externally but also domestically. Indeed, NAFTA has made it possible to expand the interaction among trade unions, NGOs and business groups in the three member states. The socialization resulting from this interaction has had positive, albeit modest, consequences for Mexico's democratic transition. In other words, although the political opening up of Mexico has been due primarily to internal factors having little to do with NAFTA, one can reasonably assume that the process has been enhanced by NAFTA (Cameron and Wise 2004, 301–323).

Finally, this study of the policies of the United States, Canada, and Mexico on the promotion of democracy and human rights in the Americas reinforces the position of the neo-functionalists, who have long held that regional integration can generate spill-over effects. Mexico's shift to a more interventionist approach in the area of democracy and human rights was certainly made easier by the ratification of NAFTA. This conclusion is in line with the assessment of most commentators, who agree that NAFTA made it possible for the three members of the agreement to enter into an unprecedented dynamic of cooperation. It seems plausible that this increased cooperation has impacted, first, on those spheres of activity – such as the environment and labor – directly related to regional trade. To the extent that NAFTA is founded on the sharing of new interests, however, it is not surprising that the effects of the agreement should extend to areas transcending North American affairs. This, at any rate, is what is suggested by the growing similarity of the positions of the US, Canada, and Mexico on the promotion of democracy and human rights in the Americas. But beyond this somewhat foreseeable result, our analysis highlights the fact that spill-over effects do not flow solely from inter-governmental exchanges. In the case that we have considered, the spill-over has largely been the result of the transnational interactions of civil society in the three countries. On the strength of this observation, one can confidently predict that the debate on the deepening of NAFTA will depend more and more on the evolution of public opinion and on civil society's ability to mobilize in Mexico, Canada, and the United States.

Chapter 6

Sleeping with the Enemy? NAFTA Partners and Antidrug Cooperation in the Americas

Guillermo R. Aureano[1]

The question examined in this chapter is: has the North American Free Trade Agreement (NAFTA) led its three member countries – Canada, Mexico and the United States – to harmonize their foreign policies on drug trafficking in the Americas? In theory, by multiplying the number of exchanges, the integration process should bring about a progressive convergence in policies, even in areas not covered by the treaties (Martin and Simmons 1999, 112). However, in regions where asymmetries are strong – as in the case of NAFTA – it would be logical to expect the weaker actors to attempt to increase their room to maneuver in fields where they are not obliged to converge.

In the area of antidrug cooperation, Canada and Mexico face a particularly dynamic and even relentless partner. The United States is the only country in the world that, for over a century now, considers the fight against drug trafficking as a major component of its foreign policy (Escohotado 1992). What is more, the two principles on which the international narcotics control system is based – prohibition and repression – were imposed on the world by American diplomacy. The inter-American antidrug system, also established under Washington's close supervision, is practically a carbon copy of the international one. Furthermore, the United States actively keeps watch to ensure that the two multilateral bodies involved in the war on drugs – the United Nations (UN) and the Organisation of American States (OAS) – dismiss all alternative solutions proposed. This extraordinary dynamic explains why the prohibitionist norms and institutions remain strong in spite of the obvious counter-productive effects they have had.

The commitment of Canada and Mexico to the fight against drug trafficking in the region is largely conditioned by their bilateral relations with the United States. In the case of Mexico, the experience has not been an easy one: it has been marked by Mexico accusing the United States of interference and Washington threatening to impose sanctions. Comparatively speaking, the disputes between Canada and the United States have been minor; the pact of non-aggression between these two countries has rarely been broken.

---

1   Translated by Karen Lang (in collaboration with the author).

The evolution of Mexico and Canada's regional policies on antidrug cooperation have generally followed different paths. In the 1980s, at the peak of former US President Ronald Reagan's war against drugs – aimed mainly at Latin American cocaine-producing and exporting countries – Mexico defended the principles of non-interference and of shared responsibility. The latter of these two emphasises the role of consumer countries – that is, those of the developed North – in the expansion of the narcotics market. But Mexico would have to wait ten years for its call for a multilateral approach to be echoed by the Latin American community.

Canada did not have to endure the hardships of regional antidrug cooperation in the 1980s. During the entire Cold War period, neither the Latin American subcontinent nor the fight against narcotrafficking were priorities on Canada's foreign policy agenda. In fact, Ottawa only began focusing on Latin America in the early 1990s. By that time, the circumstances were very different. Having learned in the 1980s that the United States would not budge in its militaristic approach to drug enforcement, the Latin American governments adopted their drug legislation to the model proposed by Washington and they accepted – without much hesitation – American aid. Also at that time, the Inter-American Drug Abuse Control Commission (CICAD), the OAS body specializing in the field, incorporated a number of American demands in its multilateral decisions. Canada arrived on the Latin American scene, then, at a time when a more consensual antidrug cooperation system – at least in appearance – was beginning to take form.

In spite of its slightly artificial character, this new turning point was comforting to both Mexico and Canada. The two countries made multilateralism one of the main pillars of their foreign policy. This strategy allowed them to justify their interventions and to increase their decision-making power at the international level.[2] Their simultaneous promotion of autonomy and cooperation reinforced their position *vis-à-vis* their all-powerful neighbor, the United States. Yet the antidrug policies did not really give them the opportunity to strengthen their leadership in the region by promoting multilateralism. The United States, which carefully avoided including security issues such as narcotrafficking in NAFTA, only allowed Canada and Mexico to promote multilateralism in drug policies on one condition: they had to respect the prohibitionist logic and American interests.

This does not mean, however, that the convergence of Canada, Mexico and the United States' foreign policies in the area of antidrug cooperation has been a smooth process. Washington continues to impose its orientations and to control any wavering by its commercial partners who, more or less enthusiastically, try to distance themselves from the United States' repressive and interventionist approach. But, in the end, it is the United States that determines which solutions are acceptable: neither Canada nor Mexico – nor any other country for that matter – have been able to drastically change the American paradigm in the war against drugs.

In order to explain the way this convergence had been modulated by the United States, it is pertinent to analyse Canada and Mexico's positions on a highly controversial antidrug assessment instrument used by the US government: the

---

2 In the case of Canada, see Hampson, Hart and Rudner (Hampson, Hart and Rudner 1999).

certification process. This analysis will pay particular attention to Canada and Mexico's participation in the negotiation that led to the creation of the Multilateral Evaluation Mechanism (MEM), a tool conceived precisely to counter the unilateral nature of the American certification process. The roles played by Canada and Mexico in another antidrug cooperation program, Plan Colombia, will then be examined. The series of hesitations that ended in the tacit acceptance of the militarisation of the Plan, promoted by the United States, provides another clear example of how harmonisation in this area was forced upon both Canada and Mexico. Finally, the last section of the article assesses NAFTA's impact on its member countries foreign policies on antidrug cooperation. But in order to be able to understand the rules of this "disciplinary" process in the framework of NAFTA, one must first comprehend the logic behind it. We thus begin by examining the origins and the workings of the international narcotics control regime and of its inter-American counterpart.

The International and Inter-American Narcotics Control Regimes

Conventional thought immediately associates drugs with prohibition, as if there were no other way to manage the consumption of mind-altering substances. The rationality used in the classification of drugs operates in the same way. In reality, however, drug prohibition and classification both have a story of their own, one that is full of conflicts and compromises. It is thus necessary to explain the process that eventually ended in a fundamentalist perception – not open to discussion – of the drug phenomenon. This perception truly constitutes the point of convergence toward which Canada and Mexico's antidrug cooperation policies are being driven.

Since the beginning of the 20th century, American political concerns – marked by heavy cultural and even racist prejudices – have dominated the establishment of an international regime that controls the production and use of certain substances (Davenport-Hines 2001; McAllister 2000; Musto 1999). The project ran into numerous obstacles in the first half of the century. European powers effectively disputed the United States' prohibitionist position right up until the time – the late 1950s – when Europe ceased to generate fiscal profits from the opium and hemp trade in their colonies. The iron will of the American government has since paid off. Three normative instruments, perfected by the UN under the aegis of Washington, currently stipulate the norms that all states must respect with regards to the production, trade and consumption of drugs. These instruments are: the Single Convention on Narcotic Drugs, 1961; the Convention on Psychotropic Substances, 1971; and finally, the Convention against Illicit Traffic in Narcotic Drugs and Psychotropic Substances, 1988.[3]

The three conventions replaced all earlier treaties. To understand their significance, one need only analyse the definition of drugs that they use, as it is the definition itself that determines what the States commit themselves to (Caballero 2000; Escohotado 1992). Sometimes referred to as "narcotics", other times as "psychotropic substances",

---

3   All three treaties are available on line at http://www.unodc.org/unodc/en/drug_and_crime_conventions.html, accessed 31 July 2006.

the drugs seem to have prompted several taxonomic hesitations that clearly bring to light the difficulties encountered during the elaboration of the treaties.

In 1961, experts were not able to clarify the concept of "narcotic", even though it was at the very heart of the Convention. The definition retained is tautological: a narcotic is any substance appearing on the list of narcotics (Article 1). Not one pharmacological or physiological principle is evoked. Thus, it is the political decision to classify a substance as a narcotic that determines its nature as such and, as a result, its prohibition. Escohotado (Escohotado 1992, III, 372) points out that no one can rationally explain why delegates labelled some products as narcotics, while ignoring others that produce very similar effects.

What is perhaps even more incredible is the omission, in this treaty of 1961, of a wide range of products that have already caused innumerable poisonings and health problems, the most common ones being barbiturates, amphetamines and neuroleptics. Nicotine and alcohol remained also unregulated. In addition to these notorious loopholes, obvious errors have been made. For example, cocaine is considered a narcotic – that is, a substance that causes drowsiness or induces sleep – which is the exact opposite of its true effect.

Pharmacologist Denis Richard concludes that, in this way, international treaties have successfully introduced an "*ipso facto* dichotomy between Western drugs, considered useful and thus legalized – as medication –, and traditional drugs from the Third World, judged useless and therefore prohibited. This explains why the cannabis plant is placed side by side with heroin" (Richard 1995, 18).

Ten years later, in 1971, the Vienna Convention on Psychotropic Substances added new controlled or banned substances to the earlier ones – hallucinogens rediscovered by the beat generation (such as LSD, mescaline and psilocybin), but also the main active chemical in cannabis, tetrahydrocannabinol (THC), amphetamines, phencyclidine (PCP), barbiturates, anorexics, and meprobamate (the "happy pill"). The gaps, however, remain just as remarkable as in 1961. A very commonly used and very toxic kind of sedatives, benzodiazepines, has not been put under any control (Hulsman and van Ransbeek 1983).

Even if the international conventions were meant to draw a clear line between the products and their possible uses, the logic underlying this division remains circular: certain substances are banned because they are addictive, and they are addictive because that is how they have been classified by the authorities that ban them following unscientific and cultural biased rules. From this exclusion of certain products comes the exclusion of all those who dare touch them, as well as the penal or disciplinary measures that states swear to subject them to.

The 1988 Convention did not propose any significant changes to the classification of prohibited substances. It does convey, however, as did those that preceded it, US concerns at that time. In the 1980s, one of the main objectives of the Reagan government was to obtain international legitimacy for his foreign policy in the area of drug enforcement. This policy was centered on militarization, extradition of drug traffickers, confiscation of drug money and the diffusion throughout the world of typical American investigative methods (Nadelman 1993), such as the "controlled deliveries". They clearly violate the constitutional norms of all countries under Napoleonic Law – the police shouldn't refrain from acting in respect of persons who are trafficking drugs or committing any other crime. In spite of these contradictions, the antidrug strategies recommended by the United States guided the drafting of the entire treaty (Del Olmo 1991).

In spite of existing doubts about the rationality and the ethnocentricity of the three conventions, they have been effectively applied and enforced for over forty years. Most countries have adhered to the treaties, either to avoid the blackmail of, or to show their allegiance to, the United States. Several organisations – both international and regional – have been mandated to supervise the application of the treaties. The UN set up the Commission on Narcotic Drugs (CND) and the International Narcotics Control Board (INCB); their efforts are co-ordinated by the United Nations Office on Drugs and Crime (UNODC). Other international institutions that also intervene in the control of multilateral agreements are the World Health Organization (WHO), the International Criminal Police Organisation (ICPO or Interpol) and the Customs Cooperation Council (CCC).[4]

To this list of international organisations must be added structures that were set up to reinforce cooperation efforts within certain regions. In Latin America, the development of this structure began as early as the late 1960s. At that time, the United States began "urging" the Latin American community to mobilize its resources for the consolidation of the international antidrug regime at the regional level. The first multilateral instrument put into place was the South American Agreement on Narcotic Drugs and Psychotropic Substances (ASEP) in 1973. It recommended that the signatory countries adopt draconian measures to eliminate the production, trafficking and use of illegal drugs. Following Ronald Reagan's 1982 "declaration of war on drugs", the OAS contributed to the establishment of a genuine regional cooperation policy that included all 35 countries in the Americas.

The first significant step towards the establishment of an inter-American narcotics control system was made in 1984. On 11 August of that year, Bolivia, Colombia, Ecuador, Panama, Venezuela, Nicaragua and Peru signed the Quito Declaration Against Traffic in Narcotic Drugs. This was followed by the adoption of Resolution 699 during the OAS General Assembly in Brasilia in November 1985. The resolution convoked the Inter-American Specialized Conference on Traffic in Narcotic Drugs held in Rio de Janeiro the following year.

The Conference in Rio ended with the adoption of the Inter-American Program of Action of Rio de Janeiro Against the Illicit Use and Production of Narcotic Drugs and Psychotropic Substances and Traffic Therein. The Program foresaw the creation of the Inter-American Drug Abuse Control Commission (CICAD). Established in 1986, this organisation's mandate is to ensure the elaboration, the co-ordination and the follow-up of measures stipulated in the Program of Action. To do so, the CICAD puts a panoply of "models" – whether they be educational campaigns, precursor chemicals control or cooperation agreements in all areas related to the fight against

---

4   In 1989, the G7 created the Financial Action Task Force on Money Laundering (FATF), which today carries out a very extensive information and surveillance mandate. This "contribution" of the G7 to the international drug control system can be also considered as an attempt by the industrialized countries to ensure themselves an extra power quota in the area of the fight against money laundering.

drugs – at the disposal of various national institutions.[5] Furthermore, the CICAD closely surveys the activities of the organisations that each OAS member country agreed to create for the purpose of co-ordinating the fight against drugs. This obligates member states to establish controls and specific measures, an obligation that is becoming more and more constraining, as the CICAD is constantly elaborating new orientation documents and establishing additional co-ordination mechanisms. What is more, the CICAD has also taken up other related issues, like small arms and light weapons, which it tries to assimilate, without too many nuances, to the drug problem.

In this way, the CICAD, which claims to represent the OAS members' collective will, actively promotes the American antidrug paradigm. This paradigm rests on the sole principle of prohibition, and it considers only one strategy – war – as legitimate. The debates on the most just and efficient way to end the drug trade are thereby limited to two imperatives: prohibit and punish. This consensus has been reinforced through the signing of several bilateral accords between the United States and each Latin American country, agreements that represent the "visible side" of US pressures.

Somewhat in the shadows of the inter-American narcotics control system are the US Drug Enforcement Administration (DEA) and US intelligence agencies (CIA, FBI, DIA). These entities have the task of catching whatever escapes the formal intervention mechanisms. The US Congress also has a role to play: each year, at the beginning of March, its members evaluate the efforts undertaken by "vulnerable" states to combat the production or trafficking of drugs. This is what is known as the *certification* process, which will be analysed in detail in the following pages. All of these measures, coercive and unilateral, condition the entire inter-American drug control system. As a result, they essentially are an operative part of the system, despite their arbitrary character and lack of transparency.

These multiple institutions and global treaties are the basis of the model for fighting drugs, as developed by the United States over the years. Together, they constitute a regime whose influence is ensured by a superpower ready to devote itself entirely to the cause. This devotion is not, however, blind. The drug problem is often used to constrain, condemn or punish countries according to the strategic interests and the rivalries of the United States at any given time. This extreme malleability of the war against drugs requires that its basic principle, prohibition, be all the more solid: it has to camouflage all of the contradictions raised by its own use as a means to political ends. This explains why Canada and Mexico, when they even slightly challenge the prohibitionist logic, have been immediately called to order.

From Certification to the Multilateral Evaluation Mechanism (MEM)

Since the 1986 modification of the Foreign Assistance Act, once a year, the president of the United States must present to the Congress a list of countries classified according

---

5   All of the documents mentioned are available on line, on the CICAD's web site at http://www.oas.org/cicad, accessed 25 April 2001.

to their commitment to the fight against drugs. The president has three certification options: *fully certified*, *certified for national interest reasons* (Natural Interest Waiver) and finally, *denied certification.* In the latter case, the sanctions imposed on the country are particularly severe: economic aid is suspended immediately and the United States sees to it that the decertified country does not receive any loans from international financial institutions. Congress has 30 days to examine the president's list.

The certification process' objectivity has often been questioned. Certain convenient omissions allow the US authorities to quietly ignore their allies' misconducts. Even when these oversights are brought to their attention, they are not given much importance. In the end, data on drug production and trafficking do not really influence the certification procedure; they are used to justify a ban on a country *a posteriori* – that is, after the decision to apply sanctions has already been made. This explains why two countries in which authorities are equally suspected of involvement in drug trafficking and money laundering can be given different marks.[6]

Such remarks are not enough to minimize the "psychological war" effect of the certification process. Each year, many nations wait impatiently for the US president's decision. While the threat of being decertified will lead some states to denounce US interference in their affairs, others adopt the measures Washington demands, or they authorize the activities of a growing number of American antidrug agents on their territory.

The certification process has not generated major tensions between Canada and the United States. The not insignificant role of Canadian organized crime in the routing of narcotics to its southern neighbor is compensated by the good relations between the two countries' police forces. The Canadian strategy on illegal drugs, which emphasizes health promotion rather than repression, has not even had to face the wrath of the United States. The limits of this tolerance, however, are quite clear. In 2002, two *ad hoc* parliamentary committees in Ottawa declared themselves in favor of decriminalizing the possession of marijuana for personal use. The White House reacted immediately. Officials warned that if Canada legalized or decriminalized marijuana, the Canada-US border would be placed under high surveillance, a decision that would have disastrous consequences on the Canadian economy. In the excitement of things, Ottawa appealed an Ontario court sentence that decriminalized marijuana possession for personal use. This gesture, which seems directed as much at US authorities as the Canadian judicial system did calm both the local judges' reformist urges and US officials' security concerns.

Only once has the Canadian government publicly stated its position on the certification process. In August 1999, the *Globe & Mail* newspaper reported the

6   The cases of Colombia and Peru illustrate perfectly the arbitrary nature of the certification process and its instrumentalization by the US government. Both suspected of collaborating with the traffickers, president Alberto Fujimori from Peru and president Ernesto Samper from Colombia were not given the same treatment. The Colombian government was systematically "decertified", while the Peruvian dictatorship had not been subject to any substantial sanctions (see Soberón Garrido 1997).

existence of rumours that suggested Washington was considering including Canada on its list of major narcotics producing or exporting countries. Such a decision could obviously greatly increase the country's risk of being "decertified". Canada's Foreign Affairs spokeswoman, Valerie Noftle, confirmed that there was some truth to the rumours. She then declared that "the drug problem is best dealt with in an international capacity, not unilaterally. It's best to tackle this issue together and not by pointing the finger at one another" (Mitrovica 1999, A1). Canada's then Minister of Foreign Affairs, Lloyd Axworthy, speculated that the rumours were a reaction among "low-level US bureaucrats to Canada's opposition to the US policy of publishing a list of countries believed to be a drug problem" (Mitrovica 1999, A6). The *Globe & Mail* article also cited anonymous American sources who claimed that Mexico had been pushing for Canada's inclusion on the US State Department's blacklist. Alfonso Nieto, press counsellor for the Mexican Embassy in Ottawa, strongly refuted these claims. He took advantage of the situation to remind everyone that "the Mexican government has strongly rejected the unilateral process of certification", a procedure that "far from strengthening the bilateral collaboration, hinder[s] the dialogue and co-operation needed in this field" (Nieto 1999, D11).

The Mexican spokesman was not lying, at least not about his government's constant criticism of the certification process. Though the US president has always "certified" Mexico, elected officials in the Congress have questioned the merits of this decision on several occasions. In 1987, 1988, 1997, 1998 and 1999, representatives went so far as to present resolutions against the president's decision. The increasing number of corruption scandals in Mexico and the constant rise in the drug flow to the United States explains, at least in part, the fact that the debates over Mexico in the late 1990s often sent the US Congress into an uproar. Also, different sources claim that ninety per cent of the cocaine sold on the American market today passes through Mexico. Not to mention the fact that Mexico's antidrug police and high-level officials' involvement in trafficking and money-laundering affairs has periodically reached what the press refers to as new all-time highs (Tirado 2002, 16–34). Such a tolerance for a country that could not satisfy US criteria on the fight against drugs can only be understood within a larger strategic framework, one that aims to maintain harmony within NAFTA and to ensure increasing US independence from oil-producing countries in the Persian Gulf (*Le Monde* 2001, 3).

The arbitrary nature of the certification process, illustrated perfectly by the Mexican case, explains why Latin American countries have been considering, since the end of the 1980s, the establishment of a multilateral evaluation procedure. Though they had sketched out the possibility several times, they have always been held up by the United States' "niet".

In order for the MEM to finally become politically and diplomatically viable, two changes had to occur. First, the large majority of Latin American governments had to adopt their antidrug policies to fit US recommendations. This phenomenon, mentioned earlier in this article, accelerated throughout the 1990s. Secondly, in June 1997, the General Assembly of the OAS approved the Antidrug Strategy in the Hemisphere, a text that clearly spells out the abandoning of all desire to pursue alternative solutions: Latin America thereby definitively renounced all possibility of contesting the prohibitionist regime. This highly symbolic gesture was of great value to US diplomacy.

Four months after the adoption of the Antidrug Strategy in the Hemisphere, during the Twenty-Second Regular Session of the CICAD, the American delegate confirmed his government's support for a proposal to create a multilateral evaluation procedure.[7] The CICAD's official documents, formerly available online, placed special emphasis on the American explicit support and, at the same time, omitted the criticisms made by governments in the region over many long years.

The opening of the US government to the idea of MEM became more apparent during the Summit of the Americas held in Santiago, Chile in April 1998. The Final Declaration mentions the notion of "shared responsibility" in the fight against drugs. As explained earlier, this principle supposes that both consumer and drug-producing countries must do their part to resolve their "common" problem. The text also evokes respect for state sovereignty and territorial integrity, as well as the principle of reciprocity. It was on these bases that the chiefs of state gave the CICAD the mandate to create the MEM.

Canada was delighted by this major breakthrough for multilateralism. Even before the Santiago Summit ended, the Canadian Minister of Foreign Affairs, Lloyd Axworthy, proposed the creation of the Hemispheric Foreign Ministers Dialogue on Drugs to accelerate the development and implementation of the MEM. Shortly after, on 8 January 1999, Axworthy officially announced the formation of the Dialogue, whose work was to be strengthened through a series of consultations held with government bodies, researchers and managers of non-governmental organizations (NGOs).

The first meeting of experts organized by the Canadian government was held in San Jose, Costa Rica in March 1999. Its objective was to analyse the pertinence of the MEM in light of the "human security" theory. This theory – dear to Axworthy – prioritizes the integrity of people and their communities. It reverses the postulates of the national security doctrine – widely diffused in Latin America under Washington's patronage – which focuses on the protection of territory and the state. The practical implications of this reversal are huge. In fact, the human security theory brings to light the role that public powers play in the emergence and the evolution of situations that compromise the well being of individuals and democratic development in the region.

The agreement among the specialists gathered in San Jose was unanimous: the human security theory allowed for the understanding and measurement of not only the negative effects of narcotic trafficking and use, but also, and above all, the impact of antidrug strategies on the effected populations' quality of life. And their assessment could not have been worse. In their view, the drug policies' most notorious consequences were: the blocking of the courts with minor offences, military and police corruption, the discrediting of the justice system and the political class, the diffusion of false information on drugs and their users, environmental destruction, marginalization of small farmers and the criminalization of underprivileged youth. Hence, the experts recommended that the MEM's indicators be used to evaluate,

---

7 The project had been presented by Honduras.

without concessions, government programs for the war on drugs, as well as the ideological and geo-strategical factors that block the search for more just and efficient solutions. In a nutshell, the experts proposed to use the MEM to determine once and for all if the antidrug policies create more problems than they solve.

This meeting greatly worried CICAD authorities, who had already put in place an intergovernmental work group on the MEM (co-presided by Jean Fournier, deputy solicitor general of Canada). The director of the CICAD, the American David Beall, who had not been invited by the Canadian government, went to Costa Rica anyway to remind participants that their proposals should be adjusted to the antidrug treaties in effect. The United States, with the decisive support of Argentina and Colombia, also made known its discontent with regard to the experts' criticisms of the prohibition and repression principles – that is, the two principles around which antidrug policies, applied and promoted by the White House, revolve.

The Canadian government eventually dismissed the recommendations of the experts it had gathered in Costa Rica. The MEM has thus finally become what it really is: a mechanism used to evaluate whether a country's national policies have been adjusted to the "truths" that Washington has succeeded in imposing throughout the years, and that today constitute the only point of reference for the war on drugs. In fact, the large majority of the MEM's indicators have been taken from the Department of State's *International Narcotics Strategy Report* (INCSR).[8] It should be recognised, however, that the MEM is an evaluation procedure that appears to be less rigid than the certification process: it takes place in a multilateral arena and does not carry sanctions. When the results obtained are judged as insufficient, the country at fault is encouraged to ask for technical assistance. If this assistance is given, however, it is highly likely that it will be tied to conditions imposed by the United States, the "donor" *par excellence*.

Only with the conditions of its application properly veiled can the MEM be considered "objective", "consensual" and "free from sanctions". In fact, the MEM, presented in official documents as a "unique" evaluation procedure, only neutralizes the unilateral nature of the US certification process in a symbolic way. The American government does not seem quite ready to give up a tool so precious and malleable to its foreign policy.[9]

In the discussions surrounding the MEM's formulation, Ottawa came upon, in an area clearly marked by the United States' unilateral decisions, a golden opportunity: it could have marked its entrance to the inter-American community by emphasizing its experience in the search for peaceful and consensual solutions. Canada gave up, however, its project of founding the MEM on the basis of the human security

---

8   The INCSR evaluates the national antidrug policies of nearly two hundred countries and territories, paying particular attention to their level of cooperation with the United States in the war on drugs.

9   In 1998, Madeleine Albright, then Secretary of State, admitted that the certification process was strongly conditioned by diplomatic interests (*Le Monde* 1998, 4). This gesture, and some less explicit ones, made some Latin American governments believe that the Multilateral Evaluation Mechanism, conceived within the OAS, was going to replace the "offensive" certification system.

theory. This project would have marked the beginning of a true revolution: it would no longer have been possible to hide the counterproductive effects of the antidrug policies defended by the United States.

Mexico followed a similar, though not identical, course. Its repeated protests against Washington's unilateralism did not stop Mexican authorities from following the American discourse to a "t", especially in all that is related to prohibition and the militarization of narcotics control (and that applies equally to both Mexico's internal and foreign policy). It also explains why Mexican officials were not too worried by the fact that the MEM reproduces, on an apparently consensual basis, the American antidrug strategy. Mexico was content with the symbolic "multilaterialisation" that the MEM supposed. What is more, Mexican delegates did not support the Canadian proposal to include in the MEM criteria that would require an assessment of the impact of the antidrug policies on the well being and the security of populations. These criteria imply a certain interference in the internal affairs of the country being evaluated, something which is intolerable in the eyes of Mexican diplomacy. In the end, Mexico preferred to avoid following entirely through with its ambitions: the multilateralism they defended only served to make American unilateralism a little more bearable.

Unlike Mexico, Canada resists the increasing security build-up and stresses that the solution to the drug problem lies more in the improvement of living conditions than in repression. But Ottawa chooses to play it safe and does not insist when the United States gives its definite "thumbs down", especially in the area of antidrug cooperation at the international and inter-American levels. In purely strategic terms, it is just not worth the risk.

The facts examined above show that, though the foreign policy strategies followed by the three countries in NAFTA were somewhat divergent, they did eventually come together. Mexico, the most adamant opponent to American unilateralism, and Canada, the promoter of humanitarian principles, have become masters in the art of "mixing apples and oranges". As soon as they see an opportunity to advance their foreign policy strategies, they do take it, but without going so far as to confront the United States.

Plan Colombia

For the past 50 years, Colombia has been caught up in a devastating civil war that appears to have no way out. The armed conflict between the leftist guerrillas and civil authorities became considerably more complex, first with the boom of the drug trade, and later with the formation of extreme right-wing paramilitary groups. Caught in the crossfire from all sides and abandoned by the government, Colombian farmers have been driven to misery. To this, one must add the constant pressure from the country that consumes the majority of the drugs produced by Colombia – the United States.

After his predecessor's failure on all fronts, President Andres Pastrana (1998–2002) resumed talks with the guerrillas. He granted the Revolutionary Armed Forces of Colombia (FARC) a demilitarized zone and took steps to initiate negotiations with the National Liberation Army (ENL). Though bold in the beginning, Pastrana would not see the process through to the end. One of the essential components of the peace negotiations and of the country's economic recovery – Plan Colombia – would be at the heart of this new setback.

According to its original version (elaborated by Augusto Ramirez Ocampo, a member of the National Conciliation Commission), Plan Colombia aimed to finance development projects related to the agreements reached with the armed opposition. These projects were mainly designed to assist the inhabitants of those regions greatly affected by the violence. Though Pastrana presented Plan Colombia in December 1998, several other versions circulated until he finally met with former US President Bill Clinton on 21 September 1999. Plan Colombia then changed its vocation. Though peace, economic recovery and strengthening the rule of law were still among the Plan's objectives, the aid promised by the American government was to be used primarily to train and equip the Colombian armed forces. From that time on, the emphasis would be placed on the fight against drugs, so as to prevent Colombia from becoming a "narco-State", as declared by US antidrug tsar, Barry McCaffrey.

In July 2000, the United States finally granted Colombia 1.3 billion dollars in aid money. Three quarters of this grant were allocated to the strictly military component of the plan: that is, for the purchase of 60 combat helicopters, the training and equipment of army battalions, the provision of sophisticated equipment to Colombian intelligence services and the delivery of chemical defoliants to be used to fumigate the coca fields. Thus, the lion's share of this "aid package" would eventually return to the United States, via contracts with the US arms industry and a panoply of private US military consultation and air fumigation companies.

After the September 11 2001 attacks on New York and Washington, US government's tone hardened even more. Washington classified both guerrilla groups and the Colombian paramilitary as "terrorists", while the American Ambassador in Bogota, Anne Patterson, compared them to the Taliban because of their links to the drug industry and their "moral hypocrisy". On 15 October 2001, the White House confirmed that it intended to resort to military force in order to end terrorist activities in Colombia. The change in policy was clear and Washington would no longer hide it. In February 2002, President Bush included in the 2003 budget proposal an additional 98 million dollars in foreign aid, to be used mainly for the protection of oil infrastructure in Colombia held or controlled by US interests. Around the same time, Pastrana's government decided, after more than three years of efforts, to unilaterally suspend peace negotiations with the FARC and the ELN. Operation "Thanatos", named after the Greek god of death, was launched, and the armed forces began once again to occupy the formerly demilitarized enclave.

In August 2002, Alvaro Uribe Velez' arrival in power reinforced the militarist option. Without hesitation, the new Colombian president began carrying out his campaign promises: he increased military spending and suspended all negotiations with the guerrillas until they put an end to their terrorist activities. But apparently this is not enough. In January 2003, in an interview with the Caracol radio station, Uribe asked the United States to deploy a military force capable of stopping drug trafficking in the Caribbean basin and in the waters of the Pacific. He claimed that "the problem in Colombia is even worse than the one in Iraq" (AFP 2003, A9). The goal of the proposed military intervention would be to cut off the guerrillas from their financial resources, the main source being (supposedly) the narcotics trade. For president Uribe, all solutions that take into account the social and economic roots of the drug trade and the armed rebellion have been dismissed for good. His choice is clear: the Colombian conflict will be resolved primarily through the use of force. And his administration does not appear to be preoccupied with a possible escalation in violence; nor do his main ally in the war on drugs – the United States.

As for Canada and Mexico, both countries were happy just watching the unfolding of events in Colombia without having to say too much. Their show of support for the peace talks did not challenge the repressive strategy promoted by the United States. The compatibility of the two – peace talks and repression – does, however, bring many questions to mind. For example, from a peace-promoting point of view, is providing arms to belligerents an efficient strategy? To what extent can a demilitarized zone encourage dialogue in the absence of international observers? Can a government that sprays fields with toxic products regain the confidence of small farmers? These are the questions that Canadian and Mexican diplomats did not even dare to formulate, in spite of their enthusiasm for and their commitment to the peace process.

Immediately after Plan Colombia was launched, Canada contributed to peace building in a variety of ways. It participated, via the Group of Ten (G10) Facilitation Commission,[10] in international efforts to aid in peace negotiations with the FARC. Guillermo Rishchynski, the Canadian ambassador in Bogota, attended a significant number of meetings between the FARC and Pastrana's emissaries. Canada was also asked to act as a mediator for the Colombian government during negotiations with the ELN. United with other donors under the banner of the Support Group for the Peace Process in Colombia – organized by the Inter-American Development Bank (IDB) and the European Union (EU), the Canadian government provided financial support to a series of initiatives aiming to strengthen the rule of law, promote sustainable development and launch social programs. Additional funds were allotted to international organizations and to NGOs through the Department of Foreign Affairs and International Trade's Human Security Program and through the Canadian International Development Agency. All of these initiatives were accompanied by numerous pleas for all actors concerned to respect the rights of the civilian population.

Like Canada, Mexico was a member of the G10 Facilitation Commission and the Support Group for the Peace Process in Colombia. Mexican authorities also gave moral and diplomatic backing to the Pastrana administration's efforts during the peace negotiations with the guerrilla groups; they did not, however, offer financial or technical support. While Mexico did in fact attempt to reserve for itself an important role in the process, its initiatives, though not lacking in audacity, failed.

Once elected president, Fox offered Pastrana his "unconditional support" for the peace process. In Fox' eyes, economic development – and thus the development of trade between the two countries – was the "best way" to achieve lasting peace. During

---

10 The Group of 10 includes Canada, Cuba, Spain, France, Italy, Mexico, Norway, Sweden, Switzerland and Venezuela.

the Group of Three's (G3)[11] meeting in April 2001, Fox and Chavez congratulated their counterpart Pastrana on his efforts to establish peace. They reminded him that Mexico and Venezuela were ready to intervene "if all concerned parties agree to make such a request". This declaration was formulated in clear and carefully chosen terms: Mexico and Venezuela would wait until all belligerent groups agreed to request their intervention as mediators. In this way, both of Colombia's G3 partners implicitly accorded the same amount of importance to all factions, and they criticized third-party countries that deal exclusively with the Colombian state.

It was most likely Chavez, and not Fox, who insisted on having the guerrilla's political status implicitly recognised. The evoking of the principle of non-interference, on the other hand, was less problematic for Mexico, as it had traditionally been part of the Mexican foreign policy "arsenal". Even so, this joint declaration by Mexico and Venezuela made it obvious that it would not be easy for Fox to fulfil his dream of becoming a privileged mediator between Latin America and the United States. Before the G3 meeting, the Fox administration had indicated to the media that it intended to propose to Colombia an antidrug cooperation program that was anti-militarist in nature and that focused on the sharing of strategic information and greater cooperation in the area of intelligence services. He also stated that Venezuela would participate in the discussions. This project, which was to be later presented to the United States, did not seem to spark Pastrana's enthusiasm and it is not even mentioned in the G3 official documents.

In early September 2001, the Fox administration sought once again to reaffirm its leadership in the efforts to resolve the Colombian conflict, even if it meant partially short-circuiting the work of the two *ad hoc* international bodies already in place (and in which Mexico participated): the Group of 10 Facilitation Commission and the Support Group for the Peace Process in Colombia. Their members, particularly those belonging to the EU (except Spain), either strongly criticized Plan Colombia or abstained from participating in it. But Mexico, far from condemning the Plan, was thinking of ways to make it more efficient. Hence Mexican officials' suggestion to US Secretary of State Colin Powell that a better "balance between Plan Colombia's military component and its social component is needed" (*La Jornada* 2001).

This push for increased efficiency was very short-lived. Following the suicide attacks on the World Trade Center and the Pentagon, Mexico revised and adjusted its foreign policy objectives in order to align itself more closely with US foreign policy. Since then, asserting Mexican leadership in Latin America and assuring its role as a "special" mediator in Colombia have become less important than showing allegiance to its powerful northern neighbor.

The Fox administration promptly understood President Bush's "make no mistake, you are either with us or you are against us" doctrine. A quick look at Mexico's action since then provides many examples of this change.[12] For instance, in the area

---

11 Colombia, Mexico and Venezuela participate in the G3.

12 Two months after the September 11 2001 attacks, Mexico became a member of the Conference of American Armies, a cold war relic that the Mexican government had refused to have anything to do with for 40 years. Besides that, Mexico seemed to have welcomed the creation of the Northern Command (NorthCom), which foresees the establishment of a

of antidrug cooperation, Mexico's decision to accept, in January 2002, the creation of a "bilateral bloc against drugs and terrorism" clearly brought it closer to the United States. Based on the narcoterrorism theory, this project implied that Mexico would not longer distinguish between the war on drugs and the fight against terrorism. To confirm this change of course, in April 2002, Mexican authorities closed the offices the FARC had opened in Mexico City ten years earlier. All of the Colombian armed group's delegates were then deported to Cuba and Venezuela. This gesture marked the end of the interest that the Fox administration had shown for a consensual and peaceful resolution of the civil war in Colombia. Furthermore, the adoption of the narcoterrorism theory renders the resuming of peace negotiations even more difficult, if not impossible. In fact, this theory completely discredits the local rebel groups by accusing them of profiting from drug money. It also adds an international dimension to a national conflict, thereby justifying a foreign intervention in the country.

In sum, Mexico gave up its attempts to ensure its leadership in the region without offending the United States. This plan, already full of nuances, was abandoned for a closer relationship free from all ambiguity with the superpower. The old approach was no longer suited to an international scene dominated by the US war on terrorism. From a political and diplomatic point of view, the time for realignment was as "clear and present" as the dangers that justified it and rendered it appropriate, even necessary.

Was there a NAFTA effect?

The United States did not wait for the creation of NAFTA to impose its concept of antidrug cooperation on Canada and Mexico. Before 1994, both countries had signed all international and inter-American treaties in this area, the drafting of these treaties having been strictly controlled by American diplomacy. Mexico, most affected by US antidrug policies, did not succeed in stopping or mitigating American unilateralism. This situation has not visibly changed since 1994. Obviously, the circumstances vary and the Americans have found, little by little, ways to hide their interventionism. But their intention to limit antidrug cooperation to repressive operations remains unchanged. The prohibitionist creed is equally well rooted, especially in multilateral arenas: any attempt to modify either one of its components is quickly blocked.

The above analyses of the certification process and the creation of the MEM do not, in fact, show any major changes. Mexico's criticisms of the certification process and Canada's desire to evaluate the true impact of the antidrug policies were ignored. Even after multiple endeavours, Canada, Mexico and the rest of the Latin American countries only obtained a minor consolation prize: the MEM. In the end, this evaluation system turned out to be nothing more than a consensual interiorization of the US antidrug model. Each country in the Americas is now obliged to measure

---

security perimeter including all three NAFTA partners under the Pentagon's control. Plus, in February 2002, the Mexican army participated in the United International Anti-Submarine (UNITAS) program, a joint military maneuvers exercise with US and other Latin American naval forces. Article 76 of the Mexican Constitution, however, prohibits its armed forces from operating abroad.

the efficiency of its efforts in the war against drugs according to criteria based on the prohibitionist logic. None of these criteria bring the repressive approach's counterproductive effects to the forefront. Indeed, this situation constitutes an undeniable triumph of "soft power". But like the carrot that needs the stick to be efficient, the United States will not abandon its good old certification process. It allows them to apply unilateral sanctions immediately (or almost), if and when deemed necessary.

The adjustments of the positions of Canada and Mexico on Plan Colombia confirm this tendency for them to align their antidrug cooperation foreign policies with the American strategy in order to protect their interests. Canada's case in this area is particularly interesting.

The Canadian government certainly did not contribute to the training of the Colombian armed forces or police corps, acts that have been harshly criticized by international organizations and human rights groups. A decision to do so would have been unjustifiable in light of the principles directing Canadian foreign policy. The government would have also had to face a public opinion that is generally not inclined to approve this type of commitment abroad. Ottawa limited its intervention to offering its services as mediator for the peace negotiations as well as its support to different humanitarian initiatives (support to displaced populations, purchasing of mobile sanitary units, aid to children affected by the armed conflict, human rights promotion and peacekeeping training). However, contrary to the European Union, the Canadian government abstained from denouncing the fact that the military solution the United States proposed was not likely to lead to lasting peace.[13] Nor did it protest when the United States bought Huey helicopters from the Canadian army with the intention to recondition and transfer them to the Colombian armed forces, an arms sale operation that Amnesty International Canada criticize immediatly. Finally, all of these contradictions were ignored in the Canadian government's response to the report of the Sub-Committee on Human Rights and International Development of the Standing Committee on Foreign Affairs and International Trade (Government of Canada – Standing Committee on Foreign Affairs and International Trade – Sub-Committee on Human Rights and International Development 2002), a document recommending that Canadian decision-makers seek alliances with countries who "encourage all parties in the Colombian conflict to pursue agreement on humanitarian principles and a negotiated solution". But it was already too late for that: the Colombian government had burned its bridges with the guerrilla groups and the US State Department had placed them on its terrorist-organisation blacklist. In other words, the issues have become non-negotiable and, as a result, dialogue is now impossible.

The path taken by the Fox administration was more sinuous, but the results were the same. The more or less veiled criticism of American aid to Colombia, which Mexico had made under Venezuela's influence, vanished completely when Mexican diplomats aspired to serve as an intermediary between the Colombian and the US governments. At that time, Mexico's objective was not to criticise the White House, but to improve the balance between Plan Colombia's military and humanitarian

---

13 The escalation in violence and the end of peace talks has since proved the EU right.

components. After the September 11 attacks, however, this unassuming objective also vanished. Mexico converted to the narcoterrorism doctrine, one that conceals the social and political causes of the armed conflicts.

Though it is true that the United States did not wait for NAFTA's inauguration to force Canada and Mexico to adopt its regional antidrug strategy, it is also true that the US government used NAFTA at its convenience to further strengthen its hegemony. This coercive adjustment process is even more striking in a context of bilateral relations. It is thus impossible to ignore the impact of this adjustment on broader regional cooperation efforts: both the disputes and the agreements clearly show that the United States will not tolerate any resistance.

The White House reaction in 2002 to the possible decriminalization of marijuana possession in Canada provides us with a perfect example of how the United States uses NAFTA as a tool to reinforce its position. As mentioned earlier, Washington made threats to Ottawa when Canadian decision-makers had judged that an amendment to the drug legislation was necessary. The White House's warnings were indeed quite severe. In July 2002, Canadian Justice Minister Martin Cauchon announced that he would introduce a bill for the decriminalization of simple marijuana possession. In mid-August, Cauchon denied that there was any pressure coming from the United States, even though John P. Walters, director of the Office of National Drug Control Policy at the White House, had just criticized the Canadian project, saying, "If you decriminalize the use of drugs, you will increase the vector through which the dependency disease will spread" (Brautigam 2002, A2). These declarations became even harsher a few days later, following the publication of the Special Senate Committee on Illegal Drugs' report that recommends the legalization of marijuana. On 17 October 2002, in an interview with the United Press Agency, Walters stressed that American authorities would not hesitate to multiply searches at the Canada-US border in order to prevent an increase of marijuana trafficking to the United States. He explained, "we firmly intend on protecting our citizens. We don't have a choice" (Bellavance 2002, A1). Given that the cross-border commercial exchanges (worth about one billion dollars per day) are vital to the Canadian economy, evoking the possibility of slowing down the circulation of goods and services is essentially the same as issuing a direct threat. Minster Martin Cauchon and Senator Pierre Claude Nolin, president of the Special Senate Committee on Illegal Drugs, minimised the importance of such an ultimatum, reminding Walters that Canada is a sovereign country. Their reminder was of no use. Walters pursued his crusade, juxtaposing criticisms and intimidations. At the end of November 2002, while passing through Vancouver, Walters condemned the Canadian initiative to open safe injection rooms – a harm reduction strategy that has already been proved effective elsewhere, namely in Europe. Later, on 12 December 2002, Walters again reminded Canada that the American government could tighten its border controls if Ottawa softened its drug legislation. Finally, on 31 January 2003, the White House expressed, for the first time, specific concerns regarding drugs arriving in the United States via Canada:

Although the United States enjoys an excellent level of bilateral cooperation with Canada, the United States Government is concerned that Canada is a primary source of pseudoephedrine and an increasing source of high potency marijuana, which are exported to the United States. Over the past few years there has been an alarming increase in the amount of pseudoephedrine diverted from Canadian sources to clandestine drug laboratories in the United States, where it is used to make methamphetamine. The Government of Canada, for the most part, has not regulated the sale and distribution of precursor chemicals. The regulations to restrict the availability of pseudoephedrine, which the Government of Canada has just promulgated, should be stronger. Notwithstanding Canada's inadequate control of illicit diversion of precursor chemicals, I commend Canadian law enforcement agencies, which continue to work energetically to support our joint law enforcement efforts (Government of the United States – White House 2003).

This warning has a political dimension that none can deny: it appeared in a very short document containing the list of countries the president proposes to Congress for de-certification because of their failure to collaborate in the war against drugs. Though Canada is not one of the countries to be banned, the fact that it was mentioned is far from insignificant. The Canadian government took note of this warning and finally abandoned its plans to soften its drug-use legislation. In the eyes of the US administration, the problem resides precisely in the decriminalization of marijuana and in the opening of safe injection rooms. Though the White House did not mention them in the text cited above, it is deeply worried that the implementation of these initiatives could provide an example of disobedience for other countries. And this type of disobedience is not a trivial matter: the decriminalization of marijuana and the opening of safe injection rooms, by attributing to users a degree of rationality that the prohibitionist approach denies them, challenge all of the principles that Washington has so fiercely defended for over a century.

We should not be misled by the fact that President Bush avoided publicly condemning Canadian harm reduction policies. Open criticism would have meant direct interference in Canada's internal affairs, an interference that would discredit *ipso facto* all possible US protests. The routing of drugs from Canada to the United States, on the contrary, is an issue that directly affects American security. President Bush therefore wins by referring to the problem of drug trafficking: it is an unassailable pretext for censuring any drug law reform. The declarations of DFAIT spokesman, Rodney Moore, confirm *a contrario* the existence of this game of veiled allusions and warnings: "The question of [cross-border trafficking of marijuana and pseudoephedrine] has not been raised in any of the recent meetings between Canadian ministers and their American counterparts" (Vallières 2003, A13). Canadian officials had perhaps been taken by surprise, but they do know that the issue at stake is not cross-border trafficking, but rather Canadian drug-use policies reform.[14]

---

14 A parallel can be drawn between the American strategy used in this case with the one that brought the Argentine government to promulgate a new law on drugs at a time when the judicial power had decriminalized the personal use of drugs. In 1989, the US Congress decided that Argentina had become a cocaine-producing country, a statement not founded on empirical information. The fear of an eventual decertification forced the Argentine government to pass a draconian law, aimed particularly at users – a law that completely stopped the legalization process initiated by the country's judiciary. In a word, just as in Canada's case, the United States used narcotrafficking in order to exert pressure on an entirely different issue, that of personal use.

Mexico did not escape the threats of a possible slowdown in its exchanges with the United States either. The Operation Casablanca affair, for instance, set off a grave conflict: it seriously endangered the "vitality" of financial flows between the two countries.

In May 1998, at the end of a three-year undercover investigation, US Customs Services arrested 162 people and seized over 100 million dollars, two tons of cocaine and four tonnes of marijuana. Fifteen executives from Mexican banks were among the arrested. They had travelled to Las Vegas and San Diego for business meetings that had actually been "set up" by American authorities in order to trap them. With three years of preparation and such promising results, Operation Casablanca was without precedent. What is more, it directly implicated three of Mexico's main banks (Bancomer, Confía and Serfín), as well as the employees of a large number of banks in Mexico, Venezuela and Spain.[15]

If the Mexican bankers fell so easily into the trap set by US Customs Services, it is because they were accustomed to collaborating with American banks in which their employees had opened correspondent accounts. These accounts enabled the banks to carry out financial transactions in countries where they are not physically present. The large international banks use them to offer a wide range of services to thousands of smaller banks: cash flow management, fund transfers, cheque clearing, foreign exchange, transit accounts for major clients, and so on. During Operation Casablanca, investigators never even bothered the American banking partners who carried out thousands of transactions for the clients of the Mexican institutions. No criminal or civil charges have been filed against them.[16]

The entire operation took place without the knowledge of the Mexican government. President Zedillo (1994–2000) did not hesitate to point out that it was a flagrant violation of the sovereignty of his country and of the bilateral treaties in effect. He even threatened to demand the extradition of the American undercover agents. The Clinton administration (1993–2001) ignored his protests and even insisted that new covert operations could be launched without notice. In such a context, as Luis Astorga (Astorga 1999) put it so well, the fight against money laundering is merely a "political weapon", easy to manipulate and morally irreproachable.

The American pressures in this case – as in many others – have had a noticeable effect on Mexico's antidrug policy, especially after Fox's arrival in power. This is exactly what the Department of State said in March 2002:

Bilateral U.S.-Mexico law enforcement cooperation has improved under the Fox Administration, through information sharing and a willingness to explore new approaches, and this cooperation continued in 2001 [...]. At the working level, the climate of cooperation

---

15 Bancomer and Serfín pleaded guilty and paid 14.6 million dollars to the American Justice. Confía, in an out of court settlement, paid 12.2 million dollars. Other banks, like Bonarte and Bital, managed to recuperate the seized money and did not have to pay a fine (*Money Laundering Alert* 2000).

16 The American regulation agency, the Financial Crimes Enforcement Network (FinCEN), only initiated consultations in order to regulate the correspondent accounts on May 23, 2002. It was forced to do so in virtue of the antiterrorist law passed by Congress in the wake of the September 11 attacks.

within the bilateral law enforcement community has improved dramatically. For the first time in recent memory, both sides are sharing sensitive information on counternarcotics cases (Government of the United States 2002c).

In reading these paragraphs, one could certainly conclude that the United States used Operation Casablanca to force the Mexican government's hand on a long list of files related to bilateral co-operation. But the instrumentalization of the antidrug policies is a much more complex – and troubling – issue. In fact, the Geopolitical Drug Observatory claims that the United States conveniently closed its eyes when the Mexican government made the strategic decision, towards the end of the 1980s, to encourage the massive recycling of narcodollars in order to generate the liquidity necessary to join NAFTA (*La Dépêche internationale des drogues* 1995). According to Fabre (Fabre 1999, 112), the United States also profited directly from this recycling, as the laundered money – from three to eight billion dollars per year – increased the Mexican demand for American goods and services. And to all this, one must still add the role of the American banks in the financial set ups that allowed the laundering of money of dubious origin coming from Mexico.

Final remarks

Behind the alignment of Canada and Mexico's antidrug cooperation policies with those of the United States lies a reality that is both complex and unstable. The three countries have different goals, which vary according to the circumstances, the relative power of each nation, and the attention paid to regional affairs. For the United States, the exportation of the prohibitionist model has proven to be a terribly efficient foreign policy tool. The war against drugs has in fact enabled Washington to instrumentalise a subtle game of permitted and forbidden complicities, of economic sanctions and undercover operations. Yet Canada cannot give in entirely: its foreign policy stresses humanitarian aims that partially bring to light the social and political problems created by the prohibitionist policies. Mexico, which does not seem too worried with the counterproductive effects of prohibition, would, however, criticize American unilateralism – that is, at least until very recently.

It would thus be false to postulate *a priori* a harmonisation in all three countries' foreign policies in the area of antidrug cooperation. The convergence is due to American pressures, but namely and above all, to the fact that a confrontation with the United States in this domain would not pay off, strategically speaking, for either Canada or Mexico. Such a conflict could risk bringing about dire consequences in many vital areas. Within this context, NAFTA amplifies both American pressures and Canadian and Mexican fears: the mere possibility of a slowdown in trade sends the "neighbors of the neighbor" into a panic. It is better to conform to the United States' regional antidrug policies than to set off an economic war.

This convergence, favored by the US decision to invest a quantity of resources – that Canada and Mexico cannot match – in the defense of the prohibitionist regime, finds its limits in differences that are not likely to disappear any time soon: for example, discrepancies in each country's views on drug use, the social roots of drug trafficking, the legitimacy of interventions in a foreign country, and so on. These limits demonstrate not only the complexity of the United States' domination in the area of antidrug policy, but also the sturdiness of the obstacles Canada and Mexico must overcome in order to free themselves from it.

Indeed, the task is enormous. It requires, first of all, increased awareness of prohibition's structuring effects: the methods and the expansion of drug-trafficking are closely related to the ban applied to them. In fact, underlying the prohibitionist logic is the creation and legitimization of institutions – national, regional and international – in charge of the antidrug war. Through their actions and their discourse, these institutions reinforce and broaden the initially imposed ban. In doing this, they contribute to the development of criminal organisations, whose profits depend exclusively on the absolute ban on the production and use of forbidden substances. Therefore, the growth of the drug industry – with its parade of violence and corruption – ends up justifying and strengthening the prohibitionist logic that starts and controls it.

Canadian diplomacy may not be quite ready to denounce this vicious cycle. It seems even less likely that Mexico will be the one to do it. The regional antidrug policy, then, will not change in the near future. Small farmers will continue to be subject to the crossfire of the traffickers, the police and the military; the fundamental rights of users will be scoffed at, and the scandals involving high-level officials will occasionally add to this drug-corruption folklore, one that no longer really surprises nor moves anyone.

Chapter 7

The Intriguing Cuban Case[1]

Hugo Loiseau

The year 2004 marked the 10th anniversary of the coming into force of the North American Free Trade Agreement (NAFTA). Indeed, the socio-economic consequences of this agreement in the United States, Canada and Mexico have been assessed on numerous occasions. However, policy convergence is rarely used in the analysis of NAFTA's influence on the behavior of its member countries in other spheres, such as foreign policy. Any integration process sooner or later reaches a threshold where policies converge. Based on this perspective, the following question should be examined: Is it possible to demonstrate a significant correlation between NAFTA and the convergence, or divergence, of the member countries' foreign policies on Cuba? More specifically, and following the example of the introductory chapter of this book, we must ask which elements converge, how the convergence occurred and how its scope can be explained. An evaluation of this scope may even reveal an alignment of Canadian and Mexican foreign policies with American foreign policy on Cuba.

To answer these questions, we will study the evolution of the diplomatic relations between the Cuban government and the governments of the United States, Canada and Mexico. Firstly, we will compare the foreign policies of the three NAFTA member countries, before and after 1994, in order to identify the changes in approach to Cuba since the creation of NAFTA. In this regard, it will be demonstrated that there is a notable convergence in the policy directions of the member states, especially with regard to their concerns with respect for human rights and the development of democracy in Cuba.

Secondly, we will examine the reasons why the member countries are taking a growing interest in these issues in order to establish a causal link between the economic regionalism of NAFTA and the convergence of the foreign policies of the United States, Canada and Mexico. However, when the causes of this convergence are examined in detail, it becomes clear that NAFTA is not a determining variable. Certainly, in the public arena, ministers will sometimes refer to the idea that democratic values underlie trade agreements, but these associations remain ambiguous and highly abstract. In fact, it is circumstantial factors, such as the behavior of the Cuban government, the attitude of political representatives, socio-economic exchanges between states, popular pressure and internal political developments, that have influenced the political positioning of NAFTA member countries towards Cuba.

---

1   The author wishes to thank Ms. Isabelle Lombardo for her invaluable help in writing this chapter.

Part One: A Comparative Study of Foreign Policies: Convergence Since NAFTA

The events of April 2003 in Cuba were a decisive moment for diplomatic relations with the government of Fidel Castro. After the sentencing of 75 political dissidents from 15 to 25 years in prison and the execution of three Cubans for an attempted highjacking, human rights and democratic development issues in Cuba became a major concern for several capitals (Government of Canada 2004). However, in the United States, Canada and Mexico, this concern had already grown in importance well before 2003. More specifically, a convergence in their foreign policy regarding the democratization of Cuba was noticeable mainly from 1994 onwards, that is, since the signing of the free trade agreement. Admittedly, the United States and Canada are a step ahead of Mexico with regard to the promotion of democratic values abroad. Nevertheless, this lag is all the more important since it shows the extent to which the political positioning of the member countries towards Cuba has converged over the last few years.

The positioning of the United States towards Cuba – a coercive democratization policy

While the United States has consistently adopted a distinct coercive approach towards Cuba ever since it gained independence in 1898, the democratization of this island country has continued to be a key issue for the Americans. Thus, regardless of the repressive nature of the measures applied, the US government has always maintained a continuous and uniform position on the subject of human rights and democratic development in Cuba (McKenna 2004, 283–284). Indeed, the majority of American foreign policy actions towards Cuba, which have sought to apply economic embargos, more aggressive military actions, travel restrictions, and so on, are almost automatically associated with the American desire to democratize the Cuban political system. Thus, it is not surprising, for instance, that the law drafted in 1992 to encourage members of the international community to limit their trade with Cuba is called the *Cuban Democracy Act* (Government of the United States 1997).

Nevertheless, it is interesting to note that the importance placed on the democratization of Cuba in American foreign policy increased, especially after the signing of NAFTA. Firstly, already in 1996, the US government drafted the *Helms Burton Act*, also known as the *Cuban Liberty and Democratic Solidarity Act*. The goal of the Act is:

> To seek international sanctions against the Castro government in Cuba, to plan for support of a transition government leading to a democratically elected government in Cuba, and for other purposes (*P.L. 927, Helms-Burton Act 1996*).

Then, to commemorate Cuba's independence, the Bush administration launched the Initiative for a New Cuba in May 2002. This policy seeks to promote a rapid democratic transition in Cuba, calling on the Cuban government to undertake the economic and political reforms necessary to organize "free and fair" elections (Governement of the United States – Department of State – Bureau of Wester

Hemisphere Affairs 2005). In addition, after the 2003 events, human rights became more of a concern and a diplomatic priority in US-Cuba relations. Indeed, the behavior of the government of Fidel Castro almost immediately provoked the expulsion of 14 Cuban diplomats from the United States. Also to be noted is the resignation of members of the executive of the most important anti-embargo pressure group in Washington, the Cuba Policy Foundation (Cuba Policy Foundation 2003). As for foreign policy, the Bush administration created the Commission for Assistance to a Free Cuba in October 2003. This group presented, once again, a plan to help Cubans undertake a transition to democracy, by listing the measures necessary to put an end to the dictatorship and establish new economic and social institutions (Governement of the United States – Department of State – Bureau of Wester Hemisphere Affairs 2005). Finally, one year later, at the UN General Assembly of October 2004, the United States voted to maintain the embargo, even though it was one of only three countries, versus 179 others, to do so (Kirk and McKenna 2005, 3–6).

Thus, it is clear that the political positioning of the American government towards the Castro regime remained closed, uniform and continuous over time. Despite the more coercive approach of American foreign policy in this respect, there is no doubt that human rights and democratic development have remained two key issues in the diplomatic relations with Cuba, especially since the signing of NAFTA. Finally, the growth of this concern has been significant considering that the Bush administration plans on spending a total of US$59 million on the "emancipation" of the Cuban population in the next few years:

> To these ends, President Bush has directed that up to $59 million be committed over the next 2 years to carry out democracy-building activities in Cuba [...] Funding will support efforts by youth, women, and Afro-Cubans to take greater action in support of democracy and human rights in Cuba and efforts by NGOs in selected third countries to highlight human rights abuses in Cuba, as part of a broader effort to discourage tourist travel and reinforce international attention on the plight of the Cuban people, including political prisoners and civil society (Governement of the United States – Department of State – Bureau of Wester Hemisphere Affairs 2005).

The positioning of Canada towards Cuba – a constructive democratization policy

In comparison to the United States, known for its coercive approach, Canada is recognized for its foreign policy of "constructive engagement" with Cuba. Rather than applying repressive measures, Canada tries first and foremost to promote the democratization of Cuba through a number of aid programs based on dialogue and sharing of Canadian values. As stated by the Canadian Department of Foreign Affairs:

> Canada has a policy of engagement with Cuba, through which we promote Canadian interests and values, including respect for human rights. Through our trade, aid, political and cultural programmes, we are able to share Canadian and, more broadly, liberal democratic values with Cuba and Cubans and to develop a dialogue on economic and social policies with current and future business and government leaders (Government of Canada 2004).

In short, the spirit of openness and the "constructive" nature of Canada-Cuba relations are traditional elements of Canadian diplomacy. A prime example is the official visit of Prime Minister Trudeau to Cuba, which carried a significant weight since it marked the first time that the head of a NATO member country decided to meet Fidel Castro (Kirk 1995, 149). Prime Minister Chrétien's involvement with Cuba is also worth noting. In 1993, for instance, he launched a program to inject funds and credits for export development, in order to stimulate investment and trade between Canada and Cuba (Ritter 1999, 21).

That said, democratic development in Cuba nevertheless became a key concern of the Canadian government, mainly after NAFTA was instituted. For instance, as of 1994, greater importance was placed on respect for human rights and democratic values in Canadian foreign policy with regard to the government of Fidel Castro. Already in 1995, the Government of Canada reviewed its foreign policy orientations and drafted *Canada in the World*, a document in which three main priorities were identified, the third being "projecting Canadian values and culture" (Deblock and Benessaieh 2001, 725). In 1997, the foreign affairs ministers of both countries, Lloyd Axworthy and Roberto Robaina, met to sign a common declaration in order to officialize the parameters of the engagement between Canada and Cuba. To this end, five of the fourteen declarations pertained to "respect for individual rights" (Ritter 1999, 21).

However, the imprisoning of four political dissidents in 1998 provoked a cooling of relations between Canada and Cuba (McKenna 2004, 294). Consequently, the visits planned on the political agenda and several bilateral co-operation projects with Cuba were cancelled (Herisman 2000, 209). It is from this perspective that, at the continental trade negotiations that took place in the fall of the same year, the Canadian government redefined its strategy towards Latin America, by reaffirming the importance of imprinting Canadian values on the institutions of the budding community of the Americas (Deblock and Benessaieh 2001, 726).

The reaction of the Canadian government to the events of April 2003 also showed to what extent human rights and democratic development have become key issues in Canadian foreign policy towards Cuba. Firstly, William Graham, the Minister of Foreign Affairs at the time, wrote to his Cuban counterpart twice to express his opposition, with other representatives following the case over the long term. The Department of Foreign Affairs affirmed:

> The Canadian government has therefore requested the release of the imprisoned dissidents, with special and immediate consideration for those in poor health. Senior officials at the Department of Foreign Affairs and Canada's Ambassador to Cuba also continue to raise concerns regarding the dissidents directly with the Cuban authorities (Government of Canada 2004).

On the international stage, these events led Canada to support a resolution of the Organization of American States in May 2003 that called for the use of "non-economic" measures to pressure the Cuban government (Government of Canada 2005b). Thus, Canada condemned this severe human rights violation, asked the Cuban government to immediately release the prisoners, and temporarily stopped all diplomatic meetings between Canadian and Cuban ministers (McKenna 2004, 295). Finally, in 2004, Canada supported a resolution on human rights in Cuba at the Office of the United Nations High Commissioner for Human Rights (Government of Canada 2005b).

In light of this information, it is clear that the spirit of openness and the "constructive" nature of Canada-Cuba relations since Prime Minister Trudeau's time must be qualified somewhat. The evolution of the political positioning of Canada after 1994 is based on a continuous trend – the growing role played by the promotion of Canadian democratic values, but also a radicalization of Canada's discourse following the events of 2003. Thus, since the signing of NAFTA, Canada's foreign policy on Cuba seems to be aligning itself increasingly with that of the United States with regard to the measures used to promote human rights and the development of democracy in Cuba.

The positioning of Mexico towards Cuba – the birth of a democratization policy

Unlike the United States and Canada, the democratization of Cuba has only been a recent concern of Mexico's foreign policy. Considering that the Mexican political regime could be described, up until 2000, as an "authoritarian democracy," where multiparty elections were not completely "free, fair, and inclusive," (Diamond 2002, 21–35) it is not surprising to find a certain lag with regard to the promotion of democratic values abroad. Nevertheless, the Mexican case remains essential to the analysis of the convergence of the foreign policies of NAFTA member states. Indeed, the situation in Mexico in particular shows the extent to which human rights and democratic development have become key priorities in the diplomatic relations between Cuba and the three member states, especially since NAFTA came into force.

During the 70 years of the Institutional Revolutionary Party (PRI) government, the issue of Cuban democratization did not exist in Mexican foreign policy. Rather, Mexico long remained faithful to the principle of non-interference in the internal affairs of states, as well as to the right to self-determination (Meyer 1991). Consequently, from the early 1960s, the Mexican government was incredibly tolerant of the Castro government and there was strong collaboration between the two countries. Thus, apart from the economic support given to the Cuban government, Mexico was long known on the international stage as one of the greatest defenders of the government of Fidel Castro. The alliance between the two states is evident, for instance, in the fact that Mexico was the only country to vote against the exclusion of Cuba from the Organization of American States in 1962. In the following years, the PRI governments always voted against any resolution proposed by the United Nations Commission on Human Rights regarding Cuba (McKenna 2004, 287). However, the signing of NAFTA marked an important turning point in Mexico's foreign policy. More specifically, since 1994, respect for human rights and democratic development in Cuba have gradually taken up a dominating place in Mexico-Cuba relations. Indeed, this development even led the Mexican government to interfere in Cuba's internal affairs.

Thus, the first diplomatic break between the two states occurred in 1999 when the Mexican president, Ernesto Zedillo, referred for the first time to the need for a democratic transition in Cuba. At the Ibero-American Summit in Havana, he stated:

> There cannot be sovereign nations without free men and women; men and women who can fully exercise their essential freedoms: freedom to think and give opinions, freedom to act and participate, freedom to dissent, freedom to choose (Smith 1999).

At the start of the 21st century, this kind of implicit reference to the importance of human rights became more of an explicit element in the body of Mexican foreign policy towards Cuba. Thus, Mexico asserted itself increasingly on the international stage by positioning itself against the policy orientations of the Cuban government. At the UN General Assembly in 2001, for instance, Mexico chose to abstain, rather than to continue to vote against a resolution on human rights in Cuba (Government of Mexico – Mexican Ministry of Foreign Relations 2001). Then, during a session of the Commission on Human Rights in April 2002, the Mexican government finally voted for a resolution by the United States concerning Cuba. To justify its vote, the Mexican Secretary of the Interior, Santiago Creel, explained: "A government can only truly be called a democracy if its leaders respect human rights" (Snow 2002). From March 2003 onwards, a more proactive approach was adopted by the Government of Mexico to promote democratic values internally and abroad. Mexico created the Government Policy Commission on Human Rights which had a mandate "to design and co-ordinate the policy and the governmental actions directed toward the strengthening of the promotion and defence of human rights" (Americas Policy Group 2004). Finally, the evolution of the diplomatic relations between Mexico and Cuba took a bitter and even repressive turn in 2004, when Fidel Castro accused Mexico of being an "American colony." He stated that "The US-Mexican border is to all intents and purposes no longer the Rio Bravo of which Martí spoke. The United States has gone much deeper into Mexico" (Castro 2004; see also Armengaud 2004, A5). Consequently, the Mexican minister of Foreign Affairs reacted harshly by ordering the immediate expulsion of the Cuban representative in Mexico.

From this perspective, it is reasonable to conclude that post-NAFTA Mexican policy regarding the Cuban government is far from what it was in the 1960s and subsequent decades. As a state that used to demand non-interference in the internal affairs of other countries, Mexico now sees itself as a responsible actor in the democratization processes abroad. This policy orientation was made clear when Vicente Fox openly stated at the National Assembly of Belize in 2005 that: "Consolidating democracy is the responsibility of all governments, the citizens in each of our countries, political parties and social organizations" (Government of Mexico – Presidencia de la Republica 2005).

NAFTA member states and Cuba – a convergence of political positioning

A comparative study of the evolution of the diplomatic relations between NAFTA member states and the Cuban government leaves little doubt that the issues of human rights and democratic development have gradually become impossible to ignore.

Admittedly, differentiations must be made concerning the terms and conditions included in the foreign policies of the United States, Canada, and Mexico. The American approach is more coercive and establishes mandatory concessions for a democratic transition in Cuba. Linda Robinson states that:

> In the fixed mindset of Washington, the embargo is a bargaining chip, something that cannot be given up until Castro's relinquishes power, or at least makes major concessions that will lead quickly to his departure. Lifting the embargo without *quid pro quo* would be, in this view, letting Castro claim victory (Robinson 2000, 118).

On the other hand, the approach of Canada and Mexico is more flexible, encouraging an increase in the "elements of democratization" in Cuba, rather than imposing a permanent and homogeneous vision of a Cuban transition towards democracy. Peter McKenna notes:

> In contrast, Mexico and Canada have refrained from linking bilateral relations to any designated set of conditions or standards. While the issue of human rights and democratic development are integral elements of their Cuba policies, they have not made cordial and productive relations contingent upon a detailed list of expected improvements (McKenna 2004, 298).

In the end, caution must be exercised in the analysis of the terms and conditions included in these approaches, in order to avoid drawing false conclusions about the foreign policies of the United States, Canada and Mexico. As stated by McKenna, human rights and democratic development remain fundamentally at the center of the diplomatic relations between these states and the government of Fidel Castro. Of course, the importance placed on these elements is more recent in the case of the Mexican government. However, a growing concern can be observed in all three governments, especially since the implementation of the Free Trade Agreement in 1994. Thus, an alignment of the foreign policies of NAFTA member states can definitely be identified through the harmonization of their political positioning regarding the democratization of Cuban society and respect for human rights in Cuba.

Part Two: The Structure of NAFTA and the Convergence of Foreign Policies

Clearly, this observation of convergence since 1994 alone is not sufficient to establish a causal link between NAFTA and the priority given to democratic values in the foreign policies of the member states. Establishing a definite correlation is rather a more complex task. As aptly explained by Michel Wieviorka:

> Within each country, it often becomes complicated to establish a strong correlation between various policies, for instance, to make economic and trade policy consistent with foreign policy. It is also difficult to reconcile diplomacy, or even a state's participation in international institutions, with increasing sensitivity of individuals to the theme of human rights (Wieviorka 1998) (author's translation).

Even if the text of the Free Trade Agreement does not address the promotion of democratic values, it could nevertheless be tempting to establish such a politico-economic correlation by focusing instead on the member states' political discourse implying that democratization is a natural process underlying trade agreements. However, an examination of the actual content and action plans of the programs related to the liberalization of trade between the United States, Canada and Mexico brings out nuances in the link between trade agreements and their impact on democratic development. In addition, when the factors in the evolution of the particular diplomatic relations between Cuba and the member states are considered, it becomes clear that NAFTA plays an indirect role in the cases of Canada and Mexico, and no role at all for the United States. Rather, circumstantial elements – including the behavior of the Cuban government, the attitude of political representatives, the socio-economic exchanges between states, popular pressure, and domestic political developments – influenced the foreign policies of the member states with regard to the Cuban government.

The case of the United States

When analyzing contemporary democracies such as the United States, it is extremely difficult to identify the multiple causes underlying the promotion of democratic values in foreign policy. Thus, with regard to the correlation between NAFTA and the promotion of human rights in Cuban-American relations, an analysis of the historical progression of this concern would be too long and inefficient. It would be more relevant to target the main factors in the recent (re)formulation of American foreign policy towards Cuba, in order to determine to what extent NAFTA has had an exclusive impact. However, considering the extent to which the anti-Castro culture, the behavior of the Cuban government and the events of September 11, 2001, have all deeply affected the American attitude toward Cuba, it would be difficult to state clearly that NAFTA is an exclusive or influential variable.

The discourse of American leaders clearly indicates that the promotion of democratic values is at the forefront in the majority of foreign interventions. However, the specific assessment of the 10 years of NAFTA by the Subcommittee on International Economic Policy, Export, and Trade Promotion barely refers to the link between trade agreements and democratic development. The idea that the benefits of NAFTA can sometimes lead to positive impacts in other areas is vaguely mentioned, such as the exchange of "ideas" and cultures in a context of "international society."

> NAFTA has provided significant benefits in other, sometimes unexpected, ways as well. The movement of goods and people creates stronger international linkages amongst our three countries, facilitating travel, tourism, and greater understanding through the constant exchange of ideas and cultures. As with the 'Great Melting Pot' concept, all NAFTA countries benefit from the increased diversity in people, languages, ideas and energy generated by an expanding international society (Wayne 2004).

Obviously, such ambiguous comments make it very risky to draw conclusions about the association between the Free Trade Agreement and the promotion of democratic values abroad. The correlation between NAFTA and the importance given to these values in Cuban-American relations is thus even more difficult to establish. It is therefore necessary to go beyond the American discourse and to examine the concrete factors that have influenced American foreign policy with regard to Cuba over the past few years.

Social pressures – a deeply anti-Castro culture   In the United States, the deeply anti-Castro bureaucratic and popular culture has been an important factor in shaping American foreign policy on Cuba. This anti-Castro culture, which underlies the general diplomatic approach to Cuba developed in the United States in the 1960s and is present to this day. Many polls conducted over this period have tracked Americans' attitude towards Fidel Castro and Cuba. In 1964, about 92 percent of the American population disliked Fidel Castro. In 1988, 89 percent of Americans mistrusted of Cuba, compared to 69 percent in 1999. Finally, in 2000, there seems to have been a return to previous levels of distrust, with 80 percent of Americans saying they had a negative opinion of Fidel Castro (Wylie 2004, 39–64).

With regard to the media, the anti-Castro culture in the United States and the consequent social pressure for democratic development in Cuba were even more evident. In 1992, Harry Tag analyzed the coverage of Cuba in the *New York Times* during the 1980s, in which he observed an increase in negative coverage of the human rights situation in Cuba. Walter Soderland undertook a similar survey of the *New York Times* coverage of Fidel Castro in 2003. Here again, it was found that the American anti-Castro culture was reflected in the media coverage: 75 percent of it was negative between 1959 and 1992, and 86 percent of the terms used to describe President Castro between 1988 and 1992 were also negative (Wylie 2004, 39–64). In light of these data, it can reasonably be concluded that the American approach to Cuba and Fidel Castro is more driven by a deeply anti-Castro popular culture than by the application of NAFTA clauses.

The Cuban government's behavior   Furthermore, this anti-Castro attitude has been reflected in American political reactions to the behavior of the Cuban government. Among other things, the development of American foreign policy on Cuba has been strongly marked by decisions made in reaction to the actions of Fidel Castro's government. This correlation between the behavior of the Cuban government and the evolution of Cuban-American diplomatic relations was also evident in the early 1960s. After the missile crisis, for instance, the American government obtained Cuba's exclusion from participation in OAS activities in February 1962. Then, in 1996, the *Helms-Burton Act* was drafted in reaction to the attack on two American airplanes by the Cuban armed forces. The mission of these airplanes, as part of the "Brothers to the Rescue" operation, was to monitor Cubans trying to cross over and immigrate to the United States. When these airplanes were used to spread anti-Castro pamphlets in Cuba in February 1996, Fidel Castro did not hesitate to have them shot down. The ensuing political crisis put pressure on the American government which felt obliged to strengthen its foreign policy on Cuba, if only on the basis of "principle." As Lane Wylie stated:

Most American policymakers on both sides of the embargo debate adopted similar interpretations of the incident. Not everyone was supportive of Helms-Burton but most felt the government had to take significant action against Cuba (Wylie 2004, 39–64).

Finally, in addition to these incidents, the events of April 2003 led to the creation of the Commission for Assistance to a Free Cuba. Once again a political crisis further emphasized human rights and democratic development in Cuba. These three examples are sufficient demonstration of the extent to which the Castro government has an influence on the direction of American policy on Cuba. Since the majority of the American government's decisions have been reactive, a correlation can be seen between all these periodic crises and the evolution of its foreign policy on Cuba.

Post September 11, 2001   Other than the diplomatic crises provoked by the behavior of the Cuban government, American foreign policy on Cuba has been affected by other events, including the attacks of September 11, 2001. Even though Cuba had not been considered as a serious threat to the United States since the missile crisis, these events fuelled the American government's suspicion about the links between Cuba and terrorism. Indeed, following the events of September 11, the United States placed Cuba on the list of countries that it considers to be complicit in terrorism, alongside other states such as Iran, Libya (before 2006), North Korea, Sudan, Syria and Iraq (before 2003). In addition, in the same spirit of suspicion, the American government became more preoccupied with the possible presence of biological weapons in Cuba. Hays sums up this tension as follows: "We need to know if a nation 90 miles from our shores is experimenting with deadly biological agents" (Hays 2002).

With regard to American foreign policy towards Cuba, it is clear that the impact of the September 11 terrorist attacks was greater and more currently relevant than the impact of NAFTA. In fact, the American anti-Castro culture, the behavior of the Cuban government, the September 11 attacks, as well as a number of other events, have been responsible for the evolution of Cuban-American relations. Nevertheless, one thing is certain. NAFTA has not been a determining and exclusive variable in explaining these relations. Thus, even though most policies promoting the democratization of Cuba have been applied particularly since the implementation of NAFTA, it would not be accurate to conclude that there is a direct correlation between NAFTA and the policy of the American government towards Cuba. It is mainly factors such as the negative media coverage of the *New York Times* and the influence of the imprisonment of Cuban political dissidents in 2003 that have contributed to the increase in the importance placed, in American foreign policy on Cuba, on human rights and democratic development.

The case of Canada

With regard to the correlation between the promotion of democratic values and trade under NAFTA, in Canada there is also a disconnection between the political discourse and the concrete actions of the government. On the one hand, the political discourse on free trade refers to human rights and democratic development. However, in NAFTA negotiations with Mexico and in assessments of NAFTA made by the government, democratic development has hardly been a priority. Thus, when analyzing Canada-Cuba diplomacy, it becomes quickly evident that NAFTA has little real influence on Canadian foreign policy towards Cuba. Rather, the attitude of political leaders and socio-economic factors related to exchanges with Cuba has contributed to the evolution of relations between Canada and the Cuban government.

The diplomatic discourse and government action From the start of NAFTA negotiations with Mexico, the government of Canada had the opportunity to make the promotion of democratic values abroad a central element of the trade agreements. However, instead of pressing to officialize this concern within NAFTA, the Canadian government chose to favor a more "natural" approach to democratic development. Among other things, Canada advocated the idea that economic liberalization would inevitably lead to the reinforcement of democracy and respect of human rights (Americas Policy Group 2004). NAFTA therefore meant a voluntary exclusion of proactive democratic development in favor of economic benefits. The Americas Policy Group states:

> During the Mulroney administration, Canadian officials resisted pressure from Canadian civil society and kept human rights out of NAFTA negotiations. The Government maintained that it would not allow alleged human rights abuses to interfere with the negotiation of the trade agreement. [...] Accordingly, no briefing notes on Mexico were prepared by the Department of External Affairs and International Trade (DEAIT) for its annual Human Rights Consultations in preparation for UN Commission on Human Rights during this period (Americas Policy Group 2004).

It should be noted, however, that in its documents on free trade, the Canadian government continues to refer to its promotion of democratic values during trade negotiations. In the 2001 report entitled *Opening Doors to the World: Canada's International Market Access Priorities*, for instance, it is stated that:

> By taking part in trade negotiations, Canada has the opportunity to get more out of the global economy all the while protecting its national interests. During negotiations, Canada promotes democratic values and principles that define our country (cited in Deblock and Benessaieh 2001, 725) (author's translation).

The above information clearly demonstrates that there is a notable discrepancy between the concrete actions of the Canadian government and its political discourse on trade liberalization. This discrepancy is present in the Canada's International Policy Statement; *A Role of Pride and Influence in the World* in which the authors highlight in the introduction the idea that economic agreements sometimes lead to the signing of agreements in other areas, such as culture and human rights. The Department of Foreign Affairs and International Trade states:

> As long as governments continue to direct procurement, set tariffs and regulations, and otherwise shape commerce, there will be agreements and understandings that underpin good commercial relations, sometimes in areas related to economic activity (e.g. trade, fisheries, environmental cooperation), sometimes in areas further removed (e.g. cultural agreements, understandings on human rights) (Government of Canada 2005a, 12).

However, when the actual agreements signed after NAFTA are considered, it is surprising to see that none of them addressed democratic development and human rights. On the contrary, the priority seemed to be on bilateral agreements on market access for goods and services, investment protection, transparency and subsidies, landing rights, science and technology cooperation, fisheries, and educational exchanges, as well as multilateral agreements on the environment and cultural diversity (Government of Canada 2005a, 12). From this perspective, it is clear that the Government of Canada has sought to emphasize a rather unconvincing link between the trade agreements it signs and the promotion of democratic values abroad. Accordingly, it follows that a correlation between NAFTA and the promotion of human rights in Canadian foreign policy, towards Cuba in particular, is just as unconvincing. It appears rather that the spirit of openness of the leaders and the socio-economic exchanges between the two countries, are the real causes of the evolution of Canada-Cuba relations.

The spirit of openness of political leaders – an influential margin of maneuver
Canadian diplomatic relations with Cuba are significantly influenced by the spirit of openness of prime ministers. Certainly, Canadian foreign policy towards Cuba was affected by events such as the imprisonment of Cuban political dissidents in 1998 and 2003. Nevertheless, it seems that the attitude of Canadian political leaders has an even greater influence because it determines the degree of receptiveness that Canada adopts in response to the behavior of Fidel Castro. Thus, unlike the more rigid and set nature of Cuban-American relations, the building and evolution of diplomatic relations between Canada and Cuba are highly affected by the personal disposition of Canada's prime ministers.

This was evident at the meeting between President Kennedy and Prime Minister Diefenbaker, in 1961, where the latter condemned the use of economic sanctions as a way to pressure the Cuban government (Morley 1987, 193). Then, the situation changed when Diefenbaker's successor, Lester B. Pearson, sought to collaborate more closely with the American government. Consequently, Pearson showed no particular interest in Cuba and the diplomatic relations between the two states were reduced. Subsequently, it was the attitude of Prime Minister Trudeau that influenced once again Canada's foreign policy on Cuba. Indeed, Prime Minister Trudeau not only went to Cuba on an official state visit, he also took concrete measures to encourage the development of Canada-Cuba relations (Kirk 1995, 149). In this manner, the political positioning of Canada with regard to the Castro government underwent cycles of cooling and warming, depending on the attitude of subsequent prime ministers like Mulroney and Chrétien, and of foreign affairs ministers like John Manley and William Graham (McKenna and Kirk 2002, 49–63). Thus, the orientation of Canadian foreign policy with regard to the democratization of Cuba was more a matter of leadership, with political positioning fluctuating over time as different people occupied the office of prime minister. This is best demonstrated by the Chrétien government's review of the policy of constructive engagement in 1999. The Chrétien government, hardened its tone by denouncing the "unacceptable behaviour of Cuba on matters of human rights." Jean Chrétien also decided to reduce high-level bilateral visits between the two countries. Officially, Canada still maintained that a "constructive engagement approach" remained "the best tool to promote Canadian interests in Cuba." However, the government's heart was no longer in it. In short, in the case of Cuba, the limits of dialogue were quickly reached (Bériault 2006) (author's translation).

Socio-economic exchanges between Canada and Cuba   In addition, despite the considerable influence of the attitude of political representatives with regard to Canadian foreign policy on Cuba, socio-economic exchanges seemed to have played an even more crucial role. Even though there were some periods of cooling relations, depending on the Canadian leaders in office, Canada has always ended up finding common ground with the Cuban government with regard to cultural exchanges and trade. As regards cultural exchanges, for instance, about 500000 Canadians visited Cuba as tourists in 2004. It is interesting to note that in March 2005, around 1.9 million Cubans participated in the "Terry Fox" marathon. Economically speaking, it is even more surprising to see that the events of 2003 had no effect on trade. On the contrary, trade grew from C$270 million in 2003 to C$322 million in 2004. Finally, in April 2005, the Cuban government lifted its ban on Canadian beef, which indicated that the relationship between Canada and Cuba seemed to be officially on the right track again. In the end, it is clear that the socio-economic exchanges between Canada and Cuba are a determining factor in the formation and evolution of Canadian foreign policy on Cuba. Accordingly, the two states enthusiastically celebrated their 50th anniversary of diplomatic relations in 2005 (Kirk and McKenna 2005, 3–6).

It can therefore be stated with certainty that these socio-economic exchanges, as well as the attitude of Canada's leaders, have strongly influenced the course of diplomatic relations between Canada and Cuba. Consequently, NAFTA cannot be exclusively and clearly associated with the development of Canada's political positioning towards the Castro government. Finally, the discrepancy between the political discourse and reality, with regard to the promotion of democratic values during negotiations of trade agreements under NAFTA, has toned down the real influence of NAFTA.

The case of Mexico

In comparison to the United States and Canada, the accelerated transition to democracy in Mexico after 2000 makes it possible to examine more specifically the impact of NAFTA on its promotion of human rights in Mexican foreign policy towards Cuba. Of course, Mexico, like Canada, favors a carrot rather than a stick policy with regard to Cuba (McKenna and Kirk 2006). The two countries' traditional reciprocal use of each others' foreign policy in the diplomatic dance (Cuba benefiting from Mexico's foreign policy diverging from that of the United States, and Mexico being able to project a foreign policy independent from that of the United States), their tacit agreement concerning non-intervention (Cuba refraining from exporting its revolution to Mexico, and Mexico discouraging counter-revolution), and especially, their long relationship of mutual respect, seem to have increasingly cooled down since 1994 (Covarrubias 2004, 3). In fact, it could be presumed that the combination of several factors such as the democratic transition in Mexico, the signing of NAFTA, and the new international realities, have had an impact on the change in tone of the Mexican government towards Cuba. In addition, contrary to Cuba, Mexico has been engaged in a process of economic opening and democratic transition since 1994. This situation is leading the two countries down very different paths.

Economic opening – the impact of NAFTA

To determine the extent to which NAFTA has influenced the evolution of Mexico-Cuba relations, we must analyze the beginning of the Mexican government's concern with opening up the country's economy and engaging in political change. Relations between Cuba and Mexico have almost always seemed to depend on their respective relationship with the United States. Thus, the signing of NAFTA by Mexico indicated that it was linking the future of its economic and trade development even more closely to that of the United States and that its interests had changed. This new attitude has been confirmed since 1994. In truth, it seems that the privileged relationship that Mexico enjoyed with Cuba was sacrificed in favor of a rapprochement with the United States on many issues, such as migrant workers and the border wall.[2]

Of course, owing to its privileged and productive trade relationship with the United States, Mexico's economic and trade interests have gradually changed since 1994. An alignment or a process of alignment can be observed between the foreign policies of Mexico and the United States. The guaranteed stable access to the American market offered by NAFTA, American investments in Mexico, the opening up of Mexico to the global economy through its search for trade partners outside its region, and the friendly relations between presidents Fox and Bush weighed heavily in the calculation of Mexico's geopolitical interests and in the re-orientation of its foreign policy (McKenna and Kirk 2006).

The direct effect of NAFTA on Mexican foreign policy towards Cuba is evident in the parallel that can be drawn between the stagnation (or even decrease) of Mexican trade interests with Cuba and the decrease of the importance of Cuba in Mexican foreign policy (McKenna and Kirk 2006). This is all the more true given the numerous diplomatic incidents that have occurred between the two countries since 1999. Examples include the Sheraton affair in 2006, the Monterrey Summit in 2002 and the meeting between Cuban political dissidents and the Mexican Minister of Foreign Affairs in 1999 (Covarrubias 2004, 3–5).[3]

Political change – instituting democratic values in Mexico   Mexico has also been opening up politically, as evidenced by the transition to democratic values. This has occurred gradually, spurred both by the demands of civil society and the slow erosion of the electoral base of the Institutional Revolutionary Party (PRI). The sometimes violent demands of civil society and the gradual progression towards the PRI defeat were two processes that started long before the establishment of NAFTA.

---

2   With the notable exception of Mexico's non-participation in the Iraq war in 2003.
3   For the recent Sheraton affair, see Ana Covarrubias (Covarrubias 2006, 8–10).

Indeed, the decrease in the popularity of the PRI could already be seen in the 1982 election results, when the PRI obtained 77.4 percent of votes, compared to 96.6 percent in 1976. Moreover, the NAFTA negotiations further accelerated this slide, because of the rise of social demands for transparency and accountability. Thus, in 1994, the PRI obtained only 48.6 percent of votes whereas the National Action Party (PAN) received 25.9 percent (Cameron and Wise 2004, 306–307). Then, in the same year, the Mexican peso crisis weakened the government even more, since it was held responsible for the poor management of the economy. It is in this context of crisis that President Zedillo tried to save the PRI's reputation by giving in to the demands of pressure groups to implement democratic reforms. This first political opening was thus marked by the allocation of state funds to electoral campaigns as well as independent monitoring of the relationship between the media and the PRI in the next elections (Cameron and Wise 2004, 320). However, as Cameron and Wise mentioned: "The opposition seized this moment, and successfully forced Zedillo's hand in securing political concessions that would quicken the pace of democratization" (Cameron and Wise 2004, 317).

Unfortunately for President Zedillo, this political opening would eventually lead to the defeat of the PRI and the arrival in power of the PAN in 2000 (Cameron and Wise 2004, 319). Thus, the election of President Vicente Fox and the PAN marked a decisive moment in the democratic transition in Mexico. On December 2, 2000, the day after taking office, President Fox signed a technical co-operation agreement with the United Nations High Commissioner for Human Rights. Two years later, the Mexican Senate also approved the establishment of an office of the UN High Commissioner in Mexico, which "worked in consultation with the Mexican government and civil society to develop a 'diagnosis' of the human rights situation in the country" (Americas Policy Group 2004, 6). Finally, the Mexican government proudly stated that today, Mexico "is experiencing an intense form of democracy" when promoting democratic values in many international forums (Government of Mexico – Presidencia de la Republica 2005).

As a result of this change in tone concerning respect for human rights and the promotion of democracy abroad, Cuba was considered in a new light in Mexican foreign policy. In terms of influence in the Americas and particularly in Mexico, Cuba was no longer the leader it had once been because it was in the uncomfortable position of being the only dictatorship on a continent in which the countries were either democratized or in the midst of a democratic transition. In addition, it is undeniable that certain diplomatic disagreements between the two countries had already occurred from the 1960s to the 1990s. The exclusion of Cuba from the Cancun North-South Summit of 1981, at the express request of President Reagan, or the accusations of spying at the Mexican embassy in Havana in 1969, are examples of these disagreements. Nevertheless, the two governments would always find an acceptable solution for both parties and their respective foreign policies would adjust in consequence. However, it seems that the pathways to solutions are currently very weak and that a slow but certain break is occurring between the two countries. The final goal of this new trend in Mexican foreign policy is still difficult to assess because Mexico seems to be playing a double game. On the one hand, Mexico seems to want to influence the Cuban political system while on the other hand, the Mexican government is seeking to reinforce the image of its democratic commitment to the rest of the world (Covarrubias 2006, 5).

Conclusion

In March 2005, President Bush, President Fox and Prime Minister Martin held a press conference to announce the signing of the Partnership for Security and Prosperity, which was intended to be a "next step" to further the trilateral co-operation of NAFTA. During the press conference, mention was made of the extent to which trade liberalization between the member countries had contributed to the promotion of "freedom, economic opportunity and democratic institutions" (*Joint Press Conference with President Vicente Fox of Mexico, President George W. Bush of the United States and Prime Minister Paul Martin of Canada* 2005). The NAFTA members are contemplating, among other things, a convergence of policies regarding national security and market competitiveness. However, when looking at the partnership's action plan, it should be noted that the situation of Cuba is completely absent from the concerns of the NAFTA member states.

What are the elements of convergence in the three countries' foreign policy, if Cuba does not even feature as a fundamental and converging concern of member states? The answer lies particularly in the increased importance given to human rights and democratic development in Cuba since 1994. However, the proper conclusion is that the real impact of NAFTA on these elements of convergence remains weak, even indirect. Certainly, it is possible to observe an increase in the importance given to democratization in Cuba after the establishment of NAFTA in 1994. However, the analysis of the concrete causes of this convergence shows that, on the contrary, NAFTA was far from being exclusively and directly responsible. In fact, it is rather circumstantial factors, including the behavior of the Cuban government, the attitude of political representatives, the socio-economic conditions of interstate exchanges, popular pressure, and internal political developments, which have influenced the political positioning of the United States, Canada, and Mexico. It can be concluded that there is no cause-and-effect link between NAFTA and the convergence of its member states' foreign policy on Cuba. Nevertheless, the Canadian policy of constructive engagement is not what it used to be, and the current relationship between Canada and Cuba has frequent ups and downs. As for the relationship between Mexico and Cuba, it has adopted an entirely new, more critical tone, and Mexico is engaged in a process of breaking from its traditional foreign policy towards Cuba. When all is said and done, it would more prudent to state that there is currently a gradual alignment of the Canadian and Mexican foreign policies on Cuba with that of the United States.

Conclusion

Gordon Mace

This book grew out of an interest in the impact of large-scale international phenomena on the behavior of state actors. As already noted in the literature (Radice, 2000: 721), phenomena such as globalization and regionalization have tended to encourage a certain harmonization of national practices, at least in the industrialized countries. In the area of international relations theories, the research programs most associated with this vision of harmonization are linked with institutionalist theories. Neo-functionalists (Archer, 2001: 140–6; Haas, 1964; Hass and Schmitter, 1964;) and sociological institutionalists (Thomas, Meyer, Ramirez and Boli, 1987; Finnemore, 1996) in particular have developed research hypotheses concerning the impact of regional or international institutions on states' preferences either through a spill-over effect or through the diffusion/iteration of norms or practices.

In this book, we have sought to test the general hypothesis that a regional institution would influence the formation of policy preferences by member states, resulting in a convergence effect. We stretched the limits of the test by choosing a regional institution such as the North American Free Trade Agreement (NAFTA) and by choosing a policy domain such as foreign policy. Why is that?

In the first instance, NAFTA is clearly a form of regionalism that is quite unique and very different from other experiences of regional integration, and in particular, from that of the European Union (EU). The main difference lies with the institutional structure. In many cases, both contemporary and historical, regional institutions play an important role in bringing member governments to harmonize some or many of their policies. At the lowest level, they can do this by offering documented advice or by suggesting how member states should proceed in specific instances. At the other end of the continuum, community institutions, such as the European Commission, adopt policies that constrain national practices or even determine the legality of national behavior with regard to regional law.

This is not the case at all in the NAFTA environment where regional institutions are extremely limited in scope. It is true, as some have pointed out (Abbott, F., 2000), that there is a certain level of delegation in NAFTA when it comes to dispute-settlement mechanisms, particularly under chapters 19 and 20. As we saw earlier in the book, however, the Commission, as the main regional institution, is an extremely weak structure with mostly secretarial functions. This means that it is not through its regional institutions that NAFTA can expect to have an impact on the policy preferences of the national governments. The convergence effect, should there be one, can only result from the strength of the regional normative order itself. Thus, it is only through the power of norms that states' preferences can converge. This is what gives the NAFTA experience its specificity as compared to the situation of the EU, creating an interesting analytical challenge.

An added difficulty stems from the choice of foreign affairs as the policy domain to be examined. While essentially a trade agreement, NAFTA also deals with related economic matters such as investments, government procurement and so on. The combination of these elements constitutes an economic framework for the management of trade and economic policies in North America. The agreement, however, does not deal in any way with foreign policy matters. Unlike in the EU, it does not include any mechanism whatsoever that would imply some form of coordination of the conduct of foreign affairs. While it is reasonable to expect some sort of linkage between international trade and other economic matters discussed in international or regional fora, one would not necessarily expect international trade to be linked with other foreign policy issues, for example, democracy. However, a linkage between economic and security matters is being increasingly promoted by national governments in the North American context.

Thus, from an analytical point of view, there would be a natural linkage between NAFTA and domestic commercial and economic policies. This would suggest a study, for example, on the harmonization of domestic regulations governing foreign investments or on the coordination of energy transport policies. However, some would say that trying to link a possible harmonization of the conduct of foreign policy with NAFTA is stretching the analysis a bit too far. Nevertheless, if NAFTA has become something of an "external constitution" for its members states, as some have argued (Clarkson, 2004: 198–228), then it is not unreasonable to expect a convergence effect even in matters of foreign policy. Proof of such a relationship would really establish the strength of the NAFTA norms while substantiating the neo-functionalist intuition of a spill-over effect of an integration process.

These preoccupations inform the design of this book. As was mentioned in the introduction, we have selected cases which represent quite a broad spectrum of foreign policy matters. They represent a gradation from matters closely linked to the NAFTA agenda, such as economic issues, to those much further from the NAFTA thematic, such as democracy and antidrug cooperation. Let us now turn to the results of this analysis by considering each policy sector included in the book.

The first policy sector examined by the contributors deals with economic affairs. We have included two case studies dealing with the Free Trade Area of the Americas (FTAA) and the three North American governments' policy preferences as regards transatlantic relations after the signing of NAFTA. In the first instance, Mace and Bélanger offer a comparative analysis of three questions that were at the center of the FTAA negotiations: the treatment regarding smaller economies; agriculture; and trade in services. Though in different ways, these questions are all closely linked to the NAFTA thematic. They also constitute an extremely interesting object of investigation because they are key elements of the difficulty to reach a trade agreement, not only in the context of the FTAA but also in the World Trade Organization (WTO) multilateral trade negotiations.

In their chapter, Mace and Bélanger demonstrate that the convergence effect did not always manifest itself, even in matters closely related to the NAFTA agenda. However, convergence in terms of policy preferences was observed in relation to the special help given smaller economies. The position of each government did evolve progressively, from initial opposition to support for a limited form of preferential treatment for smaller economies through the Hemispheric Cooperation Program. This change occurred after 1999 and represents an evolution of the policy preferences of the three governments.

In contrast, the authors found no convergence on questions related to agriculture and trade in services. In the first instance, the divergence occurred between the US position on the one hand and the Canadian and Mexican preferences on the other. In the field of agriculture, US negotiators tabled a proposal limited to market access only. Their Canadian and Mexican counterparts were not opposed to a negotiation on market access but also wanted to discuss the gradual elimination of export subsidies and state support to local farmers. In addition, Mexico wanted to include some form of preferential treatment for the smaller economies. In what pertains to trade in services, the divergence was between the Mexican position and those of the US and Canada. Ottawa and Washington favored the negative list approach while Mexico was more open to some form of asymmetrical treatment.

Consequently, the level of convergence was certainly not as high as what was initially expected. What is interesting to note, however, is that NAFTA was a conditioning factor, explaining both the convergence and divergence effects depending on what country we are looking at. The reason for this is that the Agreement played a different role in the formation of the policy preferences of each government. In the case of Canada and the United States, NAFTA acted as a normative framework pushing for a high degree of compatibility between the policy preferences put forward in the context of the NAFTA, WTO and FTAA. What explains the divergence in the preferences expressed by the US and Canada has to do essentially with domestic politics in the US and Washington's strategic positioning toward the EU and Japan in the multilateral trade negotiations. What explains the divergent Mexican position is a different type of impact of NAFTA on that government. In the case of Mexico, NAFTA's impact did not stem from its normative order but rather from a gains-related situation. Mexico, in effect, did try to position itself so as to use the FTAA negotiations to obtain results that would counterbalance what were perceived as losses arising from NAFTA, especially in the agricultural sector. So there was a NAFTA influence, but it played out very differently from one state to the other.

The other case study on trade issues also reveals a divergence in the policy preferences of member states, specifically when the overall commercial policies are examined in relation to the trade regime in the western hemisphere and the transatlantic area. Thus, Bélanger's analysis in Chapter 2 reveals divergent policy preferences: the US government favored a minimalist arrangement while both Canada and Mexico wanted a more comprehensive type of institutional structure. In its trade relations with Europe, Washington was essentially seeking an arrangement that would eliminate the irritants in the EU-USA commercial relationship. The Transatlantic Economic Partnership (TEP), signed in 1998, fulfilled this function. Canada and Mexico, for their part, sought a more comprehensive trade agreement, which the Mexican government succeeded in obtaining with the signing of the "Global Agreement" in 1997. The Canadian government, which was initially an ardent supporter of a TAFTA, finally had to resign itself to accepting a much more limited EU-Canada Trade Initiative, which was signed in 1998 and resembled the TEP.

With regard to the Americas, Bélanger pinpoints again the divergence in policy preferences in relation to the overall trade framework during the pre-negotiation as well as the negotiation period. During the pre-negotiation period, from 1994 to 1998, Washington's preferred policy option was a bloc-to-bloc negotiation between NAFTA and MERCOSUR countries using NAFTA as a model. Canada and Mexico were opposed to the bloc-to-bloc negotiation, instead preferring a stronger institutionalization of the future FTAA, an option not favored by Washington. The negotiation period, which started officially in 1998, ended with a stalemate in November 2003. The acceptance by the United States of a "FTAA light" or *à la carte* again pitted Washington against Mexico and Ottawa, both wanting to keep negotiating on a comprehensive FTAA project that would offer them more voice opportunities than the FTAA *à la carte*.

Consequently, even on foreign policy matters closely linked to the NAFTA agenda, such as trade negotiations in the Americas and the transatlantic area, the evidence does not support the "convergence hypothesis" and fails to sustain the expectations of institutionalist theories about convergence in policy preferences. Before trying to explain these findings however, let us examine the analytical results of the other case studies.

A second category of case studies involves security issues. Obviously, these are not as closely linked to the NAFTA agenda as trade negotiations are. But security and trade are not unrelated phenomena, particularly in a context of region-building. The two have been frequently associated in the literature (Buzan and Waever, 2001: 40–83; Adler and Barnett, 1998: 29–67; Schulz, Söderbaum and Öjendal. 2001) and past experiences at region-building attest to the importance of the relationship. In the case of the Association for South East Asian Nations (ASEAN) for instance, the perception of an external threat was a major factor in launching the free trade area. Moreover in European integration, the initial institutional impetus, the Coal and Steel Community, was a mechanism devised to bring together former enemies and launch a process of economic integration that in the future would reduce the possibility of conflict in the region (Moravcsik, 1998: 86–7). In the North American context, trade and security have naturally been linked closely since the tragic events of September 2001, but Roussel, Fortmann and Duplantis remind us in their chapter that trade-related security accords were signed very soon after the launching of NAFTA.

Thus, there is a link between trade and security and this relationship explains our decision to include in the book two case studies on security matters. One chapter deals with defense policies while the other concentrates on security matters with a focus on the policing functions of the state. In both cases, the authors offer a detailed examination of a potential convergence effect and its relationship with NAFTA.

In Chapter 3, Nelson Michaud analyzes the evolution of the defense policies of the three NAFTA members since 1994. From his point of view, the fundamental test of convergence lies in the passage from a bilateral to a multilateral framework for the management of defense and security policies among the three North American governments. Michaud thus starts his analysis with an examination of the NAFTA agreement. The analysis establishes that only three articles in the accord are related to security and all are oriented toward the protection of national sovereignty. There are no allusions whatsoever in NAFTA to an instrument or a mechanism geared toward the integration of defense and security policies among the member countries.

Looking then at the evolution of the security relationships themselves, Michaud remarks that the relationship between the United States and Mexico was not very strong from an historical point of view. Because of the legacy of the past, military cooperation had always been difficult prior to 2001 and military aid even diminished between 1997 and 2002. The inclusion of Mexico in Northern Command's surveillance area (NORTHCOM) is not at all related to NAFTA but has more to do with the overall fight against terrorism.

The relationship is even weaker in the case of Canada and Mexico, to the point of being non-existent. This should come as no surprise given the limited historical relationship not only between the two countries but also between Canada and Latin America as a whole. It was only at the start of the 1990s that Ottawa really institutionalized its relationship with the Americas and there was no special link with Mexico at the time, even though a Canada-Mexico joint commission existed since the mid-1970s. The overall relationship started to improve with NAFTA but not in the defense sector where there was no commonality of interests. Mexico is absent from the Canadian *1994 White Paper on Defence* and from subsequent security declarations made by Canadian authorities. When they reflect on the security of North America, Canadian policy makers seldom include Mexico in their vision of the future. This is demonstrated by the fact that none of the 44 bilateral agreements signed by the two governments between 1992 and 2004 deal with security matters.

The only substantial military relationship, from an historical as well as a contemporary point of view, is the Canada-United States relationship. This link was institutionalized during the Second World War and became stronger over the years with the membership of both countries in NATO and NORAD. But that relationship is essentially a product of geographical vicinity rather than being NAFTA-related.

Thus, even though scholars like Cope and Rochlin believe that the NAFTA environment has generated favorable conditions for military integration, at least in the Mexico-US relationship, Michaud comes to a different conclusion. He does not see a NAFTA impact on military policies in North America because he is unable to identify any manifestation of a trilateralization of defense cooperation in the region. It is possible, however, that Michaud could have come to another conclusion had he chosen a different research strategy. An examination of the content of the defense polices of the three countries over a period of time, let us say between 1985 and 2005, might have indicated, for example, that the three governments were developing an increasingly similar vision on how threats affected North America and on the nature of defense policies needed to oppose these threats.

In the following chapter on non military security, Stéphane Roussel, Michel Fortmann and Martin Duplantis also come to the conclusion that there is no real trilateral institutionalization of the management of security in North America but they do nevertheless identify some manifestations of convergence. They see convergence developing as a result of a socialization process initiated by NAFTA and reinforced by strict security preoccupation. As they point out, NAFTA has increased the focus on the border as compared to the period prior to 1994. Consequently, the agreements signed between 1995 and 1999 to monitor traffic at the borders were clearly related to NAFTA in the sense that their function was to facilitate the flow of persons and goods at the borders.

After September 2001, there was more evidence of convergence as the content of the bilateral agreements signed between the US and Mexico and the US and Canada was increasingly similar. This was true, for example, of the Smart Border Declaration. However, this increase in convergence was no longer related only to NAFTA but also to the post-2001 anti-terrorist strategy. In fact, trade and security became so intrinsically related in North America after September 2001 that it becomes extremely difficult to isolate the NAFTA influence in the socialization process leading to increased convergence. What is interesting, however, is the authors' findings concerning the emergence of what could be called "border communities" whose shared interests led them to create coalitions and harmonize the approaches used to pressure their respective governments to keep the border as open as possible. Of course, the post-2001 security trauma is the most immediate factor explaining this phenomenon but it is also very possible that the NAFTA environment created favorable conditions for the emergence of border communities. The convergence found at the local level could then become another impetus for the development of convergence between national policies.

This said, the case studies on security found in this book do not offer strong evidence to support the convergence hypothesis and the NAFTA influence in this foreign policy area. The main reason for this conclusion is that the authors of both chapters on security did not find any manifestations of a trilateralization of cooperative behavior among the three NAFTA partners in defense or non-military security matters. But as we noted earlier, a research strategy focussing more substantially on comparative analysis of the content of defense or security policies may possibly generate research results more supportive of a convergence effect. The NAFTA influence will always be extremely difficult to isolate because security and trade matters have been highly interwoven in the very specific post-2001 North American environment.

The last category of case studies involves three foreign policy issues not usually associated with the NAFTA thematic. Promotion of democracy in the Americas, antidrug cooperation and policies regarding the Cuban regime certainly constitute important components of hemispheric affairs and may possibly have been in the back of the minds of NAFTA negotiators. However, we have no evidence that they were part of the discussions leading to the signing of the agreement. Consequently, our initial expectations concerning a NAFTA-induced convergence effect were very low indeed.

Nevertheless, Jean-Philippe Thérien made some interesting observations in his analysis in Chapter 5 of the promotion of democracy. His examination of the US and Canadian foreign policy behavior with regard to the promotion of democracy in the Americas is consistent with other findings in the literature. Thérien found no evidence to support a NAFTA effect on Canadian and US behavior. Both governments were firm advocates of the inter-American regime of citizenship since the early 1990s as Ottawa and Washington each supported the steps taken to reinforce what Bloomfield has labelled the "OAS Defence-of-Democracy Regime" (Bloomfield, 1994). There was no convergence here because both governments had the same policies from the start, though possibly for different reasons, and there was no NAFTA effect since both policies predated NAFTA.

The situation concerning Mexico is very different however. Thérien observes a significant change in Mexican foreign policy in this regard after 2000 as Mexico City's traditional non-interventionist position gradually gave way to support for democracy promotion in the western hemisphere. A reluctant supporter of Resolution 1080 and an opponent of the Washington Protocol of 1992, the Mexican government became an advocate of a stronger inter-American regime of citizenship after 2000 with clear support for the Democratic Clause and the Inter-American Democratic Charter adopted on September 11 2001.

So what Thérien observes with regard to the Mexican situation is a phenomenon of alignment rather than convergence. Mexican foreign policy gradually shifted and aligned itself with that of the US and Canada as an indirect result of a NAFTA influence. For Thérien, NAFTA's effect is indeed an indirect one as its role has been more one of a catalyst: the NAFTA environment created a favorable context for political liberalization in Mexico which, in turn, brought a change in Mexico's policy regarding promotion of democracy in the Americas.

In Chapter 6, Guillermo Aureano examines antidrug cooperation, specifically the two related issues of certification and the Plan Colombia, and concludes that this is another foreign policy theme where convergence was far from a smooth process. Neither issue was foremost in Canada's foreign policy regarding the Americas but Canadian preferences in favor of multilateral solutions are a well-known fact. Mexico, for its part, has been an consistent critic of unilateral certification by the US government. This is why we can truly talk about convergence when examining the attitudes of the three North American governments toward the Multilateral Evaluation Mechanism adopted in 1999. In this case, all three governments moved from an initial divergent position to a compromise position as represented by the MEM.

With regard to Plan Colombia and the positioning of the three countries, Aureano comes to a different conclusion, identifying a phenomenon of alignment rather than convergence. Plan Colombia, in effect, is a case where US policy remained consistent. It is the Canadian and, more importantly, the Mexican governments that adjusted their foreign policy objectives, aligning them more closely Washington's policy.

Be it convergence or alignment, Aureano concludes that there was a *rapprochement* between the positions of the three North American governments with regard to antidrug cooperation after 1999. Could this particular outcome be explained by a NAFTA effect? Aureano believes so but, like Thérien in his chapter, he identifies an indirect effect. In this case, NAFTA played a gains-related role in the sense that open confrontation with the United States would not only be unprofitable from a general point of view but could even be costly in the North American commercial arena. Consequently, the NAFTA influence was there but in a negative sense. Thus, NAFTA did not positively encourage cooperative behavior in this sector but rather acted as a threat in case of non-convergence or non-alignment.

Chapter 7 offers an analysis of a quite interesting case, that is the foreign policy behavior of the three North American states regarding the Cuban regime. This makes an interesting case because the Canadian and Mexican governments traditionally supported the Castro regime while from the start, the United States adopted a punitive approach summarized by its economic embargo policy. As documented by Hugo Loiseau, Washington's policy toward the Marxist regime in Cuba remained the same over the years regardless of which political party dominated the Executive Branch. For example, the *Helms-Burton Act* came into force under the Clinton Administration while the *Initiave for a New Cuba* was put forward by the Bush Administration in 2002. Thus, Washington's position on democracy and human rights in Cuba has remained consistent from the early 1960s to the present.

On the contrary, Canadian and Mexican policy evolved significantly after 1998. Up to then, Mexico City and Ottawa had opposed US policy by supporting the Cuban regime and maintaining economic relations with Cuba while seldom criticizing the Cuban government for its attitude on democracy and human rights. It is only at the end of the 1990s that things started to change. In the case of Canada, ministerial visits were stopped and projects suspended to protest against episodes of human rights violations in 1998 and again in 2003. These events brought the Canadian government, as would be the case for Mexico, to vote between 2002 and 2005 in favor of various OAS and UN resolutions demanding respect for human rights in Cuba.

In the case of Mexico, the attitude of the government had begun to change in 1999 when PRI president Ernesto Zedillo expressed veiled criticism of the Castro regime at the Ibéro-American Summit held in Havana that year. Criticism became stronger and more frequent during the presidency of Vicente Fox culminating, in 2004, with Fidel Castro accusing Mexico of having become an "American colony" and the Mexican government retaliating with the expulsion of the Cuban diplomatic representative.

So there was a clear process of alignment of government attitudes toward the Cuban regime from 1998 onward with Canada and Mexico adopting an attitude more and more similar to that of the United States. From Loiseau's point of view, NAFTA was not a major factor in this evolution however. The US position, for instance, was developed well before the signing of NAFTA. In the case of Canada, the change of attitude, albeit more reserved than that of Mexico, had to do more with the views of the prime ministers. This factor, however, was counterbalanced by the importance of economic and social relations between the two countries which make it difficult for the Canadian government to adopt a US-style punitive approach.

In the case of both Canada and Mexico, it is clear that the behavior of the Cuban government itself has to be considered as an important factor in explaining attitudes toward the Cuban regime. But the reaction of each government to events in Cuba was different. The stronger reaction on the part of the Mexican government was influenced by the NAFTA environment but the influence, from Loiseau's point of view, was indirect, as it was for the promotion of democracy and antidrug cooperation. So there is a similarity with the case studies of this last category but the patterns are not very clear.

This is an observation that can safely be made after considering all the case studies presented in this book. The authors have indeed found a few instances where a convergence effect can be seen. This is the case for policy preferences regarding the situation of smaller economies in the FTAA negotiations and certification in antidrug cooperation. However, in other instances we witness a phenomenon of alignment, such as in policies concerning democracy promotion (Mexico), Plan Colombia (Mexico and Canada), Cuba (Mexico and Canada), and security (Mexico). Moreover, there are cases where we observe a divergence in policy preferences: with regard to FTAA negotiations concerning agriculture and trade in services, and with regard to the framework for trade negotiations in the Americas and in the transatlantic area. Finally, the case study on defense policies revealed neither divergence nor convergence.

As for the NAFTA impact, we found that there was an indirect influence in situations of convergence and alignment but it was generally impossible to assess precisely the weight of that influence and to isolate the NAFTA factor from other intervening variables. In these cases, NAFTA played a role by creating an environment conducive to policy harmonization and to the expression of similar preferences. But even on related policy issues such as those that concern trade negotiations, it is difficult to say that it is precisely because of NAFTA that convergence occurred.

We must therefore conclude that the evidence found up to now does not substantiate our initial hypothesis linking NAFTA to a convergence in policy preferences among the three member governments. Why is that and what does it mean for the study of the relationship between regionalism and the state?

With regard to the weakness of the analytical link between NAFTA and foreign policy behavior, we must recognize that our research strategy may have been original but it was evidently not optimal. There are essentially two reasons for this. The first one concerns our choice of NAFTA, which is an arrangement characterized by an extremely weak institutional capability. Our expectation was that, because of its high level of legalization, NAFTA would have a strong influence on the policy preferences of member states despite weak governance structures. The strength of the regional normative order in itself would act as a constraint on the policy choices made by the three North American governments. That this happened only in a limited number of cases is probably explained by the fact that NAFTA's inadequate governance structures do not permit the type of coordination necessary for convergence in policy preferences. Thus concluded Bélanger in his analysis of trade policies.

The other reason has to do with our selection of the foreign policy sector as the dependent variable. Even though we have chosen a fairly wide spectrum of issues, it is clear that foreign policy is not as closely related to the NAFTA thematic as, for example, domestic economic policies. While the analysis was not facilitated by the selection of this policy area, the choice was necessary to test the extension of an eventual NAFTA influence on policy convergence. Robust evidence in that direction would have clearly established the strong impact of NAFTA.

Having reached the end of the exercise, which produced mixed results, what is there to reflect on concerning the relationship between regionalism and state behavior? We have to recognize first of all that the overall picture is not completely negative. Despite the difficulties just mentioned, a good proportion of the case studies do reveal instances of convergence and alignment. In this last situation, Mexico is the country that aligns its policy preferences with the other two. This is not an insignificant fact. For various reasons, Canada and the United States have evolved similarly over the years, sharing the same values in many cases and adopting many similar policy preferences. This is not to say that there are no differences in policy preferences between the two governments as we have seen in this book, but there is a commonality of values and visions of the world which, for historical reasons, was not the case for Mexico.

Therefore, it is reasonable to expect that an institution like NAFTA will have less impact on the foreign policy values and preferences of Canada and the United States but more influence on the foreign policy of Mexico. Moreover, this is precisely what many of our research results reveal. This illustrates, at least indirectly, the influence of NAFTA as a regional institution on foreign policy behavior.

The difficulty of course, as with many research programs on the diffusion of international norms, is to capture precisely that influence or impact. How do we trace the specific process by which an institution like NAFTA influences the convergence in policy preferences when such a convergence exists? And how do we explain that in some instances a regional institution does foster convergence while in other instances it is unable to do so?

This book offers an exploratory study on the impact of regionalism on the convergence of states' preferences. The case studies included here provide some interesting insights on this research problematique. The challenge for the pursuit of such a research program, however, lies in developing a better research design. We must work at improving the research strategy so as to generate more productive definitions concerning concepts such as convergence and devising a more precise methodology to guide observation. We also need a more precise methodology to help researchers to trace the influence of regional institutions.

The relationship between regionalism and the state is a two-way street. It is a fascinating subject about which a fair amount of knowledge already exists. For the past sixty years, the literature has generated quite interesting findings on how states construct regionalism. In order to achieve a more complete understanding of this phenomenon, we must also strive to better explain how regional institutions influence the formation of policy preferences.

Bibliography

General Bibliography

Abbott, Frederick M. (2000), "NAFTA and the Legalization of World Politics: A Case Study," *International Organization* 54: 3, 519–47.

Adler, Emanuel and Michael Barnett (eds) (1998), *Security Community* (Cambridge: Cambridge University Press).

Aggarwal, Vinod K. (ed.) (1998), *Institutional Designs for a Complex World: Bargaining Linkages & Nesting* (Cornell: Cornell University Press).

—— (1998), "Institutional Nesting: Lessons and Prospects," in Vinod K. Aggarwal (ed.).

Americas Policy Group (2004), "Les droits de la personne au Mexique au 10e anniversaire de l'ALÉNA: Possibilités et défis pour le Canada," *Le Conseil canadien pour la coopération internationale*, http://www.ccic.ca/f/docs/003_apg_2004–01_nafta_mexico_human_rights.pdf, accessed 7 March 2007.

Andreas, Peter (1998–99), "The Escalation of U.S. Immigration Control in the Post-NAFTA Era," *Political Science Quarterly*, 113: 4, 591–615.

Anstis, Christopher (1999), "Canada and NATO Enlargement," *Canadian Foreign Policy* 6:3, 99–112.

Appendini, Kristen and Sven Bislev (eds) (1999), *Economic Integration in NAFTA and the EU* (New York: St. Martin Press).

Armengaud, Jean-Hébert (2004), "Castro vient à bout de la puissance du Mexique," *Le Devoir*, 4 May , A5.

Astorga, Luis (1999), *Drug Trafficking in Mexico: A First General Assessment* www.unesco.org/most/astorga.htm, accessed 30 June 2000.

Avery, William P. (1996), "American agriculture and trade policymaking. Two-level bargaining in the North American Free Trade Agreement," *Policy Sciences* 29, 113–15.

Axelrod, Robert and Robert O. Keohane (1993), "Achieving Cooperation Under Anarchy: Strategies and Institutions," in David A. Baldwin (ed.).

Axline, Andrew W. (1977), "Underdevelopment, Dependence and Integration: The Politics of Regionalism in the Third World," *International Organization* 31:1, 83–105.

Azuelos, Martine, Maria Eugenia Cosio-Zavala and Jean-Michel Lacroix (eds) (2004), *Intégration dans les Amériques: Dix ans d'ALENA* (Paris, Presses Sorbonne Nouvelle).

Bailey, John (2004), "Security Imperatives of North American Integration. Back to a Future of Hub and Spokes," in Sydney Weintraub (ed.).

Bailey, John and Sergio Aguayo Quezada (ed.) (1996), *Strategy and Security in US–Mexican Relations Beyond the Cold War* (LaJolla: Center for United States–Mexican Studies).

Baldwin, David (ed.) (1993), *Neorealism and Neoliberalism: The Contemporary Debate* (New York: Columbia University Press).

Bambas, Alexandra et al. (eds) (2000), *Health & Human Development in the New Global Economy: The Contributions and Perspectives of Civil Society in the Americas* (Washington, DC: Pan American Health Organization).

Barrera, Mario and Ernst B. Haas (1969), "The Operationalization of Some Variables Related to Regional Integration: A Research Note," *International Organization* 23:1 150–160.

Barry, Donald (2000), "Pursuing Free Trade: Canada, the Western Hemisphere, and the European Union," *International Journal* 55: 2, 292–300.

Barry, Donald, Mark O. Dickerson and James D. Grisford (eds) (1995), *Toward a North American Community? Canada, the United States, and Mexico* (Boulder: Westview Press).

Battistella. Dario (2003), *Théories des relations internationales* (Paris: Presses de sciences po).

Bélanger, Louis (1998), "U.S. Foreign policy and the Regionalist Option in the Americas," in Gordon Mace and Louis Bélanger (eds).

—— (2004), "Vers une communauté nord-américaine? Asymétrie et institutions communes au sein de l'ALÉNA," in Martine Azuelos, Maria Eugenia Cosio-Zavala and Jean-Michel Lacroix (eds).

—— (2007), "An Unsustainable Institutional Design: Incompleteness and Delegation Deficit in NAFTA," in Gordon Mace, Jean-Philippe Thérien and Paul Haslam (eds).

Bélanger, Yves (1998), "L'intégration économique continentale nord-américaine dans le domaine de la défense et l'après-guerre froide: dimensions comparatives des cheminements canadien et américain," *Arès* 16:2, 5–19.

Bellavance, Joël-Denis (2002), "Décriminalisation de la mari: Washington menace de multiplier les fouilles aux frontières," *La Presse*, 18 October, A1.

Bennett, Colin J. (1991), "Review Article: What is Policy Convergence and What Causes It?," *British Journal of Political Science* 21:2, 215–33.

Bernier, Ivan and Martin Roy (1998), "NAFTA and Mercosur: Two Competing Models?," in Gordon Mace and Louis Bélanger (eds).

Bériault, Jean (2006), "Bilan de la politique canadienne d'engagement constructif, en matière de droits de l'homme," *Radio-canada international* (published online 3 July 2006) http://www.rcinet.ca/rci/fr/chroniques/24092.shtml, accessed 26 December 2006.

Bergsten, C. Fred (2002), "A Renaissance for United States Trade Policy?," *Foreign Affairs* (published online November-December 2002) http://www.iie.com/publications/papers/paper.cfm?ResearchID=487, accessed 18 March 2003.

Bertrab, Hermann von (1997), *Negotiating NAFTA: A Mexican Envoy's Account* (Westport: Praeger).

Bhagwati, Jagdish N. and Hugh T. Patrick (eds) (1990), *Aggressive Unilateralism: America's 301 Trade Policy and the World Trading System* (Ann Arbor: The University of Michigan Press).

Bloomfield, Richard J. (1994), "Making the Western Hemisphere Safe for Democracy? The OAS Defense-of-Democracy Regime," *The Washington Quarterly* 17:2, 157–69.

Bonser, Charles F. (ed.) (1991), *Toward a North American Common Market: Problems and Prospects for a New Economic Community* (Boulder: Westview Press).

Brautigam, Tara (2002), "Dépénalisation de la marijuana: Cauchon nie les pressions américaines," *Le Devoir*, 14 August, A2.

Briceno Ruiz, Jose (2001), "El Mercosur, México y el Caribe frente al Area de Libre Comercio de las Americas," *Comercio Exterior* 51:5, 396–402.

Browne, William P., David B. Schweikhardt and James Bonnen (2000), *Chance Governs All: The Fragmented, Frustrating State of Agricultural Trade Policy in the United States,* Staff paper #2000–38 (East Lansing: Department of Agricultural Economics, Michigan State University).

Bulmer-Thomas, Victor, Nikki Craske, and Monica Serrano (eds) (1994), *Mexico and the NAFTA: Who Will Benefit?* (New York: St Martins Press).

Burrell, Jennifer and Michael Shifter (2000), "Estados Unidos, la OEA y la promoción de la democracia en las Américas," in Arlene B. Tickner (ed.).

Bush, George W. (2001), "Address Before a Joint Session of the Congress on the United States Response to the Terrorist Attacks of September 11," *Weekly Compilation of Presidential Documents* http://frwebgate.access.gpo.gov/gci-bin/getdoc.cgi?dbname=2001_presidential_documents&docid=pd24se01_txt-26, accessed 28 March 2007.

—— (2002), *The National Security Strategy of the United States of America*, http://www.whitehouse.gov/nsc/nss.pdf, accessed 5 March 2007.

Bush, Per-Olof and Helge Jörgens (2004), "Governance by Diffusion? An Analytical Distinction of Three International Governance Mechanisms," *Presentation given at the Annual Congress of the International Studies Association*, Montréal, March 17–20 2004.

Bussey, Jane (2004), "Letter Perfect? Not Yet: Hoping to Pressure Brazil into Greater Flexibility in the Free-Trade Negotiations Among 34 of the Hemisphere's 35 Nations, Some Deputy Trade Ministers Draft a Letter," *The Miami Herald*, http://www.miami.com, accessed 10 Febuary 2004.

Buzan, Barry and Ole Waever (2003), *Regions and Powers: The Structure of International Security* (Cambridge: Cambridge University Press).

Caballero, Francis (2000), *Droit de la drogue* (Paris: Dalloz).

Cameron, Maxwell A. and Brian Tomlin (2000), *The Making of NAFTA: How the Deal was Done* (Ithaca: Cornell University Press).

Cameron, Maxwell A. and Carol Wise (2004), "The Political Impact of NAFTA on Mexico: Reflections on the Political Economy of Democratization," *Canadian Journal of Political Science* 37:2, 301–23.

Carlsnaes, Walter (1992), "The Agent-Structure Problem in Foreign Policy Analysis," *International Studies Quarterly* 36:3, 245–70.

Cason, Jim and David Brooks (2002), "La Casa Blanca insta a Chávez a realizar elecciones anticipadas," *La Jornada* (Mexico City), December 14, 25.

Castro, Fidel Ruiz "Speech given by Commander in Chief Fidel Castro Ruz," (published online 1 May 2004) http://www.cuba.cu/gobierno/discursos/2004/ing/f010504i.html, accessed 26 Febuary 2007.

Centre for Canadian Studies, Mount Allison University, *La place du Canada sur la scène internationale*, http://www.mta.ca/faculty/arts-letters/canadian_studies/francais/realites/guide/mondiale/index.html, accessed 24 March 2007.

Checkel, Jeffrey (1997), "International Norms and Domestic Politics: Bridging the Rationalist-Constructivist Divide," *European Journal of International Relations* 3:4, 473–95.

—— (1998), "The Constructivist Turn in International Relations Theory," *World Politics* 50:2, 324–48.

Clarkson, Stephen (2004), "Global Governance and the Semi-Peripheral State: The WTO and NAFTA as Canada's External Constitution," in Marjorie Griffin Cohen and Stephen Clarkson, (eds).

Clarkson, Stephen and Maria Banda (2004), "Congruence, Conflict, and Continental Governance: Canada's and Mexico Responses to Paradigm Shift in the United States," *The American Review of Canadian Studies* 34: 2, 313–47.

Cline, William R. (1982), *Reciprocity: A New Approach to World Trade Policy?* (Washington, DC: Institute for International Economics).

Clissold, Gillian G. (1998), "Divergent International Perspectives on the Caribbean: The Interaction Between the Ongoing Caribbean, U.S., and European Adaptations to the New Global Economy," *Caribbean Briefing Paper* http://www.trinitydc.edu/academics/depts/Interdisc/International/caribbean%20briefings/intl%20perspective.pdf, accessed 18 March 2003.

Coalition for Secure and Trade-Efficient Borders (2001), *Rethinking our Borders: A Plan for Action*, (published online December 2001) http://www.cfib.ca/borders/6007.pdf accessed 25 March 2007.

Conaghan, Catherine M. (2001), *Making and Unmaking Authoritarian Peru: Re-Election, Resistance, and Regime Transition* (Miami: North-South Center Press).

Conference of the American Armies, http://www.redcea.org/english/home.html, accessed 1 December 2002.

Cooper, Andrew F. (1997), *Canadian Foreign Policy: Old Habits and New Directions* (Scarborough: Prentice Hall Allyn and Bacon Canada).

—— (2001), "The Quebec 'Democracy Summit'," *The Washington Quarterly* 24:2, 159–71.

—— (2002), "More than a Star Turn: Canadian Hybrid Diplomacy and the OAS Mission to Peru," *International Journal* 56:2, 279–96.

Cooper, Andrew F., Richard A. Higgott and Kim Richard Nossal (1993), *Relocating Middle Powers, Australia and Canada in a Changing World Order* Chapter 3 (Melbourne/Vancouver: Melbourne University Press/UBC Press).

Cooper, Andrew F. and Thomas Legler (2006), *Intervention Without Intervening? The OAS Defense and Promotion of Democracy in the Americas* (New York: Palgrave-Macmillan).

Cooper, Andrew F. and Jean-Philippe Thérien (2004), "The Inter-American Regime of Citizenship: Bridging the Gap between Democracy and Human Rights," *Third World Quarterly* 25:4, 731–46.

Cope, John A. (1996), "In Search of Convergence: US-Mexican Military Relations Into the Twenty-first Century," in John Bailey and Sergio Aguayo Quezada (ed.).

—— (2001), "The Western Hemisphere," *Perspectives from the Institute for National Strategic Studies* (Washington, D.C.: Institute for National Strategic Studies, National Defense University).

Cortell, Andrew P. and James W. Davis Jr. (1996),"How Do International Institutions Matter? The Domestic Impact of International Rules and Norms," *International Studies Quarterly* 40: 4, 451–78.

Covarrubias, Ana (1999), "El problema de los derechos humanos y los cambios en la política exterior," *Foro internacional* 39:4, 429–52.

—— (2000), "No intervención *versus* promoción de la democracia representativa en el sistema interamericano," in Arlene B. Tickner (ed.).

—— (2001), "La cláusula democrática," *Política exterior* 62–63, 68–71.

—— (2004), "Cuba and Mexico: Changing the Rules of the Game, or the Game Itself?," *Focal point Spotlight on the Americas* 3:5, 3–5.

—— (2006), "Mexico between Cuba and the United States...Again," *Focal point Spotlight on the Americas* 5:2, 8–10.

Cuba Policy Foundation (2003), "Statement from the Cuba Policy Foundation," (published online 23 April 2003) http://www.cubafoundation.org/index.html, accessed 15 September 2006.

Crawley, Andrew (2000), "Toward a Biregional Agenda for the Twenty-First Century," *Journal of Interamerican Studies and World Affairs* 42:2, 9–34.

Daudelin, Jean and Edgar J. Dosman (eds) (1995), *Beyond Mexico: Changing Americas* (Ottawa: Carleton University Press).

Davenport-Hines, Richard (2001), *The Pursuit of Oblivion* (London: Weidenfeld & Nicolson).

Deblock, Christian and Afef Benessaieh (2001), "Les relations économiques entre le Canada et le Mexique dans un contexte d'intégration en profondeur," *Études internationales* 32:4, 717–45.

Del Olmo, Rosa (1991), "La internacionalización jurídica de la droga," *Nueva Sociedad* 112, 102–14.

Demaret, Paul, Jean-François Bellis and Gonzalo Garcia Jiménez (eds) (1997), *Regionalism and Multilateralism After the Uruguay Round: Convergence, Divergence and Interaction* (Brussels: European Interuniversity Press).

Denholm Crosby, Ann (1998), *Dilemmas in Defence Decision-Making: Constructing Canada's Role in NORAD, 1958–1996* (London: Macmillan).

Deutsch, Karl W. (1954), *Political Community at the International Level: Problems of Measurement and Definitions* (New York: Doubleday).

Deutsch, Karl W. et al. (1967), *France, Germany and the Western Alliance, a Study of Elites' Attitudes on European Integration and World Politics* (New York: Scribner).

Deutsch, Karl W. et al. (1957, 1968), *Political Community and the North Atlantic Area: International Organization in the Light of Historical Experience* (Princeton: Princeton University Press).

Dewitt, David B. and David Leyton Brown (1995), *Canada's International Security Policy* (Toronto: Prentice Hall).

Diamond, Larry (2002), "Thinking about Hybrid Regimes," *Journal of Democracy* 13:2, 21–35.

Doern, Bruce and Brian W. Tomlin (1991), *Faith and Fear, The Free Trade Story* (Toronto: Stoddard).

Domínguez, Jorge I. (ed.) (2000), *The Future of Inter-American Relations* (New York: Routledge).

Domínguez, Jorge I. and Rafael Fernández de Castro (2001), *The United States and Mexico: Between Partnership and Conflict*, (New York: Routledge).

Donnelly, Jack (1998), *International Human Rights*, 2nd Edition. (Boulder: Westview Press).

Doran, Charles F., and Alvin P. Drischler (eds) (1996), *A New North America* (Westport: Praeger).

Doran, Charles F., and Gregory P. Marchildon (eds) (1994), *The NAFTA Puzzle, Political Parties and Trade in North America* (Boulder: Westview).

Dosman, Edgar J. (1995), "Managing Canadian-Mexican Relations in the Post-NAFTA Era," in Jean Deaudelin and Edgar J. Dosman (ed.).

Duesterberg, Thomas J. (1995), "Prospects for an EU-NAFTA Free Trade Agreement," *The Washington Quarterly* 18:2, 71–82.

Dziedzic, Michael (1995). "NAFTA and North American Security," *Strategic Forum* (Washington, D.C.: National Defense University, No. 18).

Economist Intelligence Unit (2002), *The World in 2002* (London: The Economist).

Erisman, Michael H. (2000), *Cuba's Foreign Relations in a Post-Soviet World* (Gainesville: University Press of Florida).

Escohotado, Antonio (1992), *Historia de las drogas* (Barcelona: Alianza).

Ezeta, Héctor Manuel (1992), "La inevitable (pero difícil) transición de la OEA," *Política exterior* 35, 15–23.

European Commission (2004a), *EU-Canada: Commission Agrees Design for Future EU-Canada Trade and Investment Enhancement Agreement* http://europa.eu.int/comm/external_relations/Canada/intr/ip04_297.htm accessed 8 March 2004.

—— (2004b), *Joint EU-U.S. Action Plan* http://europa.eu.int/en/agenda/tr06ap3.html, accessed 12 Febuary 2004.

—— (2004c), *The New Transatlantic Agenda* http://europa.eu.int/en/agenda/tr05.html, accessed 12 Febuary 2004.

European Communities (2000a), *Annex XV to Decision No 2/2000 of the EU-Mexico Joint Council of 23 March 2000*.

—— (2000b), "Decision No 2/2000 of the EU-Mexico Joint Council of 23 March 2000," *Official Journal of the European Communities*, 30 June 2000, Art. 37, L 157/24.

—— (2000c), "Economic Partnership, Political Coordination and Cooperation Agreement between the European Community and its Member States, of the one part, and the United Mexican States, of the other part," *Official Journal of the European Communities*, 28 October 2000, L 276/45–61.

—— (2001), "Decision No 2/2001 of the EU-Mexico Joint Council of 27 February 2001," *Official Journal of the European Communities*, 12 March 2001, Art. 44, L 70/20–21.

Fabre, Guilhem (1999), *Les prosperités du crime* (Paris: Éditions de l'Aube).

Farer, Tom (1997), "The Rise of the Inter-American Human Rights Regime: No Longer a Unicorn, Not Yet an Ox," *Human Rights Quarterly* 19:3, 510–46.

Fauriol, Georges A. and William Perry (1999), *Thinking Strategically About 2005: The United States and South America* (Washington, DC: Center for Strategic and International Studies).

Fearon, James D. (1998), "Bargaining, Enforcement, and International Cooperation," *International Organization* 52:2, 269–305.

Feinberg, Richard E. (1997), *Summitry in the Americas: A Progress Report* (Washington, D.C.: Institute for International Economics).

Finnemore, Martha (1993), "International Organizations as Teachers of Norms: The United Nations Educational, Scientific, and Cultural Organization and Science Policy," *International Organization* 47:4, 565–97.

—— (1996), "Norms, Culture, and World Politics: Insights from Sociology's Institutionalism," *International Organization* 50:2, 325–47.

Finnemore Martha and Kathryn Sikkink (1998), "International Norm Dynamics and Political Change," *International Organization* 52:4, 887–917.

—— (2001), "Taking Stock. The Constructivist Research Program in International Relations and Comparative Politics," *Annual Review of Political Science*, 391–416.

Florini, Ann (1996), "The Evolution of International Norms," *International Studies Quarterly* 40, 363–89.

Flynn, Stephen E. (2003), "Transforming Border Management in the post-September 11 World," *Governance and Public Security* (Syracuse, N.Y.: Campbell Public Affairs Institute, Maxwell School of Citizenship and Public Affairs, Syracuse University).

FOCAL (2000), "The Smaller Economies of the Americas: Making a Case for Hemispheric Integration," *FOCAL Policy Papers* (Ottawa: FOCAL).

Fogleman, Ronald R. (1996), "SICOFAA Building Trust And Confidence Throughout The Western Hemisphere," *Aerospace Power Journal* http://www.airpower. maxwell.af.mil/airchronicles/apj96/win96/fogle.html, accessed 5 March 2007.

Forsythe, David P. (1991), "Human Rights, the United States, and the Organization of American States," *Human Rights Quarterly* 13, 66–98.

—— (2000a), *Human Rights in International Relations* (Cambridge: Cambridge University Press).

—— (2000b), "US Foreign Policy and Human Rights: The Price of Principles after the Cold War," in David P. Forsythe (ed.), *Human Rights and Comparative Foreign Policy* (Tokyo: United Nations University Press).

Fortmann, Michel and David G. Haglund (2002), "Canada and the Issue of Homeland Security: Does the 'Kingston Dispensation' Still Hold?," *Canadian Military Journal* 3:1, 17–22.

Franco, Adolfo (2002), "Building trade capacity in the Americas," http://usinfo.state. gov/journals/ites/1002/ijee/ftaa-franco.htm, accessed 18 March 2003.

Frankel, Benjamin (ed.) (1996), *Realism: Restatement and Renewal* (London: Frank Cass).

Franko, Patrice M. (2000), *Toward a New Security Architecture in the Americas: The Strategic Implications of the FTAA* (Washington, DC: Center for Strategic and International Studies).

Gabriel, Christina, Jimena Jimenez and Laura Macdonald (2003), "The Politics of the North American Security Perimeter: Convergence or Divergence in Border Control Policies," *Annual Congress of the International Studies Association*, Portland, Oregon, 26 February–1 March 2003.

Gil Villegas, Francisco (1999), "Mexico y la Unión Europea: un proyecto de política exterior," *Foro Internacional* 39: 2–3, 266–94.

Girvan, Norman (2000), "Towards a Caribbean-American Strategic Alliance," in Alexandra Bambas et al. (eds).

Globerman Steven and Michael Walker (1993), *Assessing NAFTA: A Trinational Analysis* (Vancouver: The Fraser Institute).

Goldstein, Matthew (2001), "Canada: Economic Development under NAFTA, Dominant Economic Player under FTAA," *Law and Business Review of the Americas*, Winter 1, 193–206.

Gonzàlez, Carlos Pinera (2000), "Mexico's Free Trade Agreements: Extending NAFTA's Approach," in Sherry M. Stephenson (ed.).

Gonzalez, Guadalupe and Jorge Chabat (1996), "Mexico's Hemispheric Options in the Post-Cold War Era," in Gordon Mace and Jean-Philippe Thérien (eds).

Gonzalez, Guadalupe and Stephen Haggard (1998), "The United States and Mexico: A Pluralistic Security Community?," in Emanuel Adler and Michael Barnett (eds).

Gosselin, Guy, Gordon Mace, and Louis Bélanger (1995), "La sécurité coopérative régionale dans les Amériques: le cas des institutions démocratiques," *Études internationales* 26: 4, 799–819.

Government of Canada (1994), *1994 White Paper* (Ottawa: Ministry of Supply and Services).

—— (1995), *Canada in the World: Government Statement* (Ottawa: Department of Foreign Affairs and International Trade).

—— (1999), *Position initiale de négociation du Canada en agriculture. Déclaration publique* (published online 19 August 1999) http://www.agr.gc.ca/cb/news/1999/n90819ff.html, accessed 18 March 2003.

—— (2000), *Notes for an Address by Prime Minister Jean Chrétien at the Inauguration of the 30th General Assembly of the Organization of American States*, Windsor, 4 June 2000.

—— (2001a), *Canada and the Summits of the Americas: A National Report* (Ottawa: Communications Branch).

—— (2001b), *Defense Planning Document 2001*, http://www.forces.ca/admpol/eng/doc/def_plan_2001/dp01_03_e.htm, accessed 1 January 2003.

—— (2001c), *Government Response to the Report of the Standing Committee on Foreign Affairs and International Trade: Balance, Transparency and Engagement after the Quebec Summit* (Ottawa: Department of Foreign Affairs and International Trade).

—— (2001d), *Les relations entre le Canada et l'Union européenne en matière de commerce et d'investissement. Effets d'une élimination tarrifaire* (Ottawa: Department of Foreign Affairs and International Trade).

—— (2001e), *M. Pettigrew se félicite des interprétations adoptées à la réunion de la Commission de l'ALENA au sujet du chapitre 11*, Communiqué no. 116 (Ottawa: Ministère des Affaires étrangères et du Commerce international).

—— (2002a), *Canada-Mexico Cooperation*, http://www.dfait-maeci.gc.ca/mexico-city/political/bilateralcooperation-en.asp, accessed 1 December 2002.

—— (2002b), *Lieutenant-General George MacDonald – Vice Chief of Defense Staff in his testimony before the Canadian Senate Standing Committee on National Security and Defense* (published online 6 May 2002) http://www.parl.gc.ca/37/1/parlbus/commbus/senate/Com-f/defe-f/14cv-f.htm?Language=F&Parl=37&Ses=1&comm_id=76, accessed 1 December 2002.

—— (2002c), *Notes for an Address by the Honourable Bill Graham, Minister of Foreign Affairs, to the OAS Session on Following-Up to and Development of the Inter-American Democratic Charter*, Bridgetown, 4 June 2002.

—— (2002d), *Notes for an Address by the Honourable Denis Paradis, Secretary of State (Latin America and Africa; Francophonie), to the XXIX Special Session of the General Assembly of the Organization of American States*, Washington D.C., 18 April 2002.

—— (2002e), *Speaking Notes for the Honourable Art Eggleton Minister of National Defence* (published online 22 January 2002) www.dnd.ca/en/archive/speeches/2002/jan02/22MDC_s_f.htm, accessed 1 December 2002.

—— (2003a), *Canada-Mexico Relations*, http://www.dfait-maeci.gc.ca/latinamerica/canadamexicorelations-en.asp, accessed 1 January 2003.

—— (2003b), *Defense Relations*, http://www.dfait-maeci.gc.ca/mexico-city/political/defence-en.asp, accessed 1 January 2003.

—— (2003c), *Initial Canadian Offer for Cross-Border Services and Investment* (published online 14 February 2003) http://www.dfait-maeci.gc.ca/tna-nac/FTAA/ex-io-en.as, accessed 18 March 2003.

—— (2004), *Situation des droits de la personne à Cuba* http://www.dfait-maeci.gc.ca/foreign_policy/human-rights/background_documents/cuba-fr.asp, accessed 9 February 2006.

—— (2005 a). "A Role of Pride and Influence in the World," in *Canada's International Policy Statement* (Ottawa: Commerce, Foreign Affairs and International Trade Canada).

—— (2005b), *Canada-Cuba Relations*, (published online 25 April 2005) http://www.dfait-maeci.gc.ca/latin-america/latinamerica/country_info/cuba_relations-en.asp, 30 January 2006.

—— (2005c). "Fierté et influence: Notre rôle dans le monde," *Énoncé de politique internationale du Canada – Commerce* (Ottawa: Department of Foreign Affairs and International Trade).

—— (2006), The Security and Prosperity Partnership of North America: Next Steps, (published online 31 March 2006) http://www.pm.gc.ca/eng/media.asp?id=1084, accessed 24 March 2007.

Government of Canada – Canada Border Services Agency (2000), *Canada-United States Accord on Our Shared Border*, http://www.cbsa-asfc.gc.ca/general/border/menu-e.html, accessed 25 March 2007.

Government of Canada – Canada Gazette (2004), *Government Notices* 138:32 http://canadagazette.gc.ca/partI/2004/20040807/html/notice-e.html, accessed 11 March 2007.

Government of Canada – Department of Foreign Affairs and International Trade (1998), "Notes for an Address by the Honourable Lloyd Axworthy to the Canadian Institute of International Affairs 1998 Foreign Policy Conference," *Déclaration*, no. 98/67 16 October, http://w01.international.gc.ca/minpub/Publication.aspx?is Redirect=True&FileSpec=/Min_Pub_Docs/101124.htm, accessed 7 March 2007.

—— (2000), *Building A Border for the 21st Century* (Ottawa: Canada-U.S. Partnership Forum (CUSP) Report).

Government of Canada – Department of National Defence (2005). *Borderline Insecure: Canada's Land Border Crossings are Key to Canada's Security and Prosperity. Why the Lack of Urgency to Fix Them? What Will Happen If We Don't?* http://www.parl.gc.ca/38/1/parlbus/commbus/senate/Com-e/defe-e/rep-e/ repintjun05-e.pdf, accessed 24 March 2007.

Government of Canada – Privy Council Office (2003), Le Canada et le Mexique signent des accords bilatéraux (publisehd online 27 February 2003) http://www. pco-bcp.gc.ca/default.?Language=F&Page=archiveChretien&sub=NewsRelease s&Doc=canmexicobilateral.20030227_f.htm, accessed 5 March 2007.

Government of Canada – Standing Committee on Foreign Affairs and International Trade (2001), *Balance, Transparency and Engagement After the Quebec Summit* (Ottawa: House of Commons).

Government of Canada – Standing Committee on Foreign Affairs and International Trade – Sub-Committee on Human Rights and International Development (2002), "Conflict, Human Rights and Democracy in Colombia: A Canadian Agenda," http://www.parl.gc.ca/infocomdoc/37/1/fait/studies/reports/faitrp18/03-cov-e.htm, accessed 3 August 2006 .

Government of Mexico (2001), *Address by Presidente Vicente Fox Quesada at the First Plenary Session of the Quebec City Summit*, Quebec City, 21 April 2001 www.presidencia.gob.mx, accessed 1 February 2003.

—— (2002a), *Declaración del Presidente Vicente Fox Quesada sobre la situación en Venezuela*, 12 April 2002 www.presidencia.gob.mx, accessed 18 January 2003.

—— (2002b), *Palabras del Presidente Vicente Fox Quesada durante la visita que hizo a la Corte Interamericana de Derechos Humanos*, San José, 12 April 2002 www.presidencia.gob.mx, accessed 18 January 2003.

Government of Mexico – Mexican Ministry of Foreign Relations (2001), *Mexico to Determine its Position on Cuba in the United Nations Human Rights Commission*, Bulletin No. 068/01, 10 April 2001.

Government of Mexico – Presidencia de la Republica (2001), *Press Release* (published online 21 September 2001) http://www.presidencia.gob.mx/ ?Art=1891&Orden=Leer, accessed 1 December 2002.

Government of Mexico – Presidencia de la Republica (2005), *Mexico Promotes Development and Democracy in Latin America: President Fox Quesada* (published online 28 June 2005) http://envivo.presidencia.gob.mx/ ?P=2&Orden=Leer&Tipo=Pe&Art=9274, accessed 9 February 2006.

Government of Mexico – Secretaría de Relaciones Exteriores (2005), *Intervención del Secretario Luis Ernesto Derbez en el Plenario de la XXXV Asamblea General de la Organización de los Estados Americanos*, Fort Lauderdale, 7 June 2005.

Government of the United States (1997), "Cuba: U.S. Policy Now and in the Future," *Remarks by Michael Rannaberger, Coordinator for Cuban Affairs, before the Governor's Cuba Advisory Group*, Miami, Florida (published online 28 February 1997) http://www.state.gov/www/regions/wha/970228_ranneberger.html, 9 September 2006.

—— (2002a), *Address by Ambassador Roger F. Noriega, U.S. Permanent Representative to the OAS*, Washington, 16 September 2002.

—— (2002b), "Administration Unveils Comprehensive US Trade Proposal to Expand American Farmer's Access to Overseas markets," *USDA News Release*, Release No. 0312.02 http://www.usda.gov/news/releases/2002/07/0312.htm, accessed 18 March 2003.

—— (2002c), *International Narcotics Control Strategy Report 2001*, http://www.state.gov/p/inl/rls/nrcrpt/2001/rpt/, accessed 2 August 2006.

—— (2002d), "Press Conference with US Trade representative Robert T. Zoellick, Ambassador Allan Johnson, USTR Chief Agriculture Negotiator, David Hegwood, Special Counsel to the Secretary Ann. M. Veneman regarding the US agenda for the World Trade Organization negptiations," *USDA Transcript,* Release No. 0314.02, http://www.usda.gov/news/releases/2002/07/0314.htm, accessed 18 March 2003.

—— (2003a), *2003 Trade Policy Agenda and 2002 Annual Report of the President of the United States on the Trade Agreements Program* http://www.ustr.gov/reports/2003.html, accessed 18 March 2003.

—— (2003b), "Actual Language of US WTO Agriculture Proposal Presented in Geneva," *FASonline* http://www.fas.usda.gov/itp/wto/actual.htm, accessed 18 March 2003.

—— (2003c), *U.S. Advances Bold Proposals in FTAA Negotiations to Create World's Largest Free Market in 2005*, Press Release, 11 February 2003, http://www.ustr.gov/releases/2003/02/03-08.htm, accessed 18 March 2003.

—— (2003d), "USDA Official Cites Importance of Trade with Western Hemisphere, *Washington File* (published online 20 May 2003) http;//www.usembassycanada.gov/, accessed 18 March 2003.

—— (2005), *Recent Summit of the Americas a Success, U.S. Official Says*, Washington, Usinfo.state.gov, 16 November 2005, accessed 13 December 2006.

Government of the United States – Department of State (1999), *Press Briefing on Release of "Patterns of Global Terrorism 1998"*, (Washington DC: United States Department of State).

—— (2000), *Building A Border for the 21st Century* (published online December 2000) www.state.gov/www/regions/wha/0012_cusp_report.html, accessed 24 March 2007.

—— (2002), Fifth Conference of Ministers of Defense of the Americas: Declaration of Santiago http://www.state.gov/p/wha/rls/71005.htm, accessed 27 March 2007.

Governement of the United States – Department of State – Bureau of Wester Hemisphere Affairs (2005), *Background Note: Cuba*, http://www.state.gov/r/pa/ei/bgn/2886.htm, accessed 9 February 2006.

Governement of the United States – Secretary of State (2006), *Current Regulations of the Conference of Ministers of Defense of the Americas*, Title II: Principles and Purposes, http://www.state.gov/p/wha/rls/73766.htm#title2, accessed 27 March 2007.

Government of the United States – United States Mission to the European Union (1998), *The Transatlantic Economic Partnership:Action Plan*, (published online 9 November 1998) http://www.useu.be/TranAtlantic/TEP/tep119.html consulted 2004–02–12, accessed 12 February, 2004.

Government of the United States – United States Trade Representative (2002), *United States Announces Proposals for Liberalizing Trade in Services*, Press Release no. 2002–63, 1 July 2002.

—— (2003), *United States Trade Representative Robert B. Zoellick Press Conference to Announce US Proposals for Free Trade Area of the Americas*, Washington, D.C. (published online 11 February 2003) http://www.ustr.gov/releases/2003/02/2003-02-11-transcript-ftaa.PDF, accessed 18 March 2003.

Government of the United States – White House (2003), *Presidential Determination No. 2003–14*, http://www.whitehouse.gov/news/releases/2003/01/20030131-7.html, accessed 6 February 2003.

Government of the United States – White House (2007), *Quick Facts about the U.S.-Mexican Border*, http://www.whitehouse.gov/infocus/usmxborder/quickfacts.html, accessed 24 March 2007.

Graham, John W. (2002), *A Magna Carta for the Americas. The Inter-American Democratic Charter: Genesis, Challenges and Canadian Connections* (Ottawa: FOCAL Policy Paper).

Grant, Cedric (2000), *US-Caribbean Relations* (Silver City NM & Washington D.C.: *Foreign Policy in Focus*).

Grieco, Joseph M. (1995), "The Maastricht Treaty, Economic and Monetary Union and the Neo-realist Research Programme," *Review of International Studies* 21:1, 21–40.

—— (1996), "State Interest and International Rule Trajectories: A Neorealist Interpretation of the Maastricht Treaty and European Economic and Monetary Union," in Benjamin Frankel (ed.), *Realism: Restatement and Renewal*.

Griffin Cohen, Marjorie and Stephen Clarkson, (eds) (2004), *Governing Under Stress: Middle Powers and the Challenge of Globalization* (London: Zed Books).

Griffiths, Ann L. (ed.) (2003), *The Canadian Forces and Interoperability: Panacea or Perdition?* (Halifax: Centre for Foreign Policy Studies, Dalhousie University).

Grijalva, J. Ernesto and Patrick T. Brewer (1994), "The Administrative Bodies of the North American Free Trade Agreement," *San Diego Justice Journal* 2, 1–18.

Grinspun, Ricardo and Robert Kreklewich (1999), "Institutions, Power Relations, and Unequal Integration in the Americas: NAFTA as Deficient Institutionality," in Kristen Appendini and Sven Bislev (eds).

Haas, Ernst B. (1958), *The Uniting of Europe, Political, Social and Economical Forces: 1950–1957* (London: Stevens).

—— (1964), *Beyond the Nation-State: Functionalism and International Organization* (Stanford: Stanford University Press).

Haas, Ernst B. and Philippe C. Schmitter (1964), "Economics and Differential Patterns of Political Integration: Projections About Unity in Latin America," *International Organization* 18: 4, 705–37.

Haglund, David G. (2000), *The North Atlantic Triangle Revisited. Canadian Grand Strategy at Century's End* (Toronto: Irwin).

Hakim, Peter and Robert E. Litan (eds) (2002), *The Future of North American Integration, Beyond NAFTA* (Washington, DC: Brookings Institution Press).

Hall, Kevin G. (1997), "Trading Blocs to Discuss Linking Most of South America: Hemispheric Plan Prompts Meeting," *Journal of Commerce*, A1.

Hamson, Fen Olser, Michael Hart and Martin Rudner (1999), "A Big League or Minor League Player?," in Fen Olser, Hamson Michael Hart and Martin Rudner (eds).

Hamson, Fen Olser, Michael Hart and Martin Rudner (eds) (1999), *Canada Among Nations, 1999: A Big League Player?* (Don Mills: Oxford University Press).

Hay, Colin (2000), "Contemporary Capitalism, globalization, regionalization and the persistence of national variation," *Review of International Studies* 26, 509–31.

Hays, Dennis (2002), "Inspect Cuba for Production of Biological Weapons," *The Miami Herald*, (published online 29 July 2002) http://www.canf.org/News/020729newsa.htm, accessed 10 September 2006.

Heller, Claude (1999), "Los derechos humanos en la Organización de los Estados Americanos," *Política exterior* 55–6, 160–79.

—— (2000), "México en la OEA: tesis y posiciones tradicionales," in Roberta Lajous and Blanca Torres (eds).

Hettne, Bjorn (2000), "The New Regionalism," talk given at the XVIIIth World Congress of the International Political Science Association, Québec, 1–5 August 2000.

Hettne, Bjorn, Andras Inotai and Osvaldo Sunkel (eds) (1999), *Globalism and the New Regionalism* (London/New York: Macmillan/St. Martin's Press).

Higgs, Robert (1987), *Crisis and Leviathan: Critical Episodes in the Growth of American Government* (New York: Oxford University Press).

Hillman, Richard S., John A. Peeler and Elsa Cardozo da Silva (eds), *Democracy and Human Rights in Latin America* (Westport: Praeger).

Hillmer, Norman and Maureen Appel Molot (eds) (2002), *Canada Among Nations 2002: A Fading Power* (Don Mills: Oxford University Press).

Hindley, Brian (1999), "New Institutions for Transatlantic Trade?," *International Affairs* 75: 1, 45–60.

Holmes, John (1982), *The Shaping of Peace: Canada and the Search for World Order, 1943–1957* (Toronto: University of Toronto Press).

Horlick, Gary N. and Claire R. Palmer (2001), *The Negotiation of the Free Trade Area of the Americas* (Washington D.C.: O'Melveny & Myers LLP), http://www.sice.oas.org/geograph/westernh/Horloc.pdf, accessed 18 March 2003.

Howlett, Michael (2000), "Beyond Legalism? Policy Ideas, Implementation Styles and Emulation-Based Convergence in Canadian and U.S. Environmental Policy," *Journal of Public Policy* 20:3, 305–29.

Huenemann, Jon E. (2001), "The US Trade Relationship with Mexico: Where It has been and Where It Should Go," *Policy Papers on the Americas* 12:1 CSIS (published online 20 January 2001), http://www.csis.org/americas /pubs/pp_us_trade_mexico.pdf, accessed 18 March 2003.

Hufbauer, Gary C., Jeffrey J. Schott and Paul L.E. Grieco (2005), *NAFTA Revisited: Achievements and Challenges* (Washington, D.C.: Institute for International Economics).

Hulsman, Louk and Hilde van Ransbeek (1983), "Évaluation critique de la politique des drogues," *Déviance et Société* 7: 3, 271–80.

Human Rights Watch (2002), "Informe Anual de Human Rights Watch," *Gaceta: Comisión de derechos humanos del Distrito federal* February 2002, pp. 47–51.

Instituto Matías Romero de Estudios Diplomáticos (1997), *Canadá y Mexico. Los vecinos de vecinos* (Mexico: Secretaría de Relaciones Exteriores de México).

Inter-America Defence Board (2002), "Canada Joins Inter-American Defense Board," in *Latest News* (published online 22 November 2002) http://www.jid.org/news/news.asp?id=17, accessed 1 February 2003.

Jank, Marcos (2001), "United States Agricultural Protectionism: FTAA Seed of Discord," in *Foreign Trade Information System* http://www.sice.oas.org/geograph/westernh/jank2.pdf, accessed 18 March 2003.

Jockel, Joseph T. (1995), "Trilateralism and North American Defense Relations: Some Preliminary Thoughts," in Donald Barry, Mark O. Dickerson and James D. Grisford (ed.).

Just the Facts (2003), *Defence Department Programs: Military-to-Military Interaction*, http://www.ciponline.org/facts/fmi.htm, accessed 5 March 2007.

Keith, Stephen K. (2002), "A Free Trade Area of the Americas: Implications of Success or Failure for Members of the OAS," *Working Paper Series 7* (Miami: The Dante B. Fascell North-South Center).

Keohane, Robert O. (1984), *After Hegemony: Cooperation and Discord in the World Political Economy* (Princeton: Princeton University Press).

Keohane, Robert O., and Helen V. Milner (eds) (1996), *Internationalization and Domestic Politics* (Cambridge: Cambridge University Press).

Kirk, John M. (1995), "Unravelling the Paradox: The Canadian Position on Cuba," in Archibald R. M. Ritter and John M. Kirk (eds).

Kirk, John M. and Peter McKenna (2005), "A Special Relationship," *Literary Review of Canada* 13: 8, 3–6.

Kissinger, Henry (2001), *Does America Need A Foreign Policy? Toward a Diplomacy for the 21st Century* (New York: Simon and Schuster).

Klepak, Hal P. (ed.) (1996), *Natural Allies? Canadian and Mexican Perspectives on International Security* (Ottawa: Carleton University Press).

Klepak, Hal P. (1996), "Prospects for Increased Mexican-Canadian Collaboration in Security Field," in Hal P. Klepak (ed.).

Klotz, Audie (1995), *Norms in International Relations: The Struggle Against Apartheid* (Ithaca/Londres: Cornell University Press).

Knox, Paul (1998), "PM Uses Cuban TV to Push Trade Links," *The Globe and Mail*, April 27 1998.

Kourous, George (2002), *A background paper from the IRC's Americas Program: Return of the National Security State? America's Policy* (published online 18 November 2002) ‹http://www.americaspolicy.org/briefs/2002/0211security_body.html›, accessed 5 March 2007.

Krol, Ariane (2001), "Nous libéralisons le commerce, mais laissons les États redistribuer la richesse," *La Presse* (Montreal), April 22, A8.

Kubalkova, Venduka, Nicholas Onuf and Paul Kowert (eds) (1998), *International Relations in a Constructed World* (Armonk: M.E. Sharpe).

Lajous Roberta and Blanca Torres (eds) (2000), *La Política Exterior de México en la Década de los Noventa* (Mexico City: Senado de la República-El Colegio de México).

Leblanc, Lawrence J. (1977), *The OAS and the Promotion and Protection of Human Rights* (The Hague: Martinus Nijhoff).

Legler, Tom (2007), "The Inter-American Democratic Charter: Rhetoric or Reality?," in Gordon Mace, Jean-Philippe Thérien and Paul Haslam (eds).

Legault, Albert (ed.) (2004), *Le Canada dans l'orbite américaine: Mort des théories intégrationnistes?* (Quebec City: Presses de l'Université Laval).

Lindberg, Leon N. (1967), "The European Community as a Political System: Notes Toward the Construction of a Model," *Journal of Common Market Studies* 5:4, 344–87.

—— (1970), "Political Integration as a Multidimensional Phenomenon Requiring Multivariate Measurement," *International Organization* 24:4, 649–731.

Lowenthal, Abraham F. (ed.) (1991), *Exporting Democracy: The United States and Latin America* (Baltimore: Johns Hopkins University Press).

Lyon, Peyton V. and Tareq Y. Ismael (eds) (1976), *Canada and the Third World* (Toronto: Macmillan of Canada).

Mace, Gordon and Louis Bélanger (eds) (1998), *The Americas in Transition: The Contours of Regionalism* (Boulder: Lynne Rienner Publications).

—— (2003), "The North-South Dimension of the FTAA: Comparing Some Canadian, Mexican, United States' Positions," Paper presented at the *CEEISA/ISA Convention*, Budapest, 26–28 June.

—— (2004), "What Institutional Design for North America?," in Sidney Weintraub, Alan M. Rugman and Gavin Boyd (eds).

Mace, Gordon, Jacques Paquet, Louis Bélanger and Hugo Loiseau (2003), "Asymétrie de pouvoir et négociations économiques internationales: le cas de la zone de libre-échange des Amériques et les puissances moyennes," *Canadian Journal of Political Science* 36:1, 129–58.

Mace, Gordon and Martin Roy (2000), "Canadá y la OEA: Promoción de la Democracia," in Tickner (ed.).

Mace, Gordon and Jean-Philippe Thérien (eds) (1996), *Foreign Policy and Regionalism in the Americas* (Boulder: Lynne Rienners Publishers).

Mace, Gordon, Jean-Philippe Thérien and Paul Haslam (eds) (2007), *Governing the Americas: Assessing Multilateral Institutions* (Boulder: Lynne Rienner Publications).

Mackay, Donald R. (2002), *Challenges Confronting the Free Trade Area of the Americas*, *FOCAL Policy Paper* (Ottawa: FOCAL).

Macleod, Alex, Stéphane Roussel and Andi van Mens (2000), "Hobson's Choice: Does Canada have any options in its defence and security relations with the United States?," *International Journal* 55:3, 341–54.

Malamud, Andrès (2001), *Spillover in European and South American Integration. An Assessment* (Florence, Italy: Department of Social and Political Sciences, European University Institute).

Mann, Catherine L. (1999), "Liberalizing Services: Key to Faster Global Growth and the Sustainability of the US Trade Deficit," in *Testimony before the Subcommittee on International Trade, Senate Finance Committee*, Washington, DC, 21 October 1999. http://www.iie.com/publications/papers/mann1099.htm, accessed 18 March 2003.

March, James G. and Johan P. Olson (1989), *Rediscovering Institutions: The Organizational Basis of Politics* (New York: Free Press).

Marchand, Marianne H., Morten Boas and Timothy M. Shaw (1999), "The Political Economy of New Regionalisms," *Third World Quarterly* 20:5, 897–909.

Martin, Lisa and Beth Simmons (1999), "Theories and Empirical Studies of International Institutions," in P. Katzenstein, R. Keohane and S. Krasner (ed.), *Exploration and Contestation in the Study of World Politics* (Cambridge: MIT Press).

Masi, Fernando (2001), "Preferential Treatment in Trade: Is There Any Room Left in the Americas?," *The North-South Agenda Papers*: 49 (Miami: The North-South Center).

Mayer, Frederick W. (1998), *Interpreting NAFTA: The Science and Art of Political Analysis* (New York: Columbia University Press).

McAllister, William B. (2000), *Drug Diplomacy in the Twentieth Century* (London/ New York: Routledge).

McCall Smith, James (2000), "The Politics of Dispute Settlement Design: Explaining Legalism in Regional Trade Pacts," *International Organization* 54:1, 137–80.

McDougall, John N. (2000), "National differences and the NAFTA," *International Journal* 55:2, 281–91.

McKenna, Peter (1995), *Canada and the OAS: From Dilettante to Full Partner* (Ottawa: Carleton University Press).

—— (2004), "Comparative foreign policies toward Cuba," *International Journal* 59:2, 281–302.

McKenna, Peter and John M. Kirk (2002), "Canadian-Cuban Relations: Is the Honeymoon Over?," *Canadian Foreign Policy* 9:3, 49–63.

—— (2006), "Explaining the similarities and differences," *Revista mexicana de estudios canadienses* http://revista.amec.com.mx/num_11_2006/McKennaPeter_ KirkJohnM2.htm, accessed 26 December 2006.

Mearsheimer, John (2001), *The Tragedy of Great Power Politics* (New York: Norton).

Mercier, David (2000). "Le régionalisme stratégique dans les Amériques: tenants et aboutissants de l'ALÉNA vus d'une perspective mexicaine," *Études internationales* 31:1, 111–33.

Meyer, Lorenzo (1991), "Mexico: The Exception and the Rule," *Exporting Democracy: The United States and Latin America*, in Abraham F. Lowenthal (ed.).

Michaud, Nelson and Louis Bélanger (1999), "La stratégie institutionnelle du Canada: vers une 'australisation'?" *Études internationales* 30:2, 373–93.

Miller, Scott (2002), "U.S. Seeks Launch of Trade Capacity-Building Program at FTAA Meeting," in *Washington File* (Published online 1 November 2002) http:// usinfo.state.gov/regional/ar/02110101.html, accessed 18 March 2003.

Millett, Richard L. (1994), "Beyond Sovereignty: International Efforts to Support Latin American Democracy," *Journal of Interamerican Studies and World Affairs* 36:3, 1–23.

Milner, Helen V. and Robert O. Keohane (1996), "Introduction," in Robert O. Keohane and Helen V. Milner (eds).

Mitrovica, Andrew (1999), "Low funding caused U.S. drug action, B.C. says: blacklist considered, ruled out for now," *The Globe & Mail*, 16 August, A1, A6.

Mittelman, James H. (1996), "Rethinking the 'New Regionalism' in the Context of Globalization," *Global Governance* 2:2, 189–213.

Monsen, Lauren (2002), "Developing Countries need Assistance to Participate in Trade Talks, Say Experts," in *Washington File* (Published online 1 March 2002) http://usinfo.state. gov/topical/global/develop/02030101.htm, accessed 18 March 2003.

Moon, Chung-in "Market Forces and Security," paper presented at the *Annual Symposium on the United Nations System in the Twenty-first Century, United Nations University Headquarters, Tokyo, Japan, 8–9 November 1996, United Nations University's Report*, www.unu.edu/unupress/marketforces.html, accessed 25 March 2007.

Moquin, Nicolas (2006), *Les menaces asymétriques: Les initiatives du Québec en matière de lutte contre la criminalité transfrontalière* (Québec: Laboratoire d'étude sur les politiques publiques et la mondialisation). http://www.leppm.enap.ca/leppm/docs/Rapports%20securite/Rapport_3_securite.pdf, accessed 5 March 2007.

Morales, Isidro (1999), "NAFTA: The Governance of Economic Openness," *The Annals of the American Academy of Political and Social Science* 565, 35–65.

Moravcsik, Andrew (1993), "Preferences and Power in the European Community. A Liberal Intergovernmentalist Approach," *Journal of Common Market Studies* 31:4, 473–524.

—— (1997), "Taking Preferences Seriously, A Liberal Theory of International Politics," *International Organization* 51:4, 513–53.

—— (1998), *The Choice for Europe. Social Purpose and State Purpose from Messina to Maastricht* (Ithaca: Cornell University Press).

Morgenthau, Hans J. (1985), *Politics Among Nations: The Struggle for Power and Peace* (6th ed.) (New York: McGraw Hill).

Morley, Morris H. (1987), *Imperial State and Revolution. The United States and Cuba, 1952–1986*, (Cambridge: University Press).

Muñoz, Heraldo (2000), "Toward a Regime for Advancing Democracy in the Americas," in Jorge I. Domínguez (ed.).

Musto, David (1999), *The American Disease* (New York/Toronto: Oxford).

Mytelka, Lynn, K. (1979), *Regional Development in a Global Economy, the Multinational Corporation, Technology and Andean Integration* (New Haven and London: Yale University Press).

Nadelman, Ethan (1993), *Cops Across Borders: The Internationalization of US Criminal Law Enforcement* (Philadelphia: Pennsylvania State University Press).

NAFTA (1993), *North American Free Trade Agreement* (Ottawa: Acquisitions and Services Canada).

Nieto, Alfonso (1999), "Mexico denies blacklist agenda," *The Globe & Mail*, 21 August, D11.

Núñez, Col. Joseph R. (2002), "A 21st Century Security Architecture for the Americas: Multilateral Cooperation, Liberal Peace and Soft Power," paper presented at the *Integration in the Americas Conference*, 5 April 2002, (Albuquerque NM: Latin American & Iberian Institute, The University of New Mexico, Albuquerque) laii.unm.edu/conference/nunez.php, accessed 25 March 2007.

Nyahoho, Emmanuel and Pierre-Paul Proulx (2000), *Le commerce international* (Québec: Presses de l'Université du Québec).

Ogelsby, J. C. M. (1976), "Canada and Latin America," in Peyton V. Lyon and Tareq Y. Ismael (eds).

Ojeda, Mario (1984), *Alcances y límites de la política exterior de México* (2nd ed.) (Mexico City: El Colegio de México).

OAS (1993), "Declaration of Managua for the Promotion of Democracy and Development," in Viron P. Vaky and Heraldo Muñoz (eds).

—— (2000), Department of Financial Services, *Audit Book for the Years 2001 and 2000* www.oas.org/dfs/audit.htm, accessed 6 March 2007.

—— (2002), "Note From the Delegation of Mexico Forwarding the Draft Resolution 'Human Rights and Terrorism'," *Thirty-Second Regular Session of the General Assembly*, Bridgetown, 29 May 2002.

—— (2003a), *Déclaration de départ de la mission de haut niveau OÉA-CARICOM*, OAS Press Release, 20 March 2003.

—— (2003b), *"Observaciones y recommendaciones de los Estados miembros con relación al informe elaborado por la Comisión Interamericana de Derechos Humanos sobre el tema 'Derechos humanos y terrorismo',"* (Washington: Permanent Council of the OAS).Otteman, Scott (1998), "FTAA Talks Must Offer Quick Results to Keep Interest, Official Says," *Americas Trade*, 19 February 1998, 18–20.

Onuf, Nicholas (1998), "Constructivism. A User's Manual," in Venduka Kubalkova, Nicholas Onuf and Paul Kowert (eds).

Ozuna, Teofilo and Ramon Guajardo Quiroga (1991), *The U.S.-Mexico Free Trade Agreement: Natural Resource and Environmental Issues, U.S.-Mexico Free Trade Issues Paper Series* (College Station TX: TAMRC International Market Research Report No. IM–8–91).

Pansza, Arturo R. (2004), "Defienden Bush y Fox el ALCA," *El Sol de Mexico*, 13 January 2004, 3A.

Paris, Roland (2007), "A trilateral mishmash," *The Globe and Mail*, 26 February 2007, A15.

Pastor, Robert A. (2001), *Toward a North American Community. Lessons from the Old World for the New* (Washington, DC: Institute for International Economics).

Pastor, Robert A. and Rafael Fernandez de Castro (eds) (1998), *The Controversial Pivot, The US Congress and North America* (Washington, DC: Brookings Institution Press).

Pearson, Lester B. (1974), *Memoirs 1948–1957: The International Years. Volume II* (edited by John A. Munro and Alex I. Inglis) (London: Victor Gollancz).

Pinera Gonzàlez, Carlos (2000), "Mexico's Free Trade Agreements: Extending NAFTA's Approach," in Sherry M. Stephenson (ed.).

Perina, Rubén M. (2000), "El régimen democrático interamericano: el papel de la OEA," in Tickner (ed.).

Perry, William J. (1995), *New Generation of US-Mexico Cooperation and Trust*, 23 October 1995, http://www.defenselink.mil/Speeches/Speech. aspx?SpeechID=1011, accessed 5 March 2007.

Poitras, Guy (2001), *Inventing North America, Canada, Mexico and the United States* (Boulder: Lynne Rienner).

Preeg, Ernest H. (1996), "Policy Forum: Transatlantic Free Trade," *The Washington Quarterly* 19:2, 105–33.

Prud'homme, Jean-François (2003), *Mexique: l'art de la négociation politique* (Ottawa: FOCAL Policy Paper).

Puchala, Donald (1970), "International Transactions and Regional Integration," *International Organization* 24:4, 732–63.

Putnam, Robert (1988), "Diplomacy and Domestic Policy. The Logic of Two-level Games," *International Organization* 42:3, 427–60.

Radice, Hugo (2000), "Globalization and national capitalisms: theorizing convergence and differentiation," *Review of International Political Economy* 7:4, 719–42.

Randall, Stephen J. (1977), "Managing Bilateralism: The Evolution of United States-Mexico Relations," in Donald Barry, Mark O. Dickerson and James D. Grisford (eds).

Raufer, Xavier (ed.) (1998), *Dictionnaire technique et critique des nouvelles menaces* (Paris: Minos-PUF).

Reid, Scott (1977), *Time of Fear and Hope: The Making of North Atlantic Treaty 1947–1949* (Toronto: McClelland & Stewart).

Richard, Denis (1995), *Les drogues* (Paris: Flammarion).

Rights and Democracy (2000), *Rights and Democracy's Position Concerning the Ratification by Canada of the American Convention on Human Rights* (Montréal, Rights and Democracy).

Ritter, Archibald R.M. (1999), *The Human Rights and Governance Dimension of Canada-Cuba Relations, 1994–1999*, (Ottawa: Department of Economics and School of International Affairs, Carleton University).

Ritter, Archibald R.M. and John M. Kirk (eds) (1995), *Cuba in the International System – Normalisation and Integration* (New York: St. Martin's Press).

Lord Robertson (1999), "Sécurité et interdépendance," *Politique étrangère* 4, 863–66.

Robinson, Linda (2000), "Towards a Realistic Cuba Policy," *Survival* 1.

Rochlin, James F. (1997), *Redefining Mexican Security: Society, State, and Region* (Boulder: Lynne Rienner).

Rochlin, James F. (ed.) (1999), *Canada and Hemispheric Narcotrafficking* (Ottawa: Canadian Centre for Foreign Policy).

Rosenberg, Robert and Steve Stein (eds) (1995), *Advancing the Miami Process* (Miami: North-South Center Press).

Roussel, Stéphane (2002), "Pearl Harbor et le World Trade Center. Le Canada face aux États-Unis en période de crise," *Études internationales* 33:4, 667–95.

—— (2004), *The North American Democratic Peace: Absence of War and Security Institution-Building in Canada-US Relations, 1867–1958* (Montréal-Kingston:, McGill-Queen's University Press – School of Policy Studies).

Roussel, Stéphane and Athanasios Hristoulas (2004), "Letrilatéralisme sécuritaire en Amérique du Nord: Rêve ou réalité?," in Albert Legault (ed.).

Salazar-Xirinachs, José Manuel et al. (2001), "Customs Unions," in José M. Salazar-Xirinachs and Maryse Robert (eds).

Salazar-Xirinachs, José Manuel and Maryse Robert (eds) (2001), *Toward Free Trade in the Americas* (Washington, DC: Organization of American States/Brooking Institution Press).

Sanahuja, José Antonio (2000), "Trade, Politics, and Democratization: The 1997 Global Agreement Between the European Union and Mexico," *Journal of Interamerican Studies and World Affairs* 42:2, 35–62.

Sands, Christopher (2002), "Fading Power or Rising Power: 11 September and Lessons from the Section 110 Experience," in Norman Hillmer and Maureen Appel Molot (eds).

Santana Moreira, Artur Luiz (1997), *The Redefinition Of Brazilian Military Policy After The Cold War*, http://www.gwu.edu/~ibi/minerva/Spring1997/Artur. Santana.Moreira.html, accessed 5 March 2007.

Sauvé, Pierre (1997), "Regional *versus* Multilateral Approaches to Services and Investment Liberalization: Anything to Worry About?," in Paul Demaret, Jean-François Bellis and Gonzalo Garcia Jiménez (eds).

Schmitter, Philippe C. (1970), "A Revised Theory of Regional Integration," *International Organization* 24:4, 836–68.

Schulz, Donald E. (2000), *The United States and Latin America: Shaping an Elusive Future* (Carlisle Barracks, PA: U.S. Army War College – Strategic Studies Institute).

Schulz, Michael, Fredrik Söderbaum and Joakim Öjendal (eds) (2001), *Regionalization in a Globalizing World* (London/New York: Zed Books).

Seeliger, Robert (1996), "Conceptualizing and Researching Policy Convergence," *Policy Studies Journal* 24:2, 287–310.

SELA (1997), "The Treatment of Asymmetries in Regional and Subregional Integration Process," (published online November 1997) http://sela2.org/WM2/WM10i.aspx?menu=2&url=http://www.lanic.utexas.edu/sela~/AA0/EN1menu/regintdocs.htm, accessed 18 March 2003.

SELA – Permanent Secretariat (1997), "Gone with the Wind? Special Treatment for the Developing Countries," *Trends in Latin American and Caribbean Integration* 49 (published online March 1997) http://lanic.utexas.edu/~sela/ AA2K/EN/cap/N49/rcapin4916.htm, accessed 18 March 2003.

Shamsie, Yasmine (2000), *Engaging with Civil Society: Lessons from the OAS, FTAA, and Summits of the Americas* (Ottawa, North-South Institute).

Shifter, Michael (2002), "Democracy in Venezuela, Unsettling as Ever," *Washington Post*, 21 April 2002, B2.

Shifter, Michael and Sean Neill (1996), *Implementing the Summit for the Americas: Guaranteeing Democracy and Human Rights* (Coral Gables: North-South Center Press).

Shirk, David A. (2003a), "Law Enforcement and Public Security Challenges in the U.S.-Mexican Border Region," paper presented at the *International Studies Association Conference, Portland, Oregon*, 26 February–1 March.

—— (2003b), "NAFTA+Plus?: U.S.-Mexican Security Relations After the 9/11 Terrorist Attacks," paper prepared for the conference on *Reforming the Administration of Justice in Mexico May 15–17, 2003*, San Diego: Center for U.S.-Mexican Studies, University of California.

Shore, Sean M. (1998), "No Fence Make Good Neighbors: The Development of the Canadian-American Security Community, 1871–1940," in Emanuel Adler and Michael Barnett (eds).

Smith, Geri (1999), "Even Fidel's Friends Are Saying 'Enough'," *Business Week Online*, 18 November 1999.

Smith, Peter H. (1996), *Talons of the Eagle: Dynamics of U.S.-Latin American Relations* (New York: Oxford University Press).

—— (1999), "Whither Hemispheric Integration?," *Business Economics* 34:3, 38–46.

Snow, Anita (2002), "Fidel Castro says Mexican president encouraged him not to attend U.N. Conference," *CubaNews*, 23 April 2002.

Soberón Garrido, Ricardo (1997), "Entre cuarteles, caletas y fronteras…," *Cuadernos de Nueva Sociedad* 1, 81–8.

Sokolsky, Joel (1995), "The Bilateral Defence Relationship with the United States," in David B. Dewitt and David Leyton Brown.

—— (2002), *Sailing in Concert: The Politics and Strategies of Canada-US Naval Interoperability* (Montreal: Institute for Research on Public Policies – Choices).

Solana, Fernando (1994), *Cinco años de política exterior* (Mexico City: Editorial Porrúa).

Spehar, Elizabeth and Nancy Thede (1995), "Canada and Central America's Democratization Process," in Jean Daudelin and Edgar J. Dosman (eds).

SPP.GOV (2005), *Security and Prosperity Partnership of North America* (published online June 2005) http://www.spp.gov/, accessed 7 March 2007.

Stephenson, Sherry M. (2001), "Services," in José M. Salazar-Xirinachs and Maryse Robert (eds).

Stephenson, Sherry M. (ed.) (2000), *Services Trade in the Western Hemispher: Liberalization, Integration, and Reform* (Washington, DC: Organization of American States).

Stotzky, Irwin P. (2002), "Democracy and International Military Intervention: The Case of Haiti," in Richard S. Hillman, John A. Peeler, and Elsa Cardozo da Silva (eds).

Summit of the Americas (1995a), "Declaration of Principles," in Rosenberg and Stein (eds).

—— (1995b), "Plan of Action," in Rosenberg and Stein (eds).

Taillefer, Guy (2002), "Le Mexique s'affiche pro-yankee. Le gouvernement de Vincente Fox a imposé un virage de la politique extérieure qui provoque la colère à Cuba," *Le Devoir* 27–28 April 2002, A11.

Thomas, Georges M., John W. Meyer, Francisco O. Ramirez and John Boli (1987), *Institutional Structure: Constituting State, Society, and the Individual* (Newbury Park: Sage Publications).

Thorup, Cathryn L. (1995), "Building Community Through Participation: The Role of Non-Governmental Actors in the Summit of the Americas," in Rosenberg and Stein (eds).

Tickner, Arlene (ed.) (2000), *Sistema Interamericano y Democracia. Antecedentes históricos y tendencias futuras* (Bogotá: CEI- Ediciones Uniandes-OEA).

Tirado, Erubiel (2002), "Narco tráfico en la era de Fox: los límites de la ficción," *Proceso 1347*, 25 August, 16–34.

Toupin, Gilles (2007), "Partenariat nord- américain pour la sécurité et la prospérité. Des 'progrès substantiels'… peu concrets," *La Presse* (Montreal) 24 February, A20.

Unger Brigitte and Frans van Waarden (eds) (1995a), *Convergence or Diversity? Internationalization and Economic Policy Response* (Aldershot: Avebury).

—— (1995b), "Introduction: An Interdisciplinary Approach to Convergence," in B. Unger and F. van Waarden (eds).

Vaky, Viron and Heraldo Muñoz (eds) (1993), *The Future of the Organization of American States* (New York City: Twentieth Century Fund).

Valenzuela, Arturo (1997), "Paraguay: The Coup That Didn't Happen," *Journal of Democracy* 8: 1, 43–55.

Vallières, Martin (2003), "Stupéfiants: le Canada montré du doigt par la Maison-Blanche," *La Presse*, 1 February, A13.

Waller Meyers, Deborah (2000), "Border Management at the Millennium," *American Review of Canadian Studies* 30:2, 255–68.

Waltz, Kenneth N. (1979), *Theory of International Politics* (Reading: Addison-Wesley).

Wayne, Anthony (2004), "NAFTA: Ten Years After," *Testimony before the Subcommittee on International Economic Policy, Export, and Trade Promotion* (published online 20 April 2004) http://www.state.gov/e/eb/rls/rm/31645.htm, accessed 8 February 2006.

Weber, Katja (2000), *Hierarchy Amidst Anarchy: Transaction Costs and Institutional Choice*, (Albany: State University of New York Press).

Weintraub, Sidney (1994), *NAFTA: What Comes Next?* (Westport: Praeger).

—— (1997), *NAFTA at Three: A Progress Report* (Washington, D.C.: Center for Strategic and International Studies).

—— "Hemisphere Highlights," *Americas Program*, (published online February 2003) http://www. csis.org/americas/pubs/hh0302.pdf, accessed 18 March 2003.

—— (2004), *NAFTA'S Impact on North America. The First Decade* (Washington D.C.: Center for Strategic and International Studies).

Weintraub, Sidney, Alan M. Rugman and Gavin Boyd (eds) (2004), *Free Trade in the Americas, Economic and Political Issues for Governments and Firms* (Cheltenham, UK, and Northampton, MA: Edward Elgar).

Wendt, Alexander *Social Theory of International Politics,* Cambridge, Cambridge University Press, 2000.

Wiarda, Howard J. (1992), *American Foreign Policy Toward Latin Americain the 80s and 90s: Issues and Controversies from Reagan to Bush* (New York: New York University Press).

—— (1995), "After Miami: The Summit, the Peso Crisis, and the Future of U.S.-Latin American Relations," *Journal of Interamerican Studies and World Affairs*. 37:1, 43–68.

Wieviorka, Michel (1998), "Le nouveau paradigme de la violence," *Cultures et conflits* 29–30, http://www.conflits.org/document.php?id=724, accessed 7 March 2007.

Wilkie, James W., Carlos Alberto Contreras and Catherine Komisaruk (eds) (1995), *Statistical Abstract of Latin America* 31:2 (Los Angeles: UCLA Latin American Center Publications: University of California).

Winham, Gilbert R. and Elizabeth DeBoer-Ashwort (2000), "Asymmetry in Negotiating The Canada-US Free Trade Agreement, 1985–1987," in Zartman and Rubin (eds).

Wolfe, Robert (1996), "Vers l'ALÉTA? Le libre-échange transatlantique et la politique étrangère canadienne," *Études internationales* 27:2, 353–80.

Wylie, Lana (2004), "Perceptions and Foreign Policy: A Comparative Study of Canadian and American Policy Toward Cuba," *Canadian Foreign Policy* 11:3, 39–64.

Zartman, William I. and Jeffrey Z. Rubin (eds) (2000), *Power and Negotiation* (Ann Arbor: The University of Michigan Press).

Zehfuss, Maja (2002), *Constructivism in International Relations Theory* (Cambridge: Cambridge University Press).

Zoellick, Robert B. (2002), "Trading in Freedom; The New Endeavor of the Americas," *Economic Perspectives* 7:3.

Zylberberg, Jacques (1995), "La spirale du vide et du chaos: essai sur la politique haïtienne du gouvernement canadien," in Jean Daudelin and Edgar J. Dosman (eds).

Websites

(1995) "ALÉNA: unissons-nous pour faire contrepoids aux Américains, dit Chrétien," *Le Devoir*, 23 January.

(2003a) "Apoyan 15 estados revisar el agro en TLC," *Reforma* (Published online 10 February 2003) http;//www.reforma.com/parseo/ printpage.asp?pagetoprint=/ nacional/articulo/268172/de...2003–03–03, accessed 3 March 2003.

(2002), "Bob Zoellick's Grand Strategy," *The Economist* 2 March, 35.

(2001) "Canada Supports Jamaica's Call for Regional 'Adjustment Fund'," *The Jamaica Gleaner,* 2 March.

(2003) *Chile-U.S. Free Trade Agreement.*

(2003) "El campo ya no aguanta mas," *La Insignia* (Published online 16 February 2003) http://www.lainsignia.org/2003/febrero/econ_016.htm, accessed 18 March 2003.

(2003) "El TLC ha tenido efectos negativos: Canales," *El Economista*, 11 March.

(2002) *Free Trade Area of the Americas, Second Draft Agreement, Chapter on Services* (published online 1 November 2002) http://www.alca-ftaa.org/ ftaadraft02/eng/ngsve_1.asp#Future, accessed 18 March 2003.

(2002) *In the Matter of An Arbitration Under Chapter Eleven of the North American Free Trade Agreement Between Pope & Talbot Inc. and Government of Canada. Award in Respect of Damages*, 31 May. World Trade and Arbitration Materials (13): 61–155 2001.

(1999) "Interview with A.C. Morancy, Manager, Intelligence Services, Canada Customs," in James F. Rochlin (ed.).

(1995) *Joint EU-U.S. Action Plan*, http://www.eurunion.org/partner/actplan.htm, accessed 11 March 2007.

(2005) *Joint Press Conference with President Vicente Fox of Mexico, President George W. Bush of the United States and Prime Minister Paul Martin of Canada* (published online 23 March 2005) http://www.presidencia.gob.mx/en/search/?contenido=17360&pagina=1&palabras=Cuba, accessed 9 February 2006.

(1995) *La Dépêche internationale des drogues*.

(1997) "Mexico's Regional Agreements Stimulate Liberalization but Complicate Trade Regime," *SICE Foreign Trade Information System* (Published online 8 October 1997) http://www.sice.oas.org/ctyndex/wto/tprme63a.asp, accessed 18 March 2003.

(1995) *New Transatlantic Agenda (The)*, http://www.eurunion.org/partner/agenda.htm, accessed 11 March 2007.

(1996) *P.L. 927, Helms-Burton Act*, 2nd sess., 104th leg., United States (published online 1996) http://www.canadahistory.com/sections/documents/dochelms%20burton%20act.htm, accessed 9 February 2006.

(2003b) "temen 'castigo' si reabren el TLC", *Reforma* (Published online 18 February 2003) http://www.reforma.com/parseo/printpage. asp?pagetoprint=nacional/articulo/270517/de.2003–03–03, accessed 3 March 2003.

(1998) *Tratado de Libre Comercio entre la República de Chile y los Estados Unidos Mexicanos*.

(2001) *Tratado de Libre Comercio México-Triagulo Norte*, Reservas, http://www.economia-snci.gob.mx/Tratados/tlcdinamic/Texto-Tri_ngulo/texto-tri_ngulo.htm, accessed 18 March 2003.

(2003) *United-States – Chile Free Trade Agreement*, 6 June 2003, Annex I, II and III.

(2003c) "Urge Fox a campesinos a negociar," *Reforma* (Published online 24 January 2003) http://www.reforma.com/parseo/printpage. asp?pagetoprint=../nacional/articulo/263652/de.2003–03–03, accessed 3 March 2003.

(2001) "Usar parte del gasto militar de AL en combatir la pobreza, plantea Fox," *La Jornada* (Published online 22 April 2001) http://www.jornada.unam.mx/2001/abr01/010422/003nlpol.html, accessed 8 February 2002.

Index